ALL OF IT

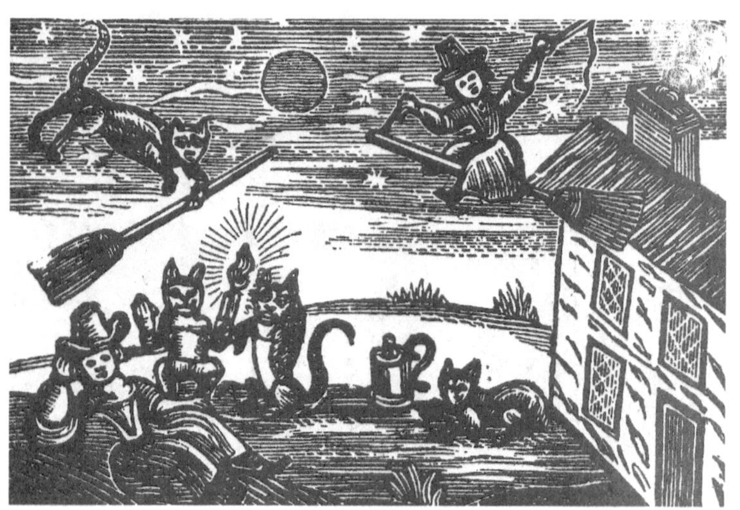

ALL OF IT

A Memoir of Love, Fear and Art

BEV AISBETT

HarperCollins*Publishers*

Some names have been changed (marked *) to protect the innocent (is anyone?) and the guilty (likewise?) and – let's be honest – to protect my ass!

Harper*CollinsPublishers***

First published in Australia in 2012
by HarperCollins*Publishers* Australia Pty Limited
ABN 36 009 913 517
harpercollins.com.au

HarperCollins*Publishers*
Level 13, 201 Elizabeth Street, Sydney NSW 2000, Australia
31 View Road, Glenfield, Auckland 0627, New Zealand
A 53, Sector 57, Noida, UP, India
77–85 Fulham Palace Road, London, W6 8JB, United Kingdom
2 Bloor Street East, 20th floor, Toronto, Ontario M4W 1A8, Canada
10 East 53rd Street, New York NY 10022, USA

National Library of Australia Cataloguing-in-Publication entry:

Aisbett, Bev.
All of it : a memoir of love, fear and art / Bev Aisbett.
ISBN: 978 0 7322 9242 3 (pbk.)
Aisbett, Bev.
Artists – Australia – Biography.
Depressed persons – Australia – Biography.
Depression, Mental – Depression – Biography.
Anxiety disorders – Australia – Biography.
709.2

Cover design by Jane Waterhouse, HarperCollins Design Studio
Cover painting: 'The Long Sunday', Bev Aisbett 2007;
all other images by shutterstock.com
All artwork is by the author; photographs are from the author's private collection.
Typeset in Minion by Kirby Jones

Dedicated to my family – of origin and of choice
and
to the beautiful monster – because he asked for it.*

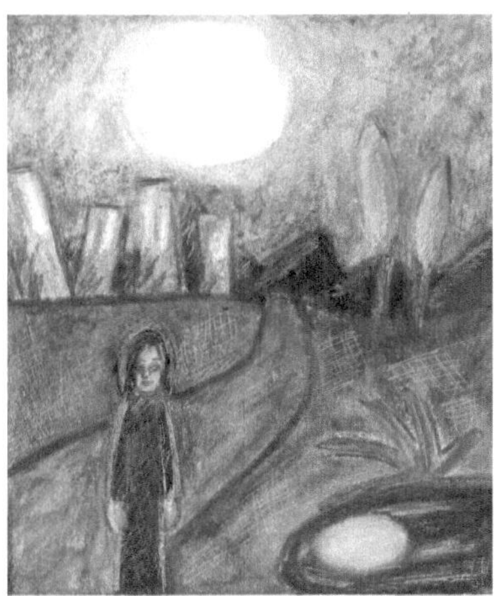

* See page 240.

Come away o human child!
To the waters and the wild
With a faery hand in hand
For the world's more full
of weeping
Than ye can understand

'The Stolen Child'

WB Yeats

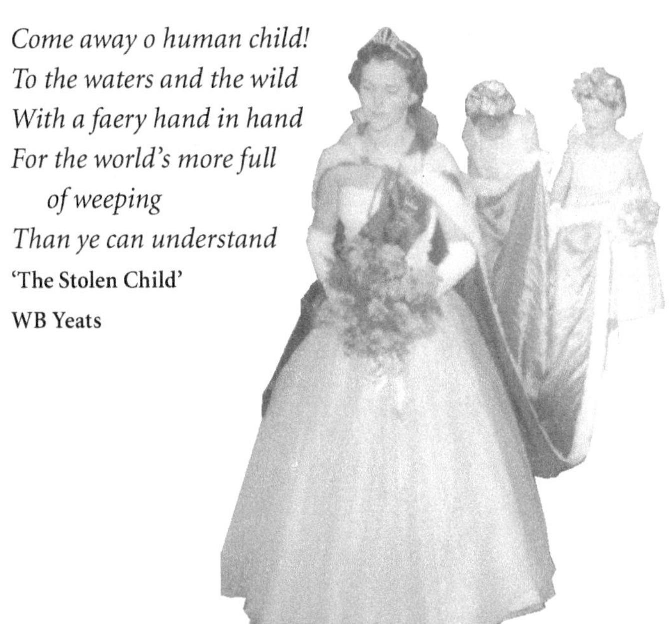

July 2010

Tomorrow, I promise myself, I will begin this book.

I am aided by my diaries – the large pile of them that record my life almost daily from 1963 and which I must now relive, step by step, like a near-death life review. Here is the evidence. Here is what was said, here is how it happened; here is what was done. Even so, these 'facts' are still my invention; my own account of 'reality'. There may be other versions, of course, but this is mine.

The truth is, I have been putting this off when it comes down to it; now that the submission – about which I had such excitement, such certainty – has been accepted, now that I have pitched this book with such brave and genuinely enthusiastic anticipation, now that I have happily crowed to people about how good it feels to be doing this (and blithely ignored their concerns that it may 'bring up stuff'), now that the contract has been signed, for which I pestered when it was slow in coming; now that all is GO!, I hesitate.

For this is my life laid bare. This is me laid bare. Here is the worst of me along with the best and it's all a bit scary but I suppose I'm used to that.

When I picture you, the reader, trying to imagine your idea of me and what your expectations might be, I wonder how you might judge me from these pages. But this is an old and unhealthy habit: not wanting to disappoint. Thought I'd left that behind; time I did. I am who I am.

Even so, there is a temptation to smooth things over; to round out rough edges and politely hide away unpleasant things; but no, I will be open and candid and as truthful as my own biases will allow. And if I reveal myself, with my human failings and vulnerabilities, what is there left to fear?

Hmm, best not to ask the Universe such a question.

LATER
I've done it! I've begun. I spent the evening lining up the diaries in chronological order (or is that disorder?). Here are the earliest years recorded in tiny notebooks with an impressive economy; written in pencil and beginning with 'Dear Diary', which I soon abandon because it takes up too much of the limited space.

14 February 1966

> *Dear Diary, Decimal Day today and I got my first ever dollar note! It was also the first day back at school. Gosh, I've got a lot of homework!*

Then, as the years go by, the journals expand in size and at their peak, become gold-edged, leather-bound tomes exhibiting an air of importance (or grandiosity) to the act of writing itself.

My journals have been my friends, witnesses, confidantes and counsellors.

They now stand in a ragged line, awaiting their turn as I plunge into the past. Do I start at the beginning or dive in at random? Does it matter?

In the end, there is only one story for each of us; played out again and again in a thousand different ways.

That story is invariably about only two things: love and fear. Where there is one, there is not the other: the Yin and Yang of life is love and fear. Should one aspire to live deeply then one will know both in equal measure.

So, I now begin. I will tell my story of love and fear; I will tell All of It and it would begin before I began.

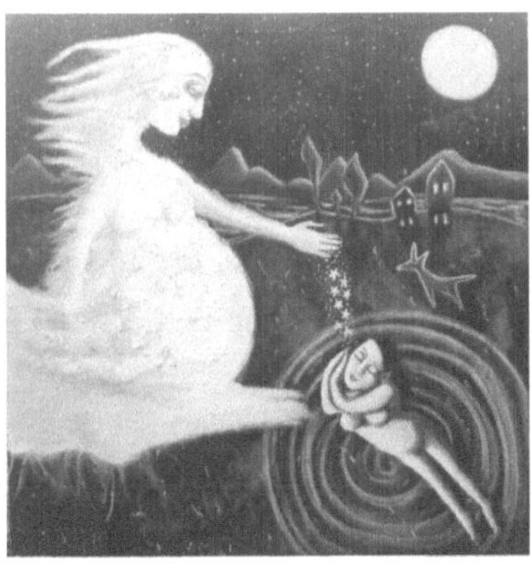

So it was agreed: I would be born into the entity known as Beverley Ellen (already a hitch – her contrary father registers the name as Beverley *Ann*: a fact only discovered 29 years later when the birth certificate is retrieved).

She would touch down on Planet Earth at 2.17 p.m. on 31 October: Halloween, which, astrologically speaking is also the Day of Attentiveness in the Week of Intensity.

Here in my hand is the Soul Contract for my mission in the physical and it is to find release; which, of course, means familiarity with its opposite, entrapment: exploring restriction to find freedom; swinging between dependency and independence. Clearly this was to be no holiday cruise.

I read the profile for this Beverley Ellen/Ann, assessing her strengths: courage (she'd need that in abundance), truthfulness (a mixed and often unappreciated blessing), reliability, perceptiveness (again, a tricky quality), resourcefulness, determination, empathy (though not always sympathy), a fine intellect and enormous creativity.

She would be youthful and spirited all her life but also child-like and even childish at times – a big learning curve there, I noted. Thankfully, she would have quite a sense of humour: dry and incisive.

The Day of Attentiveness would ensure an active radar (including a highly functioning bullshit meter) but too much alertness can cause irritation and clearly this one wouldn't suffer fools gladly; a major source of irritation because there will be so many to be found. A straight-talker, too, which might not always go down well and she could be a bit of a hot-head when she felt hurt.

'Note to self', I wrote: 'Must help her foster patience, acceptance and non-judgement.'

On the down-side there would be heavy weather: many misunderstandings, complex issues and much loss along the way. There would be confusion and feelings of hopelessness and of course, that hell-ride of anxiety. Somewhere between a blessing and a curse were two further characteristics: a heightened, almost agonising sensitivity and a most fragile, tender heart.

Seeing this formidable inventory, my hand faltered, pen poised above the dotted line.

Having had several previous turns at this location, I was well acquainted with the Earth and its unruly inhabitants; a riotous kindergarten of vandals almost incapable of living in a loving way. Oh, the place was pretty enough – in fact, looking down at it through the hole in the ozone layer on a clear day when the smog has dissipated, one might even be so bold as to declare it a paradise. The Chief Executive Officer of All Things had done a fine job in its construction. It would have been the ultimate holiday destination if it weren't for the tourists.

And now this one: all sensitivity and taking so much to heart; searching, watching, unable to rest; feeling lost and lonely much of the time, full of tears. And her love: muted by caution; expressed in practical ways, yet so deep: too deep for some and her precious gift of insight too scary for most. I almost baulked. This was going to be too tough.

How would she cope, given this strange and not-so-user-friendly set of skills?

How would she fit in? How could she be authentic? How would she deal with all that rejection?

Here was the script and it was up to her to determine which, of all possible endings, to choose. All well and good, but a happy ending was not guaranteed if she became lost in an emotional maze or stuck in some mental trap.

And here were innumerable toxic types to negotiate – charming liars, energy-suckers, bullies, users, controllers – and the snares of power games, low self-esteem, self-destruction, lack of assertion, self-pity, loss of faith, attachment to the material world and, worst of all, the black pit of despair. And all I could do to help her was to whisper in her ear now and then – 'This way, this way.'

I knew what was coming and I also knew that, when she took over, she would forget she had once chosen this, so that every blow would be unexpected, every wound would seem sudden and shocking; every loss would find her unprepared.

Even I would lose sight of this damned contract, because no-one in their right mind would ever *volunteer* for this, would they? But I had; thinking it would be exciting, an adventure; kidding myself that I'd be up for it.

And here's the thing about me: I have an inflated sense of responsibility. If assigned a duty (or rather, if I assigned *myself* a duty), you could bet your boots I would do it – even if it killed me (which of course, one day it would).

From this perspective, I felt I had a debt to clear – many, in fact – and that I was *obliged* to clear it or them; after all, this was my own karma. And the only way to do that was to strap on my sword and become the brave coward that I was.

Reluctantly, I turned to the CEO of All Things.

'I have to go back, don't I?' I asked, half-longing for a reprieve.

‘If you feel you must,’ was the reply.

I nodded, though I was secretly annoyed with the CEO for agreeing with me.

And so, with a deep breath, much trepidation and more than a touch of resentment, I signed the contract and launched myself into life as this ‘I’ called Beverley Ellen/Ann.

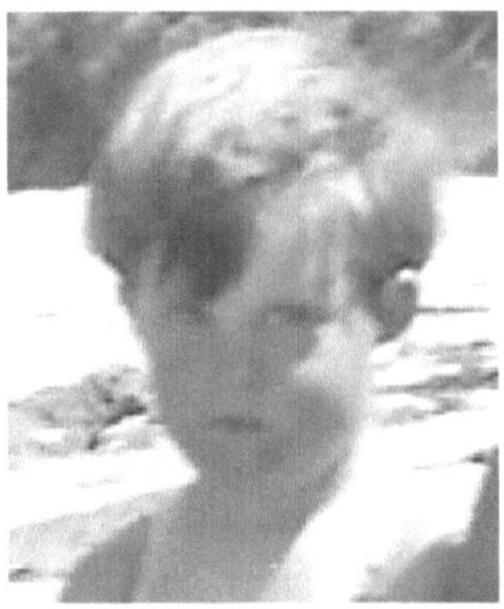

There was considerable celebration when I touched down safely at the Broadford Bush Nursing hospital one spring afternoon, healthy and whole and a whopping 7.5 pounds. Already there had already been two close calls.

During the pregnancy, there had been much debate about whether or not to proceed. It was thought that my mother had rubella and, given the risk of deformities, my father and the doctor lobbied strongly for termination but my mother had fought 'like a tigress' to keep me and won.

The first message to my tender soul was this ambivalent welcome.

A sense of vulnerability and insecurity would be born into me even before my eyes opened to the world, carried through blood and cells and nerves and the helixes of DNA which conveyed my mother's fear and my father's uncertainty to the tender bud of my being. It will whisper 'Am I really loved?', 'Am I really wanted?', 'Am I really welcome?' all my life and in reply I will hear Yes/No, Yes/No, Yes/No.

To add insult to injury, I was nearly born head-first into a toilet bowl.

Earlier in the day, my mother felt what she identified as labour pains and reported this to the nurse in charge, only to be informed that this was nonsense, that it was far too soon and my mother was clearly mistaken. Mum hobbled to the toilets, only to find that she had been right after all and consequently, she became stuck, unable to move because of the pain. By the time her cries summoned help and she was extracted from the cubicle and placed on a table, my head had already crowned.

The omens on the night of my arrival were equally inauspicious, for a pig truck broke down outside the hospital and my mother was kept awake till the small hours by a cacophony of oinks and squeals. Not only this, but the nurse had placed me in my mother's bed and, so afraid was she of smothering me, she gingerly hobbled her way along the darkened corridors to place me in the nursery in the middle of the night.

My parents, Millicent (Millie) and Arthur, lived in a small house rented from their neighbours and friends, Jess and Cyril Burge. This little house was perched on a hill opposite where the Burges' historic home, 'Glendora', overlooked grazing land for the Burges' sheep and a small creek which ran through the gully between the two properties.

Mum and Jess were particularly close, so much so that I was named after their eldest daughter, fifteen years my senior. In time, we would be known as Big Bev and Little Bev. Through this tight-knit relationship, I gained a second family.

The first visitor my mother saw through the hospital window was Jess coming down the path with her hands clasped above her head in a triumphant salute. Her gesture solemnised what was in fact a double triumph – my safe arrival and the birth of a baby girl to fill the gap left by my infant older sister, Beryl, who had died at eighteen months, during the war years.

All I knew of Beryl was a silver cup in our display cabinet, upon which was engraved her name. My parents never spoke of her and, apart from that tiny cup, it was as if she had never been. Beryl – the name of a jewel.

The Burges were a permanent and essential part of my life from my first days on the planet. My earliest memories are inextricably entwined within two locations: my family home and 'Glendora'.

I had two brothers – my own blood brother, who was twelve years my senior, and the Burges' youngest, Bill, who was ten years old when I was born.

I became a kind of 'pet' or mascot for this group of adults and near-adults and for a while my world was safe and protected with all these grown people surrounding and guiding me.

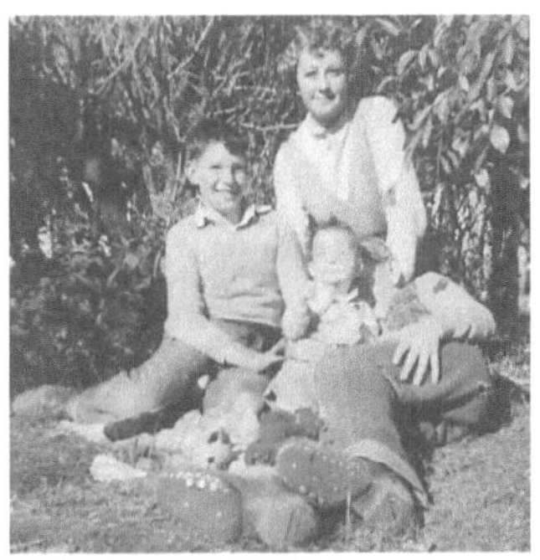

Nonetheless, my deep, ponderous nature prevailed over this sense of sanctuary and I was prone to nervous imaginings and forceful, nightmarish notions. It was as if I were super-sensitised; born without an essential layer of skin which might have anchored and buffered me better against the rigours of life.

In its place was the false foil of the legion of my protectors and without their presence, I sensed I was utterly vulnerable and defenceless. The seeds for a primal and all-pervasive fear of abandonment were spawned by my unsteady arrival and fertilised by a surplus of attention and care.

I was, indeed, true to the week of my birth – the Week of Intensity. I had one foot still firmly planted in an otherworldly realm and it seemed always an earnest and exhausting exercise to straddle this plane of esoteric wonder, while trying to accommodate the more pragmatic concerns of everyday life.

Early photographs rarely show me smiling. Instead, I am to be seen shyly and cautiously peering at the lens from beneath my fringe, as if afraid to fully reveal myself. My chin is tucked down and my head is slightly turned away as I take careful measure of the proceedings.

Thus was born a certain hyper-vigilance which would accompany me all my life. It was virtually impossible for me to detach. From my earliest days, I was a lightning rod, conducting all and any random energies around me. It would take decades before I learned how to redirect this boiling soup of sensitivities within me into something which served, rather than exhausted, me.

On the exterior, I appeared somewhat aloof, watchful and cautious; at other times contrastingly friendly, engaged and keen to please. Inside, however, I struggled mightily to make sense of the sea of feelings that often engulfed me, even in the most mundane of circumstances.

My inner world seemed to be far more complex than others'. I felt as though I was living an experience that was alien to the simple expectations of those in my small-town environment. The life I found myself living externally was too unremarkable to match the life I was living within.

Even then I felt shackled by the world and struggled to call it 'home', as if I had mistakenly landed on the wrong planet.

Despite these inner confusions, there was some comfort in the known and well-trod rituals of daily small-town life and I felt safest in the bosom of my band of protectors.

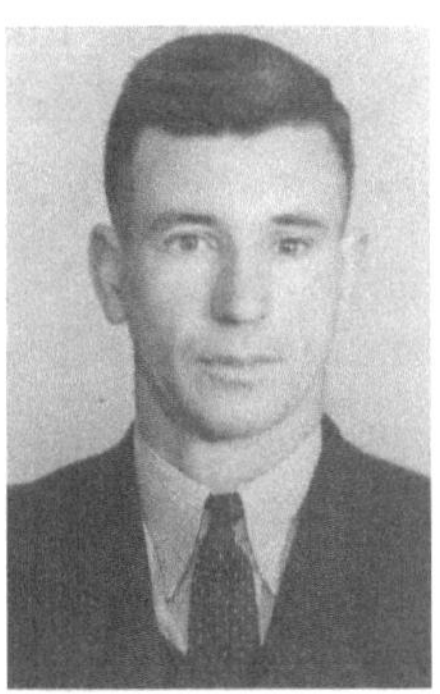

'Iron Man' my brother called him but to me he was more like the Tin Man from *The Wizard of Oz*: a good but inaccessible man whose heart had gone missing somewhere along the way.

My father, an undemonstrative, stoic and quiet man, was also a bastion of steely determination and reliable stability in an unpredictable world. True to his generation, his world was defined by manly duty: to provide for his family, make do, be frugal and resourceful. He was stubborn, fixed, practical; unable to grasp or entertain such wasteful frivolities as complex feelings.

He fulfilled his perceived duty exceedingly well and through a variety of self-taught trades. He was, by turns, a truck driver, handyman, farm-hand, motor mechanic and janitor. At home he was carpenter, builder, painter, repairer and restorer.

As it was for so many men of his time, economy and frugality were instilled in him by tough and lean early times, disciplinarian parents and the harsh years of the Depression and World War II. He had learned to *make do*; to preserve, repair and hold dear the material things which he had earned through sweat, toil and sacrifice.

Unfortunately, the skill I prized most was the one he could never master: the open expression of his love for me.

There is a favourite photograph from childhood in which I am depicted at around the age of six, wide-eyed and smiling, *beaming*, in fact, as I am caught on the downward arc of my swing. Behind me is Mount Piper, known locally as Sugarloaf, the landmark that signaled our arrival home. Also scattered in the background are the white kerchiefs of ducklings, the outhouse (the scene of many a terror-filled expedition when the wind howled and the darkness threw up unspeakable shadow monsters cast by a single candle) and my father's old Austin A30, which every summer sagged and laboured under the weight of our camping gear, as we set off for six glorious weeks at Point Lonsdale.

The tower of holiday equipment loomed precariously, well above the roofline: two wooden bed bases, mattresses and bedding (double and single), a trestle table, six folding chairs, an icebox, camping stove, kitchenware, beach umbrella, beach towels, car fridge, clothing and a tent to which my mother had added several annexes over the years on her Singer sewing machine, resulting in a marquee which would easily house the entire Moscow Circus.

In this photograph, I am wearing my favourite floral 'pinny' and I am smiling into the lens of the camera held by my cousin Betty, a helplessly thin, overly coiffed, perfectly groomed and highly nervous individual who picked constantly at unseen specks of fluff which threatened to violate her couture and who had won a local beauty pageant for all her pains.

This woman, the adopted daughter of my Aunt Lucy and Uncle Percy, was another victim of too much care. Her parents' vision of her as the epitome of grace and beauty became her duty to fulfil, despite her own enormous fears to the contrary, for Betty did not see what they saw and Betty did not love the person who looked back at her from her (ironically named) vanity mirror.

In some form of subconscious vandalism, she married a handsome brute of a man who ensured her disfigurement. He blackened her eyes, broke her nose, kicked her from one side of the house to the other and hauled her out of bed by the hair at three in the morning to make food for his drunken entourage.

Eventually, wasted and pale, she escaped this ordeal and, as compensation, later married a plain and deeply kind man who, sadly, came too late to heal her inner wounds. She died of cancer at the age of forty-three, with what was left of her peroxided hair scattered thinly on the pillow.

This photograph, however, was taken at a time of limitless possibilities and it captures the pure essence of childhood wonderment, unsullied by cares; a precious moment of abandon, taken by another adult by whom I was loved and cherished.

Most importantly, this swing was made for me by my father, by those same hands that, over all these years, I had only ever associated with pushing me off his lap, pushing me away. While I felt protected by his ramparts of stability and sturdiness, I did not feel loved by these things. I only knew that my daddy did not want to hold me and I could only conclude in my childish way that this must be because of some intrinsic flaw within me.

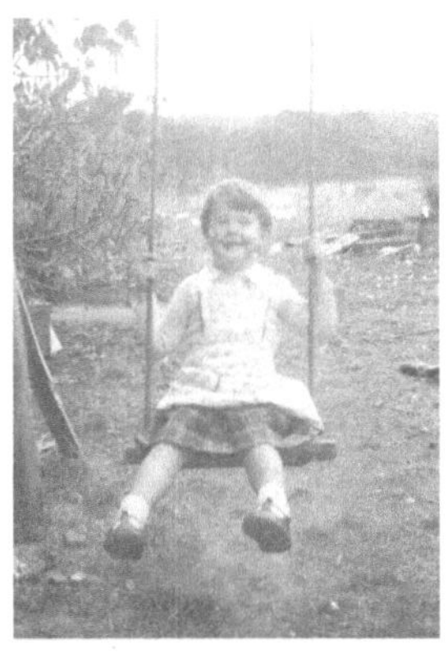

I discovered a new playmate, exactly my size. Her name was Shame and Shame whispered, 'There must be something wrong with *you*!' At first, she was no more than a vague unease, a frisson of grey; but over time she would grow to such dimensions as to steer my life along a path that was always accompanied by an undercurrent of fear and inner loathing. Shame was the soundtrack behind my life, the whispered treacheries that said I was wrong, different, unloveable and manifested in many human forms who were to populate my later life.

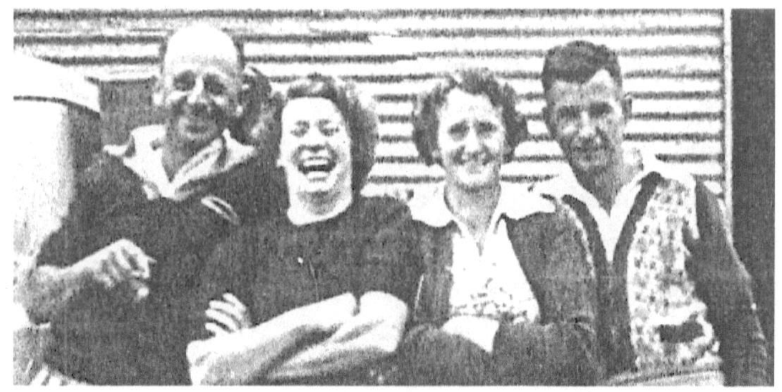

Whether Cyril Burge and my father would have chosen to be friends, or whether their friendship was by a natural osmosis of the blended families, is difficult to say. My father was a fiercely private man whose solitary nature did not encourage intimacy or mateship as a rule.

Cyril (or Geordie as he was affectionately known, for obscure reasons) was a loud, rambunctious, mischievous foil to my quiet, withdrawn, no-nonsense father. As a child, I found Cyril a little frightening with his brash and rough-edged ways, so unlike my quiet and restrained father. He frequently used words like 'bloody' and 'bastard', which I was firmly instructed to ignore.

On the other hand, Jess became something of an idol and a surrogate mother to me. A strong, practical, determined woman, she held me in thrall with her tinkling, wicked laughter and her solid and focused presence, which contrasted with my mother's more petulant and changeable nature.

Her children were brought up briskly and with little fuss, in the manner typical of a farmer's wife who fronts life's challenges with a jutted chin, yet her nurturing side often surfaced in surprising ways and she spoiled me rotten.

She fostered an orphaned joey found in the fields next to its dead mother. The joey hung in a hessian sack next to the ever-blazing combustion stove and was fed from a baby's bottle. The cat, however, was not extended the same generosity. When it was found sleeping in the front-loader washing machine, it was given a few spins to teach it what was what.

Whenever I stayed at 'Glendora', my freshly laid breakfast eggs were accompanied by a sentry line of buttery toast 'soldiers' and at other times there would be some heavenly scented treat fresh from the combustion stove awaiting me. At night, during these stay-overs, I would share a double bed with my namesake. The eerie creaks and moans of the old house caused me to twitch and turn in my attempts to sleep, for which Bev would gently but firmly chastise me with 'Bevie, lay still!' and I obediently lay stiff as a board till my muscles ached. To me, Bev was a placid, calm angel, and a natural nurturer whose innate maternalism was well suited to her career as a mothercraft nurse.

Later, at the age of eight, I was her flower-girl – an esteemed role that was so eagerly awaited; the excitement so fuelled by all the feminine preparations, I thought I would burst. There were the fittings for the dresses with Mrs McPherson, the elderly dressmaker – her house redolent with the ever-present waft of 4711 eau de Cologne – who engineered miracles from shushing layers of fabric: whispering tulle and lace and dainty teardrops of pearls painstakingly sewn onto the bride's gown. With a mouthful of pins, she tweaked the tiny pink rosebuds that adorned my headdress, which was itself shaped like a cup of petals that was to crown my newly permed curls.

Bev was marrying Norm, an army cook from Queensland, who, soon after, would leave for a tour of duty in Vietnam. Norm was a handsome, dark-haired man with a wonderful sense of life and fun.

On the day of the wedding, the heavens conspired to create a downpour of such Biblical proportions, the house was soon surrounded by a muddy bog. Norm valiantly carried me to the bridal car to spare my dress and spotless shoes but Bill, who was groomsman, did not fare so well. In his haste he slipped in the mud at the gate of my parents' house and fell head-first into the mire in his brand-new suit while, at the same time, badly gouging his leg on a rock.

My mother and Aunt Lucy had little time for sympathy. Bill was unceremoniously stripped of the suit and stood there nursing his wound, along with his modesty, while the suit was quickly cleaned and pressed. He was dispatched with a firm warning that he was not to limp, even if his life depended on it.

Too soon, the magic day ended and it was time for the bride and groom to depart. The entire company formed a circle for the farewells and, as was the tradition, linked hands and sang 'Wish me luck as you wave me goodbye', wherein Vera Lynn urged us to not shed a tear and remain in good cheer.

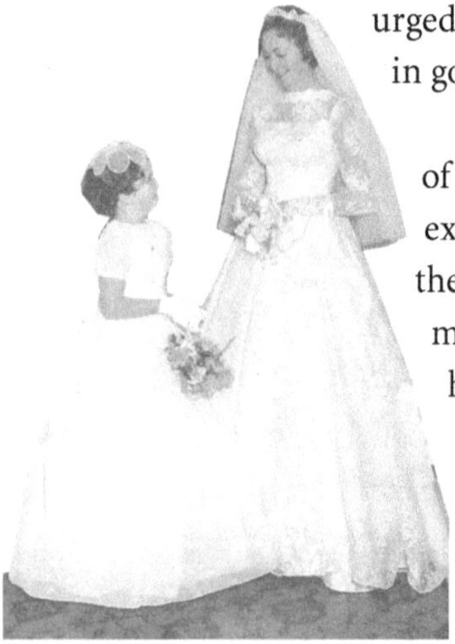

But I did shed a tear. The strains of the song, the intoxicating excitement and the departure of the princess of my childhood had me weeping till I thought my heart would break.

Norm survived Vietnam physically unscathed but Bev was beside herself with fear during his absence. She worried herself into a stomach ulcer and became frightfully thin. By then she had given birth to Mark, the child Norm would only come to know upon his return.

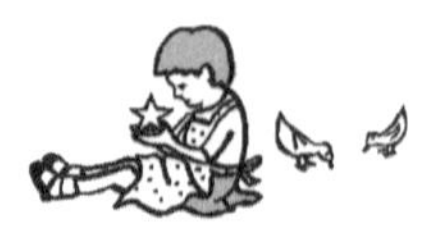

I loved the woolshed. I loved it when it was clamorous with activity; the muscular shearers bending to their task with fierce-set faces and sweat-slicked arms as they plied their whirring shears to the yielding fleece.

The wall-eyed sheep, lined up like asylum inmates shuffling to their fate, bleated pitifully as they surrendered their pink and vulnerable undersides to the blade. Carved open, their white vests fell to the floor in curly capes, exposing grotesquely cadaverous bodies beneath. Bewildered, quivering, the denuded beasts staggered away, sometimes aided by a kick to the rear, as the next was tackled roughly to the ground between the shearer's legs.

I skulked around the edges, my presence tolerated but not encouraged; a child – worse, a *girl*-child – intruding into this holy bastion of maleness. I remember the men in their greasy blue singlets, or rather, the sense of these men but not their faces. There was no kind stranger here. I was just the little spy and they a faceless, nomadic mob, anonymous as the sheep they shore.

And I loved the woolshed when it was empty, after the men had suddenly departed. The silence still echoed with their presence, as if the riot of noise and bluster of the preceding weeks had left an energetic imprint on the air that lingered long after the last blade fell silent.

I loved the tick and groan as the old building settled back on her haunches, the whistle and shriek as wind fluted through chinks in the boards and the tiny percussions of pine needles and branches on the old tin roof.

But most of all, I loved the woolshed on party nights, when fairy lights trailed along the roof-line and tables groaned with country fare. I would gaze with faint horror as the corpse of one unfortunate beast rotated on the barbecue spit from early afternoon as it would for hours, legs splayed; the stump of its neck skewered by a steel rod which exited disgracefully at the other end.

At sunset, a procession of finned, candy-coloured cars wound its way along the dirt track and parked haphazardly on the grass verges beside the shed. From them emerged women with towering beehives, skirts flaring like mushrooms and vertiginous high heels. Teetering and preening, they plucked their way across the grass, aerating the soil with their progress.

Their escorts, in thin-legged pants, spear-toed shoes and white shirts grappled and tugged at unfamiliar ties which would soon be abandoned altogether and with these arrivals came a tide of chattering, ascending excitement which caught me in its wake.

I remember the Twist and the seesawing twirl of skirt and petticoat, the Limbo and its acrobatic gyrations beneath a broomstick; men drinking from brown bottles and young women clustered into whispering coteries while their older counterparts transported towering plates back and forth throughout the night.

Thrilled and enthralled, I arched my back and pulled in my little round tummy under the broomstick as the adults applauded. I drank fluorescent-coloured cordial and allowed myself to be navigated awkwardly around the dance floor by some calloused adult hands, sometimes balancing on the toes of large male shoes, proud in my party dress, yet shy in this strange configuration.

I played in concert with the wild and alien creatures that were other children, excited to be included in the pack, but in my insular world of adults I was at the same time awkward and unfamiliar with the unspoken rules of a tribe that had been toughened by an upbringing that involved sharing with siblings.

Delighted to be accepted, I became drunk with it: giggling too hard, hurling myself around the room screaming in a game of chasey, stuffing myself with unladylike handfuls of food and shrieking at the top of my lungs as we popped a balloon behind the startled head of an elderly lady. Finally, exhausted, bloated and mildly nauseous, I sank against my mother's side, willing my eyes to stay open, engaged in a losing fight between lingering excitement and consuming fatigue. The party was over. Soon, I would be carried to the car and ferried home, full of pretty dreams.

But there was a shadow that for now was just out of sight.

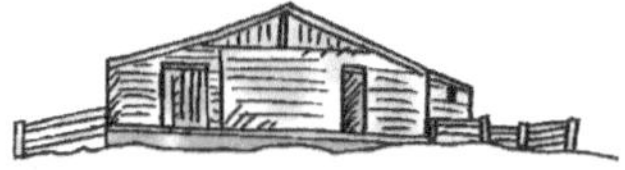

I search my childhood for clues but none seem to readily explain such ongoing unease, pointless distress and ferocious terror that plagued me in adult life. I had good parents with an average but not excessive number of neuroses; I was not beaten, starved or locked in a cellar. I had a nice, pretty bedroom and nice, pretty frocks and a pet cat and a mother who cooked nice food and a father who worked hard to keep us in a nice house and a brother who teased me but loved me nonetheless. My childhood was filled with people and life and things to look forward to.

When I was eight, my parents moved into the township and, for the first time, I had the experience of being in a neighbourhood. The phone rang often and a steady stream of visitors bearing cakes and preserves appeared, calling 'Yoo hoo!' at the screen door; there were hours spent sitting and talking on someone's brick fence or riding bikes in lazy circles out on the street.

In summer, there were entire days spent diving, swimming, splashing and ducking (or being ducked) at the local pool and telephone calls begging the manager to re-open after dinner if the temperature remained over 85 degrees. There were camping holidays or trips to country locations for picnics and Sunday drives with the men in the front seat of the Holden and the women and children consigned to the rear. There were fetes and fairs and balls and barbecues. There were dolls and playhouses, teddies and tea-sets. There was Sunday School and singing solo in my best dress at the annual concert. And later, there were best friends and boyfriends and a boarder, the daughter of an itinerant bridge-builder, who became my little sister for a year.

And yet, there was also an unease, lurking always in the background. Sometimes it loomed large; at others it fell out of sight but never completely disappeared.

Could it really have been my uncertain arrival that made my existence thereafter seem so treacherous?

Ann, my therapist, thought so. I saw her weekly for over a year to unravel the most stubborn remaining knots in my psyche that had been left too long and tightened onto themselves. 'A trauma in the pre-language stage has one of the greatest impacts on the sense of emotional security in the individual – greater even than trauma that may be experienced by an adult as a result of war, accident or abuse, simply because all the *feelings* are absorbed but there are not yet the means to interpret or articulate them,' she explained.

I search the Internet and find evidence from a variety of sources suggesting that one's time in the womb is not an unthinking coma of sweet oblivion but is deeply impacted by any number of stresses to which the developing foetus may be exposed:

> *The earlier the trauma during womb life the more disastrous the effects. That is our important secret.*
> **Arthur Janov, PhD. Extract from www.primal-page.com**

> Foetal life *is not drifting on a cloud, [but is] as eventful as the nine months that come after birth. The foetus is not unaware of itself, or of the emotional response of the mother to its presence, but acutely conscious of both and their interaction.*
> **Frank Lake, MD, *Mutual Caring*, Emeth Press, Lexington, 2008. Extract from www.primal-page.com**

Not only this but I discover that stress, trauma and pain in infancy reduces one's tolerance to these in the future and can also weaken the body's defences.

> *Dr Janov writes that someone can be born with all kinds of allergies. A history of emergency clinic visits for all kinds of infections, asthma, breathing problems, and in general, having a very deficient immune system is not uncommon.*
>
> *To understand the origins of much ill health in youth, middle age and old age, we need to go back in time and direct our attention to those early months in the womb. When we do, we often find out that the mother-to-be was quite anxious and/or depressed.*
>
> **Extract from www.primal-page.com**

Reading this, it all starts to make sense.

Even now, I'm trying to shut the gate after the horse has bolted, as if I can fix things from the arse end of the problem, by taking a supplement or eating the right food or whatever.

Just last week, I had (yet another) CT scan for (yet another) sinus infection after (yet another) allergic reaction and (yet another) flu that began in autumn, raged through winter and never really went away.

I have had tissues stuffed up my sleeves as far back as I can remember. I recall my mother complaining as her washing was once again turned into lamingtons by one she had overlooked.

I recall feeling tired and ratty to some degree all my life and realise that irritation by life in general is now firmly implanted in my DNA; it has been virtually impossible for me not to be irritated physically, intellectually or emotionally in some way. My barriers were down from the moment I slipped off the landing bay and it is only with years of emotional sandbagging that I have any barriers at all.

'Poor old me!' I now think, having blamed myself mercilessly for being too touchy, too easily aroused, when the pressures of life were often simply too overwhelming, too confusing and, like a porcupine rolling into a ball with its spikes up, I protected myself in the only way I knew how. And without adequate filters, any opportunist: a bug, a bugbear or a bugger, would be only too willing to take advantage.

I look at my childhood and, not only is there the trauma of my unsettled womb-life but also a further shadow: someone trusted, who got his rocks off with nasty masturbatory games at my expense when I was eight. I never told – sworn as I was to secrecy, I was too frightened of blame to disobey – and as the years progressed I sometimes wondered did it really matter after all this time? And that was the question my brother asked when I finally confided in him decades later.

Of course! Why should it matter? It's not like there was *penetration*! Just some young guy foolin' around, experimenting; no real harm done. What's the big deal? Why then, forever after, did I sleep on my stomach with the blankets over my head, one hand over my mouth (*Don't tell!*) and the other protecting my groin?

Why then, on those occasions over the years when we happened to attend the same events, did I feel myself stiffen; the unspoken words snagging angrily in my throat: *Don't think I've forgotten, mate!*

Why did sex, after the first rush of love, sometimes feel pneumatic, controlling, intrusive, predatory?

But hey, no big deal! So I stayed quiet, for I knew his tribe were more fierce in their loyalty and pride than mine and I knew that to speak would be deemed the greater crime, in the end.

Tuesday 3 August 2010

This morning I have woken in a palpitating and unsettled state, as if my subconscious has been hard at work in my sleep, frantically sorting through all the back-files for the next spook to be put to rest and flagging this particular candidate for further evaluation before final eviction. Somehow.

This acknowledging, allowing, accepting and releasing will never be finished; there will always be the next thing and the next, layer upon layer and these things only arise when you're up for it, though that may seem far from true in the thick of some desperate internal battle or the depths of a musty bog-hole of depression.

My brother was right I suppose. It only matters if I let it matter. But was this whole of it? Was there something more, now hidden from memory? Sometimes there is a knowing – a ferocious *YES* – tiny glimpses, fleeting and intangible but the only hard evidence is the greatness of the fear.

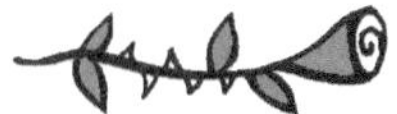

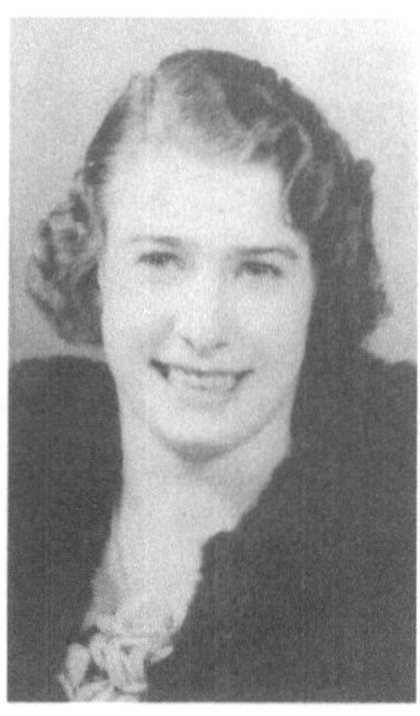

A rivalry common to country women was based on who was the best cook in the community and my mother and Jess both vied fiercely for this prestigious position, each with her own specialties.

No doubt I owe my slight childhood obesity (generously named puppy fat) to these cook-offs. My earliest memories are redolent with the sights and smells of sponges, caramel tarts, butterfly cakes, lamingtons, scones, nut loaves, lemon meringue pies, tea cakes and trifles.

Millie and Jess presented to me two contrasting images of womanhood and, because I loved both in equal measure, I emulated them in equal measure; thus I am hard and soft, practical and indulgent, masculine and feminine, forthright and flirtatious, no-nonsense and neurotic, persistent and procrastinating, mature and immature, determined and tentative, independent and accommodating.

The friendship of these two women was the song that ran behind my life; their love and influence forging my dichotomous nature. For my mother, the playfulness and easy exchange of laughter and knowing asides with Jess, the familiarity and camaraderie, were an antidote to the restrained and dutiful life she lived with my father.

My mother, a bright, sociable, impulsive and deeply feminine character, reminds me now of a vibrant, multi-hued butterfly, pinned by the wings to a man who was ever old, a father figure to her childlike ways, a prosaic pragmatist, prone to sarcasm and putdowns, a man twelve years her senior whose sober, sensible, yet unimaginative character threatened to drain all the colour from her kaleidoscopic inner world. She coped by flitting and fluttering from one gay bloom to the next, through engaging in any and all of the social events that made up small-town family and community life in the 50s and 60s.

A birthday party or afternoon tea (of which there were many) was made more memorable, more 'pretty' in my mother's care. The best floral china cups and saucers, lace place cloths and tiered cake stands with their tantalising cargo would emerge; the silverware, polished and gleaming, was released from its wooden case; the house, cleaned from top to bottom, was offset by an artful floral display and, beaming at the centre of a nest of chattering, nattering ladies in high heels, perms and beehives would be my handsome mother, her broad mouth curved into a crescent, erupting now and then into devilish laughter that rippled infectiously around the room.

It was as if she felt that Fate had dealt her a far inferior role than she was destined to fulfil. She gathered friendships like wildflowers and in no time had people under her spell, making them feel as though they were desperately interesting and important, while flirtatiously raising her pinky when sipping tea or smiling sweetly enough to harden the hardest heart. But she also carried the air of someone frustrated to be playing to this small, incestuous arena, as if she was really meant for a far more sophisticated audience than small-town Broadford, population 3,600.

In Millicent's secret thoughts her talents were wasted on this bunch of unrefined yokels, when she could have been holding court with some debonair jet-setting crowd, just like in those

Cary Grant movies where women wear furs and diamonds and have men eat out of their hand and drink champagne from their shoe.

She reminded me, during those soirees, of a southern belle at a cotillion – charming, seductive and being forceably gay. But when the last car drove away, her light went out along with the spotlight. Cinderella returned to her true roots, the pitifully poor and uneducated farm girl who had slept in an apple box as a baby and was woken by a rat gnawing on her cheek, and who was sent out at thirteen to find work – as my father had been at the same age. She found work as a housekeeper for a wealthy family and, no doubt, it was in these environs that her fantasies of a higher social station emerged.

It was in the midst of her dreary day-to-day life that her full character was revealed and an impetuous and petulant streak would assert itself, which confused and confounded me. The line became blurred between best friend and authority figure and a war of wills was fought between us, which would often lead to seismic eruptions, especially through my moody teenage years. It was Mother who disciplined me. The ultimate threat was always 'Wait till your father gets home' but this was mostly an empty threat.

I encountered a new experience of intimacy – that the capacity to love was proportionate to the capacity to hate and I loved and hated my mother by turns with equal intensity, but one thing that was never in doubt was the powerful and ever-present force that she represented in my life.

Even as an adult, I seldom made one major decision without mentally seeking her approval. There were few areas of my life over which she did not hold dominion but she was also my ultimate confidante, my sounding board, my Mother Confessor and my best friend. She was the sun, the life force, the shining hope, the magical goddess who held me to her voluptuous bosom and caused my deep, dark, Gothic fears to run from her light. But she was also the soft prison, who held too tight, who confided too much, who conspired with me and divided my loyalties.

Above all, she was my foothold on a life that, as the years progressed, became more and more difficult to negotiate. The torrid force of my emotions, the growing stockpile of hurts, rejections and losses would see me reeling to her knee for comfort. But it was this very succour that left me without armour and bound me to her.

Upon her death, at 65 – too early, too soon – mixed within the anguish and grief, I came upon a new emotion: a strange and guilty sense of liberation.

I had been cast adrift, yet sailed free.

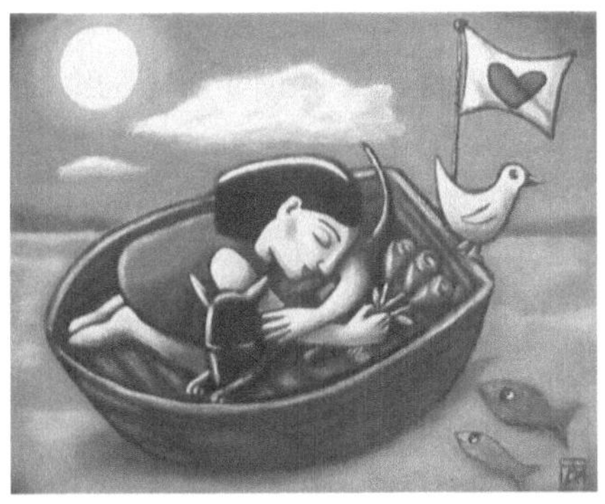

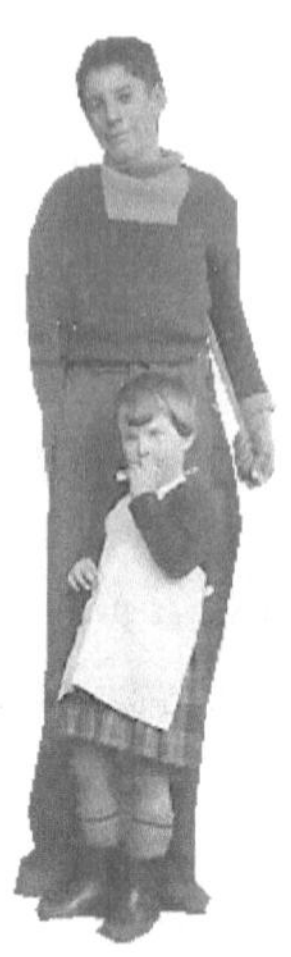

I loved my big brother. He was like another daddy to me – a daddy who did all the things that my real daddy didn't do. He read to me, played with me and taught me how to draw. He liked to teach, especially little kids; it was in his blood and it was inevitable that he would ultimately choose teaching as a career.

He built a wooden toboggan and we hurtled down the hill as I sat squeezed between his legs. I was scared but I knew I was safe if he was there behind me. He shared secrets with me, like the time he drove me fast around the slippery hairpins of Murchison Road to Strath Creek in his FJ. He was hooting and hollering and with the windows down the wind was whipping our hair and I truly thought we would fly, that we would soar up and over the gum trees and away in our blue boat on wheels.

'You musn't tell!' he yelled over the roar of the engine but I was so excited and proud I blabbed the minute we got home and he was roundly hauled over the coals. Even so, he forgave me.

He teased me, though, calling me Puddin', which made me mad, and I'd race at him in a fury and then he'd tickle me, which made me madder still and we'd wrestle till my mother intervened. Some guys called him Aisie, so I will, too.

Aisie told me one night that my hairclip would give me moonstroke and I ran bawling indoors, terrified that I had unwittingly fried my brains as we sprawled out under the stars to escape the heat of the house on a summer night.

Sometimes I watched him in cycling races, flying around the track in a blur of hard breaths and wheels which whirred like dragonflies. His face, tight and grimaced low down near the handlebars, was intense with concentration and his legs seemed as big as tree trunks, powering past.

One day, he had a bad fall. I caught a glimpse of him lying on his bed and a flash of red before the door was quietly closed to me as my parents inspected the damage. I loitered outside, caught between fear and curiosity, imagining the gore and grisliness of the business going on in that room, till eventually my parents reappeared and reassured me that he would survive, but he never raced again.

He tried again and again to win me a teddy bear I had my heart set on at a carnival, spending too much of his meagre wages in the effort, till my father called a halt. I wailed as we walked away but that Christmas, under the tree, was a beautiful teddy bear, just like the one at the fair.

He left home when I was four to train in Bendigo as a schoolteacher and then began a round of rural placements, which included his first year teaching Grade One at Broadford Primary School when I was in Preps. His dual role as brother and teacher confused me. I could not bring myself to call him Mr Aisbett, nor did it feel right to call him by his first name, so I refused to call him anything and avoided him as much as possible.

In the following years he was assigned to schools throughout rural Victoria and I only saw him on school holidays. In a way he then stopped being my big brother and became something else – a special visitor who arrived in a wave of giddy anticipation and left for another world a few weeks later.

Occasionally he brought home young women who were exotic and intriguing, with their towers of fairy floss hair, billowing skirts and high heels which made dents in my mother's linoleum. I hovered around, peeking through the crack in the door as they were entertained in the lounge room, dancing to Bill Haley and sipping soft drinks or shandies from frosted glasses, leaving lipstick on the rim. I saw it as my duty to report any indiscretions to my mother, who was discreetly busying herself in the kitchen and, occasionally, I noticed strange kissing going on which was nothing like the kisses that my brother gave the rest of the family.

On one occasion he and a mate were set for a night at the drive-in with twin sisters, the daughters of family friends, with whom we were staying for the school holidays. For some reason, my brother was coerced or ordered to take me along.

The movie was so scary I spent the night cowering under the dashboard with my eyes closed and fingers in my ears. I wanted to go to the toilet but the others were too busy pashing and ignored my pleas. I held on as long as I could but it was too late. After much swearing, gagging and covering of noses by the occupants of the car, I was ordered to hold the offending underwear out of the car window all the way home, which not only brought any of my brother's amorous ambitions for the night to an inglorious halt but also ensured that we were both to face my mother's wrath when we walked through the door on our return.

Eventually, he brought home someone called Eileen and there was an excessive amount of kissing all round at her arrival. She even kissed me like she knew me. Everyone was misty-eyed and gushing when she held out her hand to show off her new diamond ring.

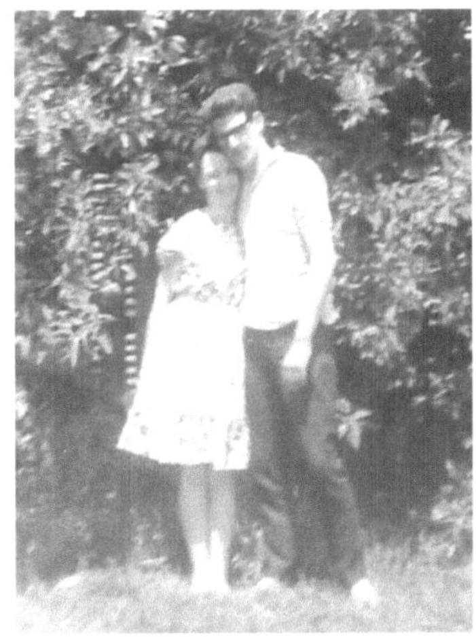
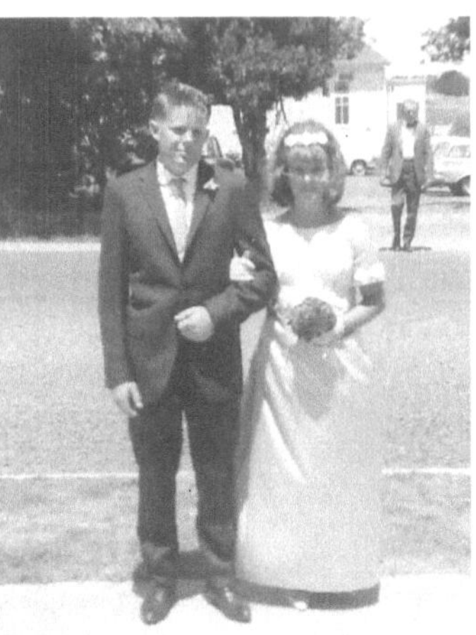
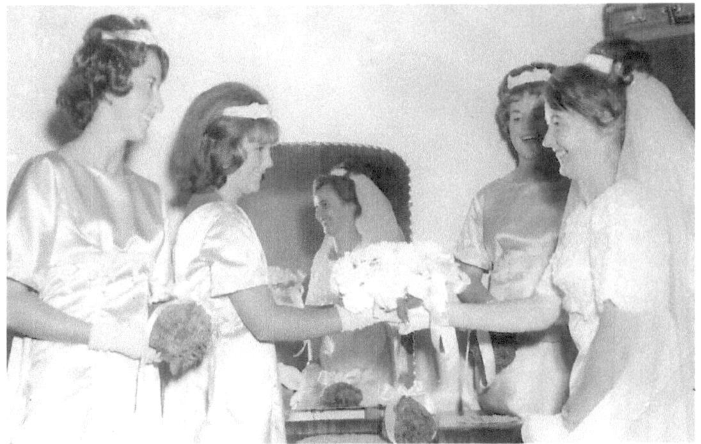

I was 'junior bridesmaid' at their wedding, awkward and excited at the age of thirteen, with an equally awkward and somewhat reluctant teenage partner in tow, who had been recruited from family friends for the occasion.

Because of the gulf of our years and the long absences, I did not have the chance to come to know my brother as a brother; to evolve with him as siblings in a long unfolding of shared memories and secret codes. By the time the gap was closed by my own adulthood, he and I were both set on different courses. My brother had become a Husband and a Father and there was no immediate prospect of my having either of those in my life.

The bond between us was our name, this name that somehow carried a distant discord, as if tainted by some long-ago sadness that lingered still within the sharpness of the A or the snakelike S, or the final bett that became a but – '*Life is good, but …, I am happy, but …, I am loved, but …*' So much so, that my brother always unconsciously ended his sentences this way.

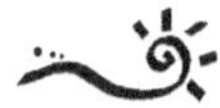

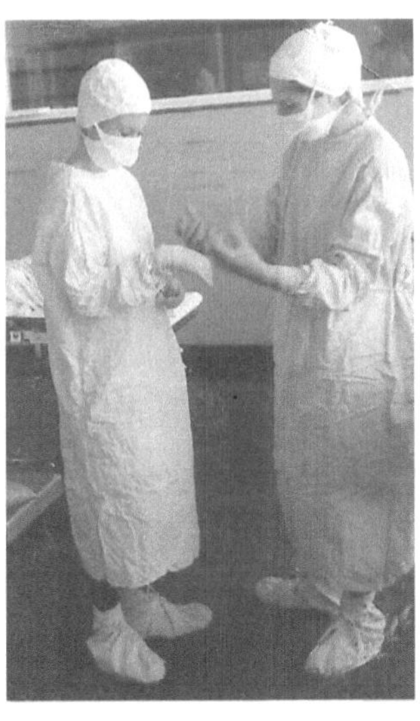

Though I had been an excellent student, my parents were struggling financially and asked if there was some career that I felt I could do at my Form 5 (Year 11) level of education. I was keen to move to the city for a big adventure, so I did not fully take into consideration the frustration that I would later feel as a result of not having taken my education to the higher level that I was easily capable of.

Surprisingly, I actually liked my dentist – having undergone extensive orthodontic work – and the dentist I saw on our trips to Melbourne was an extremely kind and gentle man. These trips usually coincided with treats such as a restaurant lunch, a movie and shopping in the Big Smoke, so clearly, the positive associations were high.

As a result, I opted to enrol for training as a dental nurse at The Royal Dental Hospital of Melbourne, thus turning my back not only on small-town life but also on any aspirations I might have had to pursue a more creative or intellectual path.

The move to Melbourne was a rude shock. No longer did people smile or greet me in the street. I spent the first few years of my young adulthood bored and restless in the company of elderly ladies in two boarding houses, the first of which had been arranged to ease my transition to the city, whereas it had the opposite effect of leaving me feeling lonely and alienated.

Worse still for me was the fact that many of my schoolfriends, as well as newcomers from other classes, were encouraged by my mother to visit in my absence, as she and my father both worked at the high school as janitors and my mother had befriended the kids there, some of whom were virtual strangers to me. I felt as though my mother had substituted these kids for me in my absence and that, as a result, I had been left out in the cold.

A year later I met a slightly older engineering student called Greg. Greg rode a motorbike and I was often the fearless pillion gripping on for dear life while he and his mates raced around the hairpin bends of the Boulevarde in the staid and leafy suburb of Kew.

Greg and I saw each other for a year, when unexpectedly he announced that he had decided that it might be best if we parted because he had to study for exams and would not be able to see me for several months. Naturally, I told him that I would wait for him. 'You'd do that for me?' he asked. 'Of course!' But he insisted that the separation was necessary. Several months later, one of my friends ran into Greg. He was engaged.

This was an early and significant chapter in what was to become my 'Abandonment Story'. There would be many more chapters to come.

Eventually, I moved out of the boarding-house situations when my second elderly landlady could no longer tolerate my pop music and late-night rousings after I had gone out and forgotten the key. I moved into a ramshackle bungalow behind an equally ramshackle house rented by an eccentric couple and their gaunt, vacant-eyed child. Gordon often knocked on the door with a bottle in hand and took great delight in shocking me by telling me that his wife shaved her pubic hair into a heart shape. They supplemented their dole payments by phoning tow truck companies when there was a collision on the main intersection near our property, which was quite a lucrative pursuit, as, without traffic lights on the four-way intersection, there were prangs several times a night.

I recruited a dental-nursing friend, Sue, to be my flatmate and soon our bungalow became the venue for many legendary parties and late-night visits by no doubt randy dental students who fancied their chances (but failed the bet). Given that our neighbours often invited themselves to these events, noise was not an issue.

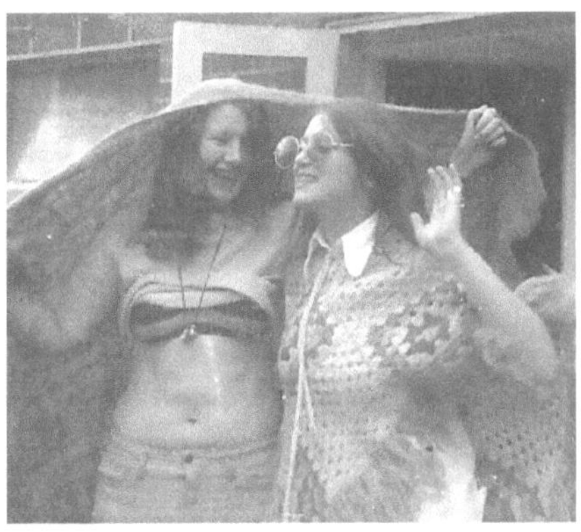

With this new popularity, my sense of freedom expanded and I began to enjoy city life, heading out with a gang called the 'Brighton Crowd' on all sorts of strange expeditions, dreamed up by one or the other of the group, including the 'Great Yabbie Catching Competition'.

My crazy Irish friend and workmate, Geraldine, eventually moved in with me after Sue's conservative parents dragged her home again and we began seeing Julian and Rob, friends from the Outpost Inn, our regular blues and folk haunt in the city.

This led to experiments with marijuana supplied by the boys and a trip to experience a key event in 70s history, the Sunbury Festival, which was Victoria's 'Woodstock'. Just like its American forebear, the festival was 'Three Days of Peace, Love and Music' on land provided for the event by a local farmer. It was the hippie dream, featuring some of the finest musicians of the era.

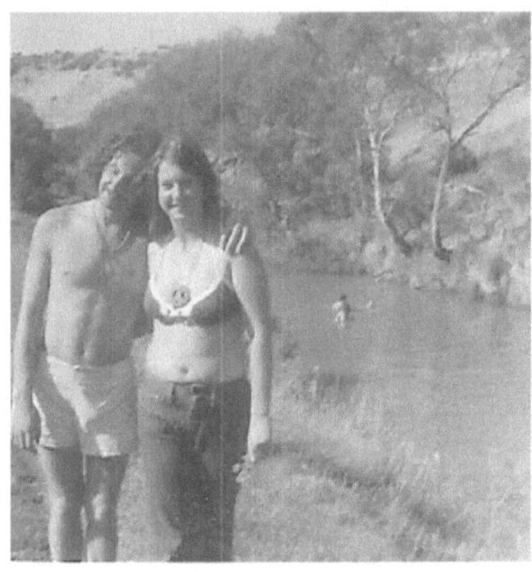

Not long after, Julian ended our relationship, then Geraldine's parents, also concerned about the goings-on in our grungy flat, ordered her home. I was devastated.

I suppose one could call my reaction to Julian's, then Geraldine's, departure as 'separation anxiety'. I wept fretfully when Geraldine left and clung hysterically to Julian at the eleventh hour in a desperate hope that he would reconsider. It must have taken great strength on his part to walk away.

I then moved into a flat in East Melbourne, in a building mainly occupied by middle-aged hermits, not far from my cousin, Betty, and opposite my old dentist friend, who, in my naivety, I saw as a substitute family figure until it became painfully apparent that this was not the case. This was a far cry from the fun and excitement I had so recently known. Living alone seemed the only option but I was not suited to such solitude and, now located some distance from my friends, my evenings and weekends were often unbearably empty.

Eventually, I met Gary, who worked in the Public Service (Pensions A–K) but who had aspirations to be a drummer, which he did in time realise.

Within twelve months, I received a phone call from my old schoolfriend, Marg, offering me a place in a communal house (previously an old shop) with six others in Carlton. I now found myself deep in the heart of 'Hippiedom' and I loved it. Carlton, which was then Melbourne's Haight-Ashbury, was abuzz with all that was of the time.

Not having been reared with siblings, I had little prior experience of being in the bosom of a large family group such as this household represented. I revelled in the stimulation and variety the household afforded and felt affirmed by being included, though I often chafed on some of the others, unused as I was to the dynamics of communal living.

We often hosted huge, all-night parties at the house and the air was thick with the smell of wine, cigarettes and joints. We went to uni gigs, crawling along stoned at 20 km/h in someone's ancient car. These events were truly 'psychedelic' with dim lighting, projected images of multi-coloured bubble shapes on the walls and the intoxicating experimental music of the time. It was not uncommon in those days to simply walk into someone's house, if they looked like a 'head', and share a joint, food or even a bed with them before heading back to your own place.

A powerful memory of this time is of walking along Lygon Street in a batik kaftan, my long hair held back from my face with a leather thong and hearing for the first time the din of clocks on Pink Floyd's *Dark Side of the Moon* as I walked past a record shop.

Something new and exciting was unfolding and it was symbolised by the audacity of the music. It was our time and there would be no other like it and it would be worshipped and emulated in fashion, song and film for decades to come and there would even be some who would never leave it behind.

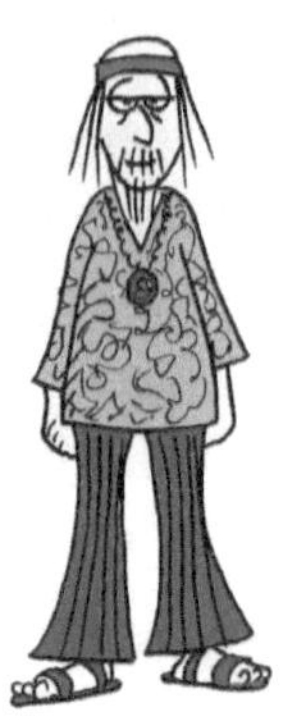

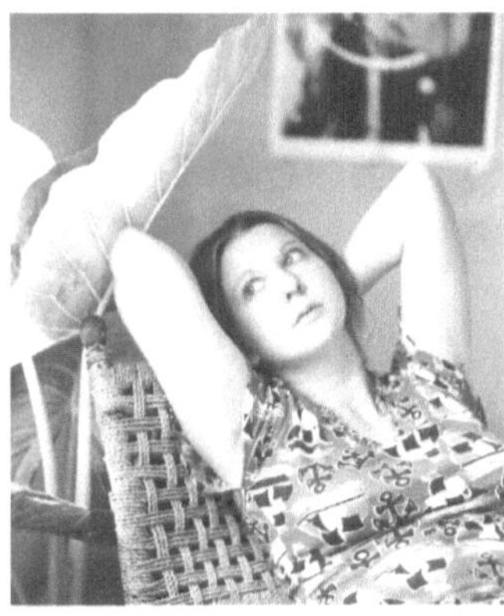

The changes and expansion in my domestic world were beginning to highlight the shortcomings of my career choice. At the dental hospital I was subjected to the same, if not a greater institutional hierarchy than I had known in my schooldays and with my rebellion and revolution in the air, I was soon chafing against the rigid and authoritarian structure of the hospital system.

The times were instead calling for freedom and expression and I began to experiment with art, as I had done from my earliest years, and found great release and pleasure in doing so. It was evident that I had a certain gift and a good eye but I had never really thought in terms beyond my own tinkering.

One of the members of Gary's band (who were now playing four nights a week at Lazar's Restaurant) was studying photography and I often trailed behind him like a puppy on his excursions, soaking up the excitement of a life making art that I so envied and secretly wished for myself.

Both Gary and I were photographed by Dave and for my twenty-first birthday he presented me with a portrait he had taken one stoned Sunday of dress-ups, which depicted me as the Joel Grey character of MC in the film of that year, *Cabaret*.

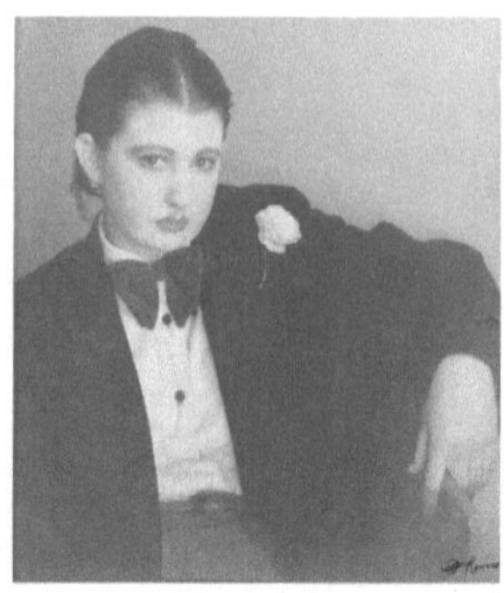

It was also David who convinced me to submit my humble folio of drawings to Prahran College of Advanced Education and, to my great surprise, I was accepted into the Art and Design Course, majoring in photography. However, when I delivered the news, my parents were less than thrilled by my announcement that I was leaving dental nursing to do art.

Having come from impoverished backgrounds, my parents were keen that I pursue a trade that would provide well for me until I inevitably met and married someone who would take over that role. That I would step out into such risky territory after four years of training was both shocking and treacherous to their way of thinking. Art was, at best, a hobby and their disappointment in my decision, while based on reasonable concern for my wellbeing, was yet another handicap to my shaky belief in myself. I longed for them to share in my excitement and when they did not, it placed a strain on our bond.

Eventually, being a 'muso's widow' became wearing and Gary and I started fighting frequently and eventually drifted apart. A year earlier we had become 'engaged', even announcing it to our parents, but luckily it was a passing youthful fancy that had no grounds in reality. The idea had simply dissolved over time.

I moved into another shared household in Fitzroy and began my new life as a student at the age of twenty-one. I loved being a student; especially a student surrounded by art. I realised that this is what my heart had been waiting for and I now knew why I had been so determined to follow some inner pull, despite my parents' disdain.

My teachers were of the highest calibre in their fields: Paul Cox (film director), Athol Shmith (renowned fashion photographer) and John Cato (highly awarded landscape photographer).

I subsidised my studies by working several nights a week in various strange jobs, the worst being on a process line in a slipper factory, where I was required to snip the loose threads left after the slippers had been sewn. I lasted only a few weeks there before my brain turned to porridge.

My next job involved delivering meals in a private hospital. Many of the patients were elderly and in advanced stages of dementia (one ninety-year-old woman declared, 'I know why you've got me in here! I'm pregnant and no-one has told me!'). It was not uncommon to deliver the food only to discover that the recipient would never be eating a meal again.

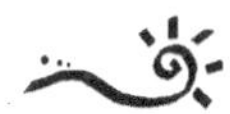

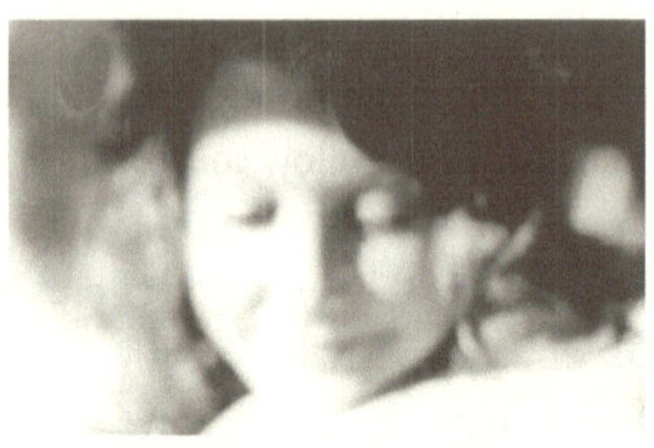

If ever I wish to invoke a good feeling, I invariably take myself back to a single day – in fact a single hour – in the summer of 1975.

Why my psyche has chosen this as its retreat is unknown to me, for there is nothing particularly extraordinary about this day. There have certainly been more momentous hours in my life but this one small fragment of a time, so long ago, remains a symbol of sweet contentment and peace.

I am gently swinging in a hammock on the front porch of an old farmhouse on the back road from Hastings to Rosebud. I have a Tequila Sunrise in my hand and I am gazing off across the parched land to a bank of scrappy eucalypts that border the road along the fence line. I am watching the sun flick and fleck in dappled patterns through the leaves and I can hear the lazy drawl of a crow lulled by the somnolence of summer heat.

The air chimes with stuttering cicadas and above, the sky is a seamless, sacred blue dome of perfection as the dry, crisp grass prostrates itself beneath a sudden wind shift from the north. From within the house, I hear Van Morrison playing. This morning I had woken for the first time to his musical poetry/ poetic music and had fallen into a trance just like Madam George. Now it winds along the hallway and out the open door to float and dance through all my senses till I am swept away by *the loves to love the loves to love the loves to love …*

Inside I can hear my friends Paul, Johnnie, Pat, Reinholt

and a strange, pale creature called Lori (Reinholt's girlfriend), a vegetarian who contrarily subsists on nothing but eggs.

All is well. I am drunk on the day. All possibilities are launched before me like the cluster of birds that now banks in a white curlicue into the sky. I do not even care to name these possibilities for, in the precociousness of my youth, I take for a fact my birthright to a good life. How could my life be anything other than a delight?

Just look at this day: the glory of it, the heady, heavy, heat-hazed perfume of it, the hymn of it, the perfection of it, for there is only this now and the music and the sway of the hammock and a delicious, carefree confidence in the constancy of this present abundance, in the certainty that peace and love are my entitlements and joy my true and natural state.

Paul and Larry were Canadian friends from Vancouver who were travelling around Australia. Paul had hooked up with Johnnie two nights before and when they visited me, I hitched a ride to the farmhouse on the back of Paul's motorbike.

Late that night, I had been suddenly seized by an urge to present myself in Paul's bedroom. There I stayed and in doing so I would soon join him and Larry on a wild adventure across the then unpaved Nullarbor to Perth in a Morris van complete with tie-dyed cushions and my own paintings of Emerson, Lake and Palmer's record cover armadillo/tank on the back and William Blake's *Ancient of Days* on the side.

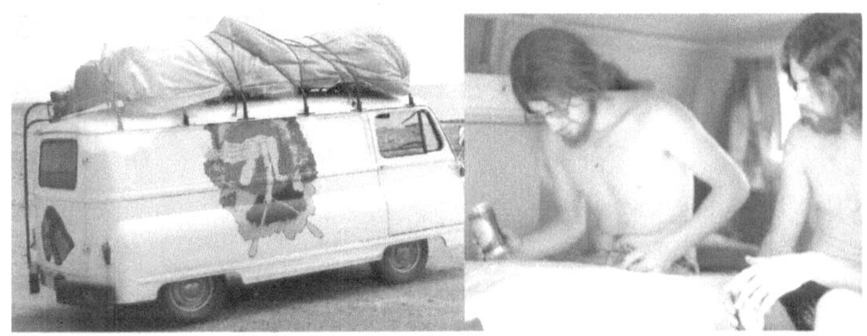

It was part of the liberation of those times to unquestioningly obey the whims and desires of the moment. We explored and played with childlike and innocent spontaneity, however transient our interludes turned out to be. We were guided by a principle of freedom and it was intoxicating and exhilarating to throw off the stifling and claustrophobic social mores of the previous decades' prim and parsimonious view on life, love and above all, sex.

The times invited us to dive in and swim with the currents of our true nature – to trust, rather than analyse; to accept rather than judge. We danced and played in this new and intoxicating stream. Life was an adventure and the world was our playground.

We were high on life but wanted to be higher still, sensing that there were planes of experience undreamed of that were yet within our reach. With a little help, we could straddle the Universe and unlock its mysteries and its secrets, so tantalisingly woven through our music, our art, and our mystical gypsy attire.

We read Carlos Castaneda, Timothy Leary and Hermann Hesse, which further piqued our curiosity and our desire to search within. We sought the keys to unlock our perception and the keys came in kilos in zip-lock sandwich bags and matchboxes and small foil packages or tiny dots on tissue paper; or for some, freedom came at great cost: via a steel spike and a ripe blue vein.

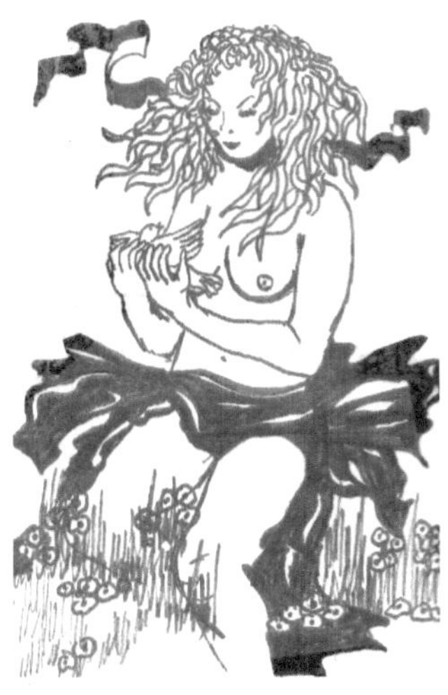

My three-month summer in Perth was so filled with joy, friendship, adventure and freedom that I was crestfallen when it came time to return to Melbourne. Not only was I saying goodbye to friends and a place where I felt part of a 'family', I was also saying goodbye to Paul, who was continuing on his travels.

As we drove to the airport for my first-ever flight, while watching an ascending plane I was broadsided by a surge of nauseating fear as it dawned on me that I was soon going to be locked into a steel capsule and jettisoned into thin air with no way out.

Distraught from the goodbyes and fighting an escalating claustrophobia, I took my seat next to two elderly ladies. Before long, the doors were clamped shut and as the metal coffin began to taxi along the runway, I was seized by a full-blown panic attack. 'I have to get out! I have to get out! Get me out, now!' I panted, pointlessly fumbling with the safety belt.

'Oh no, you can't get out, dear,' one of my companions offered helpfully, which only set me off again. Once airborne, I summoned an attendant, who moved me to another seat and sat with me till I calmed down enough to complete the flight.

Interestingly, in years to come, I would fly again without any fear; in fact, I would fly all the way across the world, but on this future occasion, it would be because I *wanted* to.

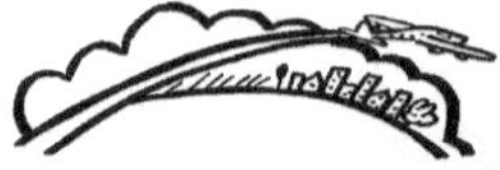

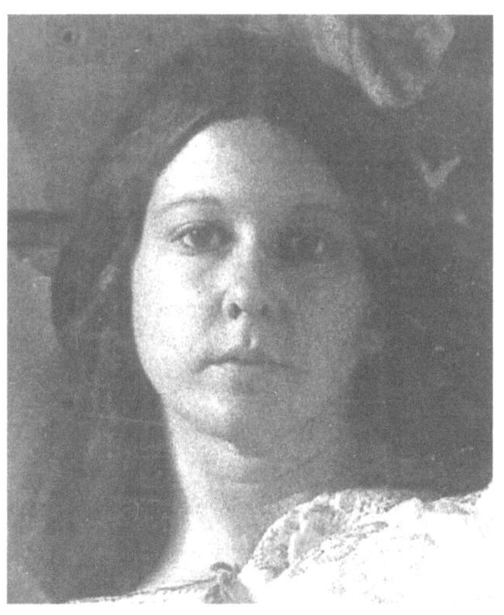

As the weeks of that blissful summer drifted into memory, the leaves outside my window drifted earthward with the first prickles of autumn tweaking the air and I found myself slumped in a persistent melancholy.

Though I knew Paul was destined to continue on his journey, the bond between us, to my mind, over-rode any practicalities. Why wasn't he fighting to stay with me? Larry had returned to Melbourne for Ilona, the girl he had met in Perth. Why hadn't Paul done the same for me?

I haunted the letterbox, hungry for slim hope. Mail came sparingly – Paul was never a good correspondent – and was more often postcards; which spoke only of travel news and day-to-day events, crammed into a few lines.

I replied with dismal poem letters that betrayed my melancholia.

Sunday 28 March 1975

Easter, schmeaster,
Holiday, schmoliday
Getting better, getting worse,
Who knows?
Empty house,
Sleeping cat
I've got a cat,
How about that?

... Don't know if I feel anything
Right now
I think of you and wonder
What tomorrow will bring
And that's the thing
The sting
I don't fucking know.

I had moved into a new household, ideally located immediately opposite the college, sharing with students who were a couple, which only heightened my sense of loneliness, especially when their seismic sex resounded through the house on frequent occasions.

My temporary salvation came when I befriended members of another group household who lived in a two-storey Victorian terrace on busy Punt Road, a few blocks away. I visited frequently; in fact, I virtually lived there. Being once again part of a 'family' lifted my spirits and restored some of my delicate balance.

Friends of this household were living the country life with their baby in rural Daylesford, west of Melbourne and a group of us visited one weekend. The final leg of the journey involved a bone-shattering, bumpy trip in a single-carriage train, then a long walk from the station along a dirt road, with our shadows stretching out before us, lit by the late-afternoon sun.

The weekend was a tonic; long, lazy walks through the autumn leaves, singing songs by the fire, feasting on home-made vegetable pie and sharing a bath, having boiled and hauled just enough water for one bath among five people. We also sampled the local 'magic mushrooms', known as Blue Meanies. My first experience of these was, indeed, magical. I felt invincible and all-knowing. My second was to be the start of a terrifying ongoing nightmare.

Having just found a delicate emotional balance with my Punt Road family, I was to take another blow. An official letter arrived, informing me that there had been an administrative error regarding my student allowance and I had been overpaid and, though technically it was not my fault, I was required to repay $2000 covering the two years of my studies.

Having stretched my finances for the trip to Perth, this meant that my meagre savings were all but wiped out. I had no choice but to leave college and the life I felt was my true path.

Several weeks later on a grim, overcast and steely day, which also happened to be my friend Laurie's birthday, I made a fatal mistake when I shared with him some of the now dehydrated mushrooms as a birthday treat.

My instincts were telling me that something was not quite right that day. I felt a sense of foreboding that I could not quite shake but neither could I pinpoint its source. Having eaten the mushrooms, we wandered to Punt Road. The air was dense with humidity and there was an ugly and ominous quality to the overcast sky. Upon arrival, we found the members of the household scattered around the upstairs living room listening to Pink Floyd; then I felt the drug kick in.

The music began to take on a sinister edge and the room yawned around me, becoming suddenly vast and cavernous while my friends seemed strangely inaccessible and coolly remote. I stumbled out to the balcony and looked down at the passing traffic and all I could perceive of the people passing in their cars was that they were heartless robots, automatons who stared coldly ahead devoid of compassion or humanity.

Then I was struck by a devastating epiphany which lanced me to the very core. In one dazzling revelation, I realised I was *alone*; deeply and profoundly alone; alone in this body, this mind, this life; alone to face my fate, alone to face my ultimate death.

No-one could reach in and take away pain, fear or loneliness. No-one could save me from my fate, whatever that might be and somehow I sensed that it would be a twisted fate that awaited me, full of sharp edges and sorrows and aching confusions.

Alone, I was trapped in my difficult psyche from which there was no rescue; no lover, mother, father, or God could protect me from this *I* that I was and this *I* was fearful, overwhelmed and *abandoned* in the Universe. This *I* was damned.

Never did I feel fear so intensely as in that moment, when wave after wave of anxiety consumed me, so powerful that I thought I would faint from sheer terror. It was a tsunami of fear and I found myself locked into a surreal dream from which I could never awaken, for that dream was life itself.

You can't get out, dear! I heard again the old woman's voice and this time I knew what those words meant, in the deepest sense; that even if this life was unbearable, I was trapped in its dream. Life, or death – there was no way out. Hour after hour, panic surged through me. My friends tried to calm me but I was unreachable. They assured me that it was just the drug and that all would be well when it wore off.

But it wasn't. Not the next day, nor the next, nor the next. I had glimpsed the abyss; there was no turning back. I had entered the world of anxiety and I could barely function with the eerie sense of disconnection that had overtaken me. My heart thundered in my chest and I was consumed by a nameless, shapeless dread for which I could find no comforting antidote. I could not define the malaise that I felt but I had stumbled into a cold and barren outland from which I feared I would never return. I often felt a rush of fear so great that I would cry out, alarming and confounding my housemates.

Soon after, we were forced to vacate the house, which was something of a small relief to me. I hoped that a change of scenery and occupants would snap me out of whatever constituted this freakish state that I was living in.

Larry and Ilona agreed to share a new house with me and two other people and on many a night, they comforted me as I sat rocking beside their bed.

Tuesday 11 August 1981

I watched the film Sybil *tonight, which was based on the true story of a woman with 16 different personalities. It took me back to 1975, when I was fighting my own madness.*

That time seems like another world to me now – being so crippled by fear that I could not leave the house. I would pace around long after the others were asleep, unable to sleep or I would sit by Larry and Ilona's bed, rocking back and forth, my arms locked around me, whimpering 'Help me, help me.'

Sleep did not come easily at either end of the day. Nights, I would lay there feeling every nerve ending in my body. I had to have a candle burning by the bed because the darkness swallowed me so. Dawn brought only the pain of consciousness.

My mother brought me a bunch of dainty purple flowers. I put them on my dressing table and watched them in the flicker of the candle's flame. I remember how I was so touched by their fragile beauty – but even the momentary comfort they gave was tinged by sorrow, for I knew that they would wither and die and all the mirror would then reflect was the person who had become a stranger to me, a child trapped and whimpering for release.

Life itself was a chain – I had no choice but to exist, on and on, to exist in fear, for eternity it seemed.

Fear of fear itself made me claustrophobic. I was afraid simply because I drew breath. Yet death offered no respite: the great unknown, greater and more forbidding than this living hell where I hovered like an Earth-bound ghost. I could not believe that death would be any kinder to me than the world.

Friends became a burden of my own guilt. I feared that I would drive them away with my crazy pain and a few I did.

I sketched a woman with a head encased in an iron box, trying to find her own reflection in a mirror. I clawed at the plaster of my bedroom wall one night, as if I could break down the wall that blocked me from inner peace.

Today, I have forgotten what that fear was like. It is as if it was a great pain; too much for my psyche to recall, in the same way that the pain of childbirth is forgotten after the event. I am describing something that happened to someone else, long ago.

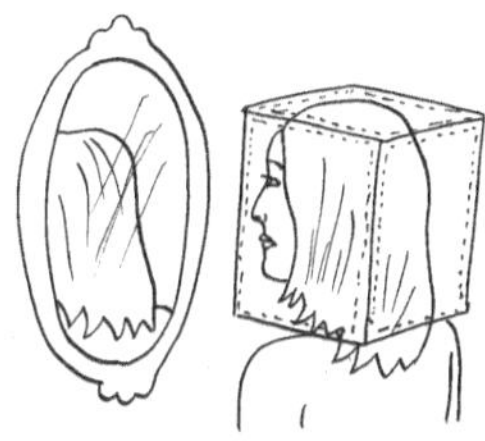

In the end, I was so distraught that Larry wrote to Paul and urged him to return in the hope that it might lift me out of my misery before it was too late.

I sought psychiatric help from the Malvern Clinic but turned on my heels when the caricature of a psychiatrist appeared and promptly berated me for being late. A short, stumpy woman in a savagely cropped bob, tweed skirt and sensible shoes, glasses perched on the end of her nose and a clipped German accent, she conjured in me an idea me that if I followed her through those doors, I would not return in one piece. Here was the feared bureaucracy of our times. After all, I had seen *One Flew Over the Cuckoo's Nest*. I didn't want shock therapy or a lobotomy.

It was my brother who eventually led me to my salvation. One of his teacher colleagues had been training as a counsellor and he asked if she would see me.

Wednesday 16 June 1975

Last night, I rang the counsellor Aisie told me about. I was in such a terrible state she urged me to come immediately. I didn't take much convincing. Larry drove me to see Jan, my very own Dr Wilbur.

I remember little of that hour-long journey, except that it was raining and already late. But I do know that the person who travelled back along that dark road, not long before dawn, was someone clutching a tiny hope, a tiny shining thing, that with time would grow. Much time.

Jan introduced me to Transactional Analysis, which is based on identifying and moderating the inner voices of Parent, Adult and Child and aiming for the balanced perspective of the adult. This wonderful woman gave freely of her time over many weeks until I began to find my feet under her guidance. I learned that my self-talk swung wildly between the two extremes of admonishing Parent and fearful or precocious Child and that what was mostly missing was a moderator, the Adult, which would provide perspective and balance, once I consistently tuned in to its middle-ground view.

The profound philosophical ponderings that had so overwhelmed me were downgraded to more manageable concerns, with a realisation that it was best not to burden myself with things beyond my control. Instead, Jan encouraged faith and hope in the future which, even though a concept that for me was still more wishful thinking than belief, was still preferable to downright terror.

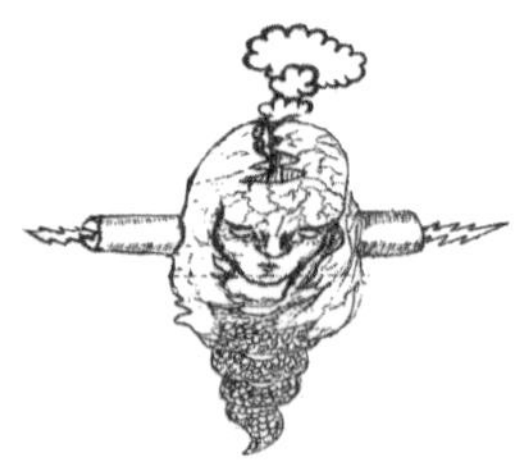

Paul's return was supposed to be temporary, as he was on his way to New Zealand, but in the end, I travelled there with him for a year. The stability of a relationship further calmed my fears and my anxiety slowly subsided.

In its place were the wonders of this breathtakingly beautiful country as we travelled around the North Island prior to settling in windy Wellington on the bottom-most tip, where we lived and worked in a fairly uneventful way until, in the last weeks prior to our return to Melbourne, we decided to travel around the spectacular South Island.

The relationship had paled for me in recent months. Having regained my strength, I was again hungry for life and felt too young to be confined to a settled life with one person. There were adventures awaiting me that I had been denied through my affliction and I yearned to explore this new freedom.

An American artist crossed my path halfway through the trip and my desire to break free surfaced in a rush of hedonistic impulsiveness, which meant that it was Paul who was abandoned this time. The irony of this did not escape me. I had longed for Paul to return to me yet when he had done so, I felt trapped in mediocrity.

I felt ashamed. I knew my behaviour was fickle, unkind and selfish. It seemed I was never satisfied, always seeking drama and excitement in any form, yet I could no more change this aspect of my nature than change the colour of my eyes.

It was to be my destiny that I would not find what I sought from one source. I feared that I would never find it at all because my needs and nature were of such changeable stuff. Something that gave me peace and pleasure one day would chafe and irritate the next. Deep down, I was motivated by a fear of finding myself in the trenches of tedium that I saw as settled domesticity; a fear informed by my mother's quiet desperation and the deadening of her bright spirit that marriage and the mundane had cost her – and it terrified me.

But I was not running from Paul or my parents as much as I was running from what I saw as a life lived small and this was not so much a matter of choice but a calling of Fate that I was obliged to follow.

I Google Paul S on the Internet, on the off-chance he may pop up and if so, I imagine he will most likely be back in his beloved Canada. I am astounded by the synchronicity of things. I find him running a vineyard with his wife in Tasmania, just over an hour from Hobart, where I will be visiting for the opening of my latest exhibition in a month's time.

> Date: Monday, 4 October 2010
>
> Subject: Hello from a ghost from hippie days
>
> Hi Paul,
>
> I'm sure this email will come as a surprise (if not a shock) but I happened upon a picture of you (long story) at your vineyard (congratulations!) and I thought, good grief, it is actually you (still recognisable!) and I thought, what the hell, I'll send this off, see what happens.
>
> I'll actually be coming to the Apple Isle in November – Hobart – I have some paintings at a gallery there and if you have forgiven me for being such a selfish little turd 30 odd years ago, it would be a lovely thing to catch up on all these years (well, I hope it would).
>
> If not, totally fine.
>
> All the best,
>
> Bev

I see no reply for ten days. My default guilt rises. Have I not been forgiven, even after thirty-four years? I then open my Junk Mail folder and discover that Paul had answered, almost immediately.

Date: Wednesday, 6 October

Re: Hello from a ghost from hippie days

Hello Beverly, I can almost see you cringe at that name or have you changed?

Great to get your email, have often wondered where you were at and how you were doing. Its been a little while since the last time we saw each other, so much to catch up. My story is pretty mundane but really enjoyable. After swearing off Aussie women and Scorpios, who should I meet a few months later in Thailand but Louise, an Aussie Scorpio!

We travelled together and ended up getting married in England to keep the immigration people happy and thirty two years, three kids and a granddaughter later I'm growing grapes in Tasmania. It would be very fine to catch up and I could fill in some more details and find out about you. Saw your web page and so proud to see you doing so well.

Do you still drink wine? If so you will be coming to the right spot.

Cheers Paul

I smiled to myself. So he married the right woman after all.

His warm reply was generous in itself but in a phone call soon afterwards, Paul also offers to pick me up from the airport and invites me to stay at the vineyard.

I recognise him immediately, despite the grey peppering now much shorter hair; it is that same kind face that I knew long ago. We exchange an unusual hug, as it must be – a combination of the warmth of past shared intimacy and the coolness of establishing our new status as platonic friends.

We set off in the little red van with the winery logo (designed by Paul's son) on the side, to wind through spectacular landscape which features an almost complete complement of natural elements; as if, when designing Tassie, God couldn't decide which attractive feature to leave out, so threw them all into this one small island.

Paul's hometown is a sleepy harbour in the off-season but will soon be thronging with summer tourists. The vineyard is picturesque, leading down a hedge-lined slope which affords a view of the sea in the distance and mountains hugging the harbour and is garlanded by Louise's horticultural touches: irises, roses, azaleas, red hot pokers and the tantalisingly named naked ladies.

Louise arrives home from work. I greet her with, 'Hi Louise, lovely to meet you. Thanks so much for having me stay.'

'Um hmm,' she replies.

It is not quite the response to put me at ease but, strangely, I am not as thrown as I might once have been. I am here on a quest to like myself and to accept these good people who have welcomed me into their home as they are. I will take it as it comes.

Over the next days, I come to know that this is just Louise's understated way. There are none of the usual embellishments, there is the same 'Um hmm' in response to any compliments or niceties and one night, when I have washed all the wine glasses from a progressive dinner at their house which has proceeded on to the next location, there is no conventional thank you, just a comment the next day to the effect that I am welcome to wash glasses anytime I feel like it.

I observe that for once I am actually okay with being emotionally 'left to myself' as it were and am pleased to find that, at last, my ego is occupying the back seat more and more these days.

Of course, as is the case any time I get comfortable with the idea that I have something sussed, my ego is again challenged a few days later, when Paul takes me to see Port Arthur. As we wind through wild, craggy and strappy landscape, I tell him that now I have come to know her I like Louise very much.

'I found people's reactions interesting when I told them about this visit,' I say. 'A couple of old-school types couldn't understand how I could even contemplate visiting an old boyfriend who was *married.* "My wife would never hear of it!" one said. "She would have had a fit!" Others were more open but still thought I was being rather brave. Only a few of the more enlightened had no issue with it at all. The way I see it, after thirty years in a relationship, surely you'd be fairly insecure to feel threatened, wouldn't you?'

'Hmm, well, it was a bit tricky for Louise, your coming,' Paul says.

'Really?'

Yet again it occurs to me how differently I see things at times.

'You know you were Beverley Bitchface for a long time?' he says.

Bitchface. The word clatters around the car and lands in a wasp-sting in my stomach. Is that who I still am? Is that who was invited to stay? Am I a private joke, whispered about under the covers when I have gone to bed feeling happy about how well we've all gotten on? Did he turn from my email and say, 'Hey, I've just had a message from Beverley Bitchface!'?

I say nothing, even though I can hear Paul scrambling to back-pedal through my silence. I need time to let this work its way through my internal computer – sorting through the files for the most ego-less, self-loving response.

I open the folder marked Paranoia and decide that, yes, there is a bit of that. Next I add the thick folder marked Guilt to the pile, then Precious, then finally shuffle through a few in the Other People section, trying to decide which is my stuff and which is not.

We wander through the gloomy ruins of the convict settlement and though I am engaged by the outing – the atmosphere, the grim history and our small talk – the comment has lodged itself and I know it will sit there, undigested, until I talk it through.

On the way back, I finally speak up.

'Umm, having a wee bit of trouble processing the Bitchface thing, Paul.'

I explain how it felt like a slap in the face, given that this was for me a journey intended to knock off any sharp corners and to write a new and healing chapter. To my annoyance, I find myself crying – just a little – not so much over this but for all the times I have felt the brunt of another's disdain in the past.

Paul, in his quiet and even manner, explains that the nickname was actually Louise's term and that it had been no more than a kind of knee-jerk protective device aimed at the unknown ex-girlfriend who had broken her man's heart.

The talk cleared the air. I felt another old insecurity release and dissipate and was thankful that this had led to my being relieved of a further layer of toxic dross.

That evening, Paul drove into Hobart for a meeting, which left Louise and me together. Surprisingly, Louise began to open up. 'Has he changed much?' she asked.

'Not really,' I replied, before I had fully assessed where this question might be leading. 'I don't think people do change that much on a fundamental level.'

'Well, I think perhaps I've helped him become softer and he has made me stronger,' she said. 'I mean, that brutal bluntness – his whole family are the same – I spent the first three months that we were together in tears.'

I smiled. 'Funny you should say that. As a matter of fact, just today, I was in tears myself.'

And so I told her about the Bitchface thing and suddenly, all the walls came tumbling down as we fell into the eternal roles of women sharing our frustrations about men. Soon, we were laughing and chatting like old friends and Louise was proudly showing me special keepsakes and mementos around the house.

'I must admit, I did behave appallingly back then.'

'Like a Bitchface,' she said and we both laughed.

'Yes, like a Bitchface.'

'You'll have to dream up a nickname for me,' she said.

But when it came to it, I knew I wouldn't. Some things you simply don't push.

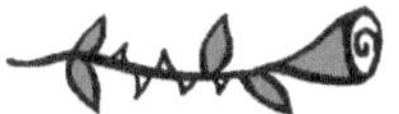

1963

I'm lying in bed and I can see through to the kitchen and there are all the things which will look ordinary in the morning but just now they don't look right; they're kind of creepy.

I feel sort of scared and I don't know why.

The house is quiet. I heard Mum and Dad go to bed a while ago and I should be asleep but I can't stop thinking and now I'm thinking about Death.

I keep thinking about how it goes on and on and on forever, for eternity *and even if I don't want to die, there's no escape, I can't stop it happening and I can't get out and there's nowhere else to go and I'm stuck, there's no way out and now I'm really scared, I'm so scared ... MUM!!*

'Again?' she says when she comes into my room and sits on the bed. She's yawning. I must have woken her up.

I nod, because I can't speak yet. My heart is thumping too hard.

'I don't know why you worry so much about this. You have your whole lifetime ahead of you.'

She strokes my hair and I feel a bit better.

'Besides,' she says, 'it's not as scary when you get older.'

'Really?' I say.

'I promise. Now go to sleep.'

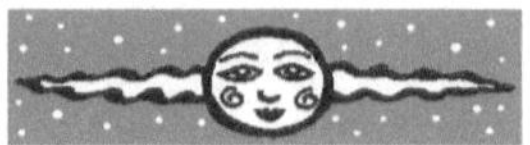

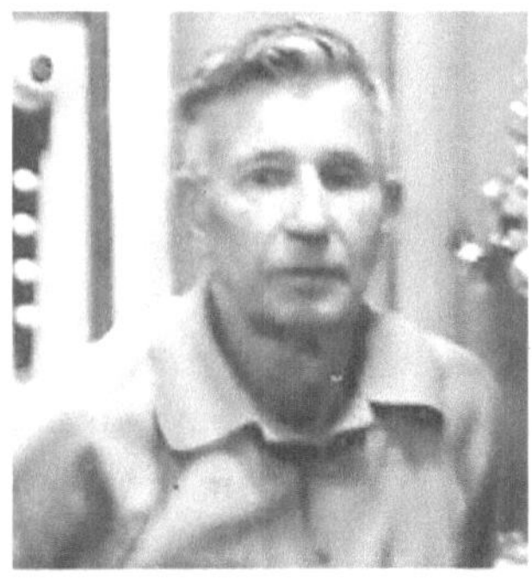

What a strange dream I'm having: someone banging on wood and ringing a bell – four bangs, two rings, sharp and impatient – but now I'm waking up; it's someone at my door.

It was still night, though the sky was now a cobalt blue instead of black – almost dawn. Who could it be at this hour? I stumbled to the door to find my brother, bleary-eyed and pale on my doorstep.

'Dad's gone,' he said.

Still half asleep, I found the phrasing confusing. Gone where? Where would he have gone? And then the reality slowly seeped through to my consciousness. My father was dead.

On Tuesday, 15 February 1978, just over an hour away from me, my father's death had come and gone without my knowledge as I had no phone in my top storey Art Deco flat which overlooked the palm trees along the St Kilda Esplanade.

As we drove out of the city towards the seaside town of Rosebud, popular with retirees like my father ('God's Waiting Room,' I had often quipped), a soft dawn spread its watercolour palette across the sky. I felt strangely calm and disconnected. Wasn't I supposed to be feeling something else? Grief? Pain? Anguish?

No longer would I see this small, wiry, impenetrable man who had been such a shadowy figure in my life. He had always seemed old to me. Twelve years older than my mother and patriarchal in manner, he seemed almost like a parent to her and a grandfather to me.

It had never been clear to me just how he felt towards me. I had been held at arm's length from his heart. I could not recall ever hearing him say he loved me and the pain burned deep within that I had been pushed away. This wound would cause me to seek him out again and again in the men in my life, in my psyche's desperate attempt to heal through a different outcome.

Upon arrival, we found my mother in the front garden, pacing and wringing her hands, eyes wide and verging on panic. I went to her and she gasped breathlessly over and over again, 'What am I going to do?'

I had no answer for that. Live. Grieve. Sell the house. Move on and marry again at the age of sixty, as it transpired.

Over the next hours, visitors came and went, including Jess, and my mother received them with the expression of a frightened deer. In an attempt to be helpful, I made a hippie vegetable soup which Jess took one sniff of and immediately dispatched to the back of the fridge. Soon after, it had disappeared completely.

My brother told me that he and my mother had rushed my father to the hospital during the night in terrible pain. Stoic to the end, he had ordered them from his bedside at the last. He wanted to die as he had lived: alone with his thoughts and without emotional fuss.

My mother had had no prior inkling of just how ill he was – another secret he had kept to himself – except for one occasion the previous week, when she had heard strange, small thuds emanating from the bathroom when he had gone to have a shower. When she investigated, she found him trying in vain to lift his foot over the lip of the shower recess.

But she also told me of a rare moment of tenderness a few days prior to his death, when he had been gazing out at the garden and suddenly turned to her with a look of wonder and softness such as she had rarely seen in him before.

'Darling!' he said. 'Look at the dew on the leaves! It's like diamonds!'

Later in the day, I wandered down to his shed. The light danced with dust motes as it filtered in lasers through the cracks in the boards. I stood in the cool semi-darkness of the room, feeling the silence of the stilled tools, regarding the curls of shaved wood, the jars of screws and nails labelled by his own uneducated hand, observing the dirt floor made smooth and solid by a thousand footsteps; the saw, the hammer, the vice, the drill – and I suddenly understood what I had failed to see before – that *this* was his love for me, right here in this humble shed.

It was the doll's house, the pram and the swing, the cubby house, which was the shell of an old car, hauled and hoisted on a home-made pulley and dragged for yards to be located at the side of the house where the wisteria grew.

It was the rides home from the school dance, the repair of my first car, the new teenage bedroom, built by his hand as I sat and watched him work and convinced him to hammer in time with the Beach Boys' 'Good Vibrations' on the radio and the delight when, just this once, he let himself play with me as the hammer banged out two beats in unison.

And it was then that the tears came for my father, my dad, the simple son of a dirt-poor family from Dimboola, this brave, honest and uncomplaining man with one glass eye who had come into this world to be no more nor less than he had been – a provider and protector, which he had been to the letter and which he had been through his love for me.

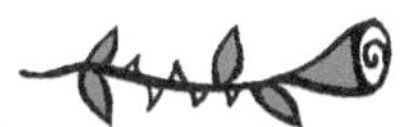

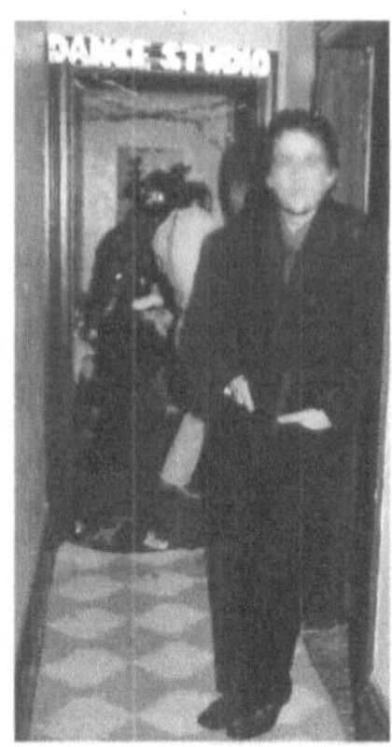

I will call him Mr M, though RM Esquire may be a more accurate and descriptive term for such a character.

Mr M was two years younger than me but seemed much older. He dressed like my father might have: in tweedy jackets with leather patches on the elbows, plain business shirts and a neatly trimmed beard and tidy haircut. The only nod to his youth was a pair of flared jeans and Cuban-heeled riding boots. Even so, he stood out from the rest of us who were starting to emerge from long hair and Indian peasant shirts into the edgy black uniforms of the punk era.

I don't recall the exact time and place of my first encounter with Mr M, apart from it being in the unsettled days of my return from New Zealand and the inglorious end of my time with Paul S. What I do recall is being simultaneously fascinated and bemused by this strange man who spoke like a BBC radio announcer, was witty in a self-deprecating, cynically academic way, who employed quaint and theatrical mannerisms bordering on fey, yet treated me as if I were the embodiment of a goddess, whose every whim it was his duty as a mere male to fulfil.

He was an outsider, as was I, though his difference was more like eccentricity, but I was drawn to the challenge of his intellect and identified with his variance from the norm.

Thursday 1 January 1981

We began the New Year and the new decade with an ill-fated night out with a group of friends, racing from party to nightclub to bar, arguing all the while about where to celebrate as the night edged closer to its finale.

Eventually, we stumbled into 'Bananas', a seedy, tired-looking establishment, populated by the same set of New Year's Eve desperados as we were.

However, I was determined to salvage the night as best I could and dance my way out of the black mood that had engulfed our little entourage: one couple were arguing, Mr M was proceeding to get as drunk as possible, one of our party had fled the scene completely and my date for the night kept telling me to 'Cheer up!', a phrase which can turn me to violence.

After a few more champagnes and considerable determination, I at least managed to see in the New Year with a smattering of enthusiasm but each time I looked at Mr M, I could not help but feel a surge of sadness and pity.

He was so desperate to enjoy his night out but seemed marooned on the edge of the fun and sense of belonging he so yearned for.

He was trying so hard; too hard, as usual and was being ignored, as usual. I wonder how it is that he has landed himself in the position of a secondary human being in most people's eyes. It really is sad. I am his only true friend, it seems, yet even I am guilty of taking him for granted at times.

Back home at the end of the miserable night, Mr M is drunk and in tears. He knows he doesn't fit in the way that others do so casually. He misreads and overcompensates, ladelling on the charm, becoming a parody of himself as he ramps up the intellectualism, not registering that others have long drifted away into a fog of bored indifference. How our innocent crimes condemn us!

I wanted to rescue him from his loneliness – to be the friend who knew him as no other might care to – and in return, he seemed willing to wade through my own complexities and I thought perhaps we could look out for each other, like brother and sister.

Besides, I also needed a new flatmate.

So began the most bizarre four years of my life in his company.

While Mr M often bugged me with his faux poshness and an inertia which tethered him to one epic tome after another, as he sat squinting at the pages and smoking till the early hours, he appealed to and respected my intelligence, and his learnedness fostered in me a love of art, music and literature that would be an influence for the rest of my life.

Mr M and I shared three houses, in the last of which was finally revealed the lost and lonely sham that was the man I thought I knew; I discovered that his life was a complex fictional construction masking a deep sense of failure which would ultimately lead to his breakdown and psychiatric care. Mr M had always been somewhat creative with the truth but soon the lies piled one upon the other. Unbeknown to me, he was in terrible debt, yet he left for work each morning and returned with stories of his day at the office, so I was none the wiser. Soon after, there followed a series of perplexing phone calls from several of my friends. The sneaking suspicion that all was not right, nor true, in the world of Mr M was brought to a climax over a period of weeks.

Tuesday 30 April 1981

The phone rings: Peter, who I haven't heard from in months. M had been around there last night. I might have known something was up, as M only visits those who are really my friends, if he wants something. Sure enough, he was after a loan. No less than $1500, in fact. He told Peter he was making a film, of all things. Peter refused him the money, thank God.

Soon after, the phone rings again: Julie this time, wanting to speak to M. Noting the agitated tone in her voice, I ask if M has hit her for a loan. Yes – this time the figure was $600, and she had agreed to lend it to him. I have no choice but to warn her.

I come away feeling sad and torn: torn between protecting my friends and being the traitor who went behind M's back. I feel afraid for him, that he may actually be going a little crazy. I have noticed a slight unravelling for some time. Now it seems to be slipping into more sinister territory.

Mr M's 'eccentricities' were converting to outright weirdness. He had slept on the floor on two oversized cushions I had given him for temporary use for over three years. He wore the same three sets of clothes in rotation. His few friends had now drifted away and he sat up till all hours, reading, reading, always reading.

It pains me to think that soon he may not have a friend left in the world. I am forced to admit that I cannot save him from himself: frustrated that he cannot see; that he actually believes in this parody of himself, as if he is doing no harm. He has become a cardboard cutout, a fictitious character of his own creation, who is leading the good person inside on a desperate and dangerous dance, where each invention must grow bigger in order to maintain the myth.

Friday 1 May 1981

When I went in to wake M this morning, he said he had been discharged from hospital at 5 a.m. after being mugged and robbed but I didn't know if I could believe that. It seemed every bit as extraordinary as so many of his other stories. I dropped open-ended clues that I knew about yesterday's events but he feigned innocence. I went to work in a solemn mood.

When I came home, he was predictably seated at the dining room table reading a spy novel. Given my inside knowledge, I decided to raise the issue of the unpaid borrowings.

What ensued was quite dramatic. He broke down.

When he eventually recovered he seemed disorientated, but finally acknowledged that there was a problem and it was a big one.

This showdown seemed to have at least jolted him out of his inertia. He promised faithfully to settle all of his debts and began searching for a job in earnest. One day he proudly declared that he had secured a position as a stand-by television announcer for ABC television and even demonstrated his technique with a program promotion and a notification of a break in transmission.

Given his splendid diction and dulcet tones, he seemed perfectly suited to the job, though I found it odd that I seemed to miss his announcements whenever I watched the ABC, which he put down to his 'standby' status.

Each morning, he rose early, showered, shaved and, dressed in jacket and tie, bade me farewell as he went off to work.

Sunday 5 September 1981

Tonight, a phone call from Ruth: 'I must ask you. Can I trust M? I've heard that he is a liar, and I just lent him $800.'

Oh God, not again. In a bizarrely synchronised twist, no sooner had I hung up the phone when the doorbell rang and a policeman stood on the doorstep. He had come regarding parking fines under my name.

M had helpfully offered to pay the fines for me one day (using my money) at the police station he was to be later passing.

I felt anger surge through me. Slamming into his room, I did something I never thought I'd do – I went through his papers. There, I discovered an unpaid gas bill and a disconnection notice due in days, the parking fine notice from the police, money in arrears for TV rental, all of which I had given him to pay, and the final straw – dole slips, dating back months.

Fuming, I investigated further. I rang the ABC and they had never heard of him, of course. The dole office informed me that he had been registered for months and the estate agents reported crossly that we were close to eviction for consistently late rent, even though I religiously handed over my share each month.

I was in a cold, white rage by the time he came home. I do not recall ever before being so angry. He sat with his head down before admitting everything.

'Where did you go each day?' I asked.

'I was trying to get job interviews.'

'You have to do that to stay on the dole anyway! Stop bullshitting me! Where did you really go?' I yelled.

'Okay, yes, all right. The truth is, I sat in the park all day, reading a book till it was time to come home; that is, the time I'd come home if I had a job,' he said and smiled crookedly at his small attempt at levity. 'I also had to check the mail before you saw the dole cheques … I'm sorry,' he added limply.

'I want you out! Now!' I said and, as if he had been expecting this, he immediately rose and walked heavily to the door. As I watched him leave, it was as if he had shrunk; broken and ashamed, he slouched down the hallway and disappeared into the night.

I remained sitting for a long time, trying to grasp the tower of lies that had just come crashing down around me. I had to get out, to walk, think, calm myself. When I returned around midnight, I found him sitting morosely on the doorstep.

'Can I speak with you?' he asked. I nodded and let him in.

He told me that after he'd left, he had rung a personal emergency service which referred him to a psychiatric unit where he was told that had he not appeared that night, he would have deteriorated to the point where he would eventually have not left his room. A further appointment was arranged, along with some tests.

I agreed that he could stay the night while I mulled things over. As usual, when I was faced with multiple options, confusion tended to win. I wondered whether I should be more sympathetic. He had nowhere to go, poor bastard. He was not well. Maybe now that he had finally faced up to it, with professional help he could start to sort things out.

But my trust had been badly broken. I felt used. I prided myself on always being honest and truthful with others and here was someone trusted who had stolen from me, a fact I found impossible to overlook. I decided I would give him time to find his feet, then go through with him leaving. It seemed the best solution.

Sunday 20 September 1981

M leaves tomorrow. These have been strange times. Today was very hard. I realise that he is going to leave a gap in my life; that despite the problems, it's hard to imagine my life without him after all this time. He has almost been family – the eccentric cousin, the wacky uncle.

He too was all over the place emotionally today: lost and on the verge of tears. I felt so utterly helpless to ease the pain that he was going through, and will go through for some time. I identified so strongly with that absolute desolation: the realisation that you are truly alone in the world.

I couldn't bear it for a while: I sat on the back step and cried; mourning for my gentle friend who has fucked up his life so badly that even I have turned him away. I can only take a deep breath, bid him goodbye and wish him well.

But I am forced to acknowledge that with his leaving also goes a four-year security blanket, hassles and all. I realise now how he sheltered and protected me, how he seldom asked that I stand on my own two feet and how much I came to rely on this. Though at times I had felt resentment for his weakness to my whim, overall he protected me from the big bad world.

I thought I was independent but on reflection, he ran errands for me, made sticky business enquiries for me, fed the cats for me, consoled me when I was down and nursed me when I was sick. And here he was, also ill but I could not manage alone financially and was now myself in debt, because of him. How ironic that he came as Ratso, from Midnight Cowboy *at my 'Hollywood' Halloween/ Birthday party.*

When he left that day, I felt as vulnerable as if I were alone in the woods at night in hostile territory – left to fend for myself – as indeed I was. And it was clear why I had let this ridiculous farce go on for so long; why I had chosen to ignore the blatant warning signs and had not been sensible and asked for paperwork; for I had been privy to the loving, gentle and kind-hearted nature underneath his pompous bluff that few others ever took the chance to see.

For a while I regretted having made this decision and was cast into a deep depression for hours but having begun, the story had reached its climax and had now arrived at its dismal finale. But there was still the matter of many debts, including money I would desperately need in the coming months and money I would need to pay my way across the globe one as-yet-unforeseen day in the not-too-distant future.

Months on, friends reported that Mr M was still inventing reality, still dodging bullets, still owed half of Melbourne and was still pushing his luck. Sadly, I remained on the list of debtors, months after he had promised to pay me back.

Eventually I was paid but only after long months of hunting parties, angry showdowns and bitter confrontations which meant that any remaining compassion I might have felt had run completely dry and which left both of us feeling hurt, angry and betrayed; each in our own way.

Many years later, I saw him at a party. 'I don't know you anymore,' he said. I had to agree.

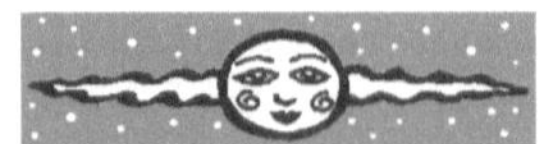

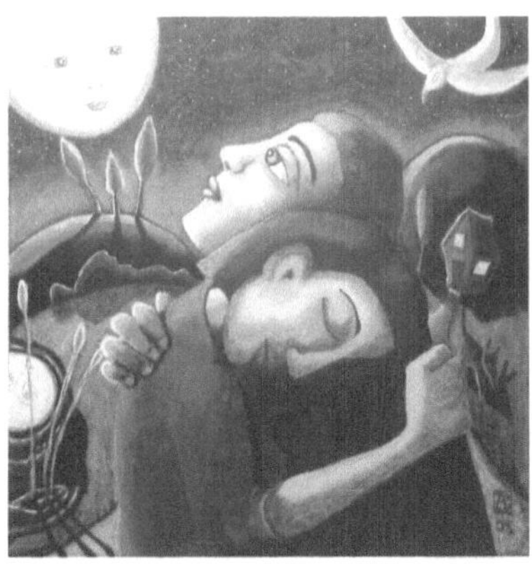

In happier days, Mr M had been virtually joined at the hip with his friend D, a handsome, warm and totally engaging young man who brightened the room with his welcoming and friendly manner; this belied a dark and brooding talent for theatre which would one day be internationally recognised.

At the time, D was in a relationship with an actress, R, who lived nearby but there was a deepening bond between D and me that at first I interpreted only as friendship but which was steadily evolving into something that was harder to define, or deny. D began spending a lot of time at our house, hanging out with M and me and then more often just with me, talking for hours at a time.

One summer afternoon, I had been inspired to decorate our old Kelvinator fridge. As I painted, D sat at the kitchen table, watching me work and chatting easily as we always did. Then I noticed a pause in conversation and looked up to see him gazing intently at me. The look was unmistakable. It spoke of love.

I missed him when, soon after, he departed for three months in England, waking late for the flight and hastily ramming a meagre selection of clothes into a shoulder bag before racing to the airport – and nearly dying of hypothermia on his arrival in freezing London as a result.

Letters came from D, addressed to both of us; then one letter came addressed solely to me. In it was a poem of love and longing, describing a tug-of-war between heart and head and written just before his departure but sent from the safety of distance a month later.

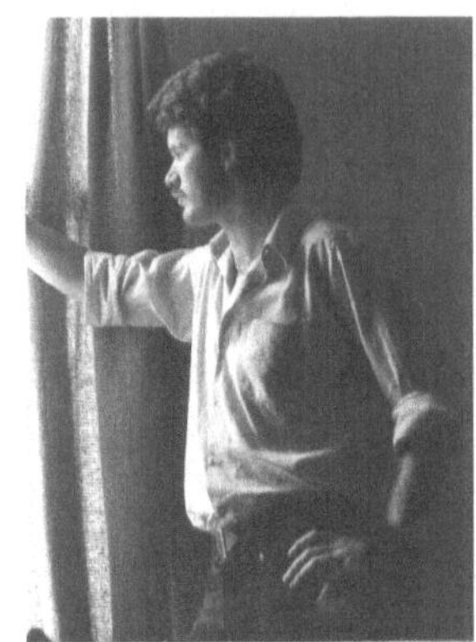

Nonsense thinks 'love'
And cries it out.
The thud of that old word,
Against the heart,
against the head,
against the walls that send it back,
to silence.

And the nonsense one loves you;
and feels you know it,
somehow feels you know it
and fears you know
and hides inside sense ...

His letter opened the way and now that love was declared, it was no longer a hidden secret to others, to our hearts, or to each other; it was now a beautiful fact and a force that, once named, became unstoppable.

He ended his relationship with R soon after his return. She seemed to right herself after the break-up with astonishing speed, wishing us well and maintaining a close friendship with D, bonded as they were by their mutual love of theatre. I was staggered by her resilience and what I perceived as grace at the time.

My own introduction to the stage was at one of D's parties with his drama school friends, where guests were required to put on an ad-lib performance on the spot. I have no recollection of what I came up with that night, but the mixture of exhilaration, fear and elation was addictive.

D also brought with him a world of books and theatre and as a couple, we often visited D's circle of intelligentsia, on which occasions deep discussions unfolded on great writers and literary giants of the past. At those times, I felt once again the sizeable gap between my world and theirs, as the conversations excluded me by way of my limited education.

After one such evening, I asked D to bring me 'every book I should have read by now'. The next day he arrived with a sports bag full of books. For the next weeks or months, I entered the worlds of Dostoyevsky, Camus, Sartre, de Beauvoir, Kafka and others, working my way through the entire contents of the bag. And so was born a writer.

To my surprise and delight, D invited me to join him and two theatre graduates, including R, to form a theatre group. We were to perform a trilogy of edgy and 'punk' pieces: Peter Handke's *Self Accusations*, which required us to bark a list of rules at the audience; Sam Sheppard's *Rock Garden*, a minimalist interpretation of family dynamics; and the grand finale, *Your Children*, the transcript of Charles Manson's defence statement.

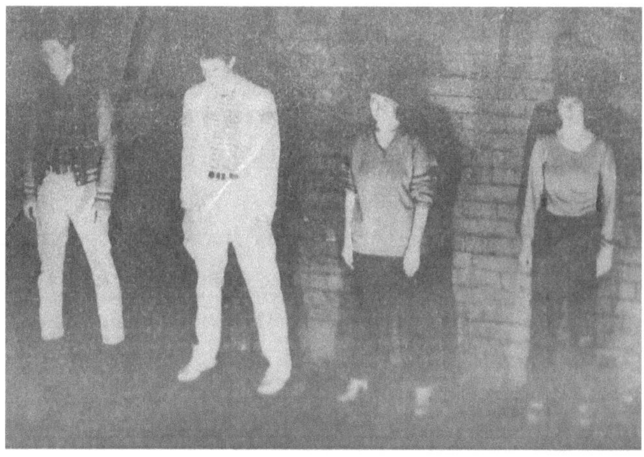

However, the production was fraught with the shifting dynamics of the triumvirate of D, R and myself. While R had initially appeared gracious in the surrendering of her personal relationship with D to a purely professional basis, in my naivety, I did not see the seductive web that was being cast by her aspirations. I also had no sense of the depth and power of a creative union, nor that, in the end, art would win over heart.

D was Tracey to her Hepburn, Bergman to her Ullman, Pollock to her Krasner. She was the Muse and nothing could stand in the way of great art; least of all, this naive little ring-in with her unworldly romantic delusions. As the season progressed, D pulled further away from me and I was helpless to understand this pull, let alone stop it. My tears only served to enrage him and underlined my own shallow comprehension.

R had no car, so I often also chauffeured her home, en route to my house. On one last, fateful occasion, as we drew up outside R's house, D exited the car with her.

'Where are you going?' I asked and I could hear the mawkishness in my voice and hated it for being there.

'For God's sake, we're just going to work!' he said and slammed the door.

And in my heart, I knew then that it was over.

I actually physically felt that heart splinter inside me. I felt those thousand little pieces, like shards of glass, piercing me to the very core.

Above all, I felt I had been condemned for the crime of simply loving him. What had I done wrong? I simply could not grasp how this man, who I knew had loved me with equal passion, could so completely withdraw his affections for a two-dimensional mistress of paper and words, floorboards and footlights and a thousand faceless 'lovers' in the dark.

By now the production had gained some recognition and included performances at some of the leading Melbourne venues: La Mama and in the last days of the once famous and now defunct Pram Factory in Carlton. I dutifully appeared for each performance and remembered my lines and went through the actions but I was an automaton and at the end of the night, drove home alone with my stomach in knots, tears bleeding the traffic and streetlights into a meaningless blur of misery.

On the last night, after almost a year of performances, the ensemble prepared to celebrate. I walked directly to the exit.

'Thanks for *nothing*,' I said.

I was mad with pain. I could hardly bear the emptiness of opening my eyes to the day. I felt so raw and ragged without him. Yet it was more than the man I loved who had been wrenched away: he took with him the awakening of my spirit to a new song; an awakening of creativity and its ever-changing colour that had now been cast to grey.

Discarded like an old rag, I knew that this wound in my splintered heart would never quite heal but instead become a ridged scar that would always remind me: 'I am not good enough.'

The father in one's life represents one's sense of achievement, and here was another 'father' who had pushed me away. My old self-loathing surfaced and boiled into grief and pain and self-directed anger. But grief also released my creativity, which became both my salvation and my weapon, as I began to write from the heart of my sorrow.

The following year, I wrote a short story 'South', which poured forth from the deepest and darkest part of my soul and with which I lured D to my door one last time in the faint hope that the pain and longing so raw on the page might open his heart to me once more.

... I dreamt I saw you on that train. As clear as day you were sitting in that proud way of yours, carving tattoos with your eyes into the night.

And I was hiding behind dark glasses; in case you should see me; in case you should know that I was dreaming of you ...

Excerpt from 'South'

Bev Aisbett 1980

Published in *Carringbush Writing*, 1981

He listened intently from a chair on the far side of the room as I read it to him. 'Bloody genius,' he said when I had finished.

He left me with the highest compliment but still he left me.

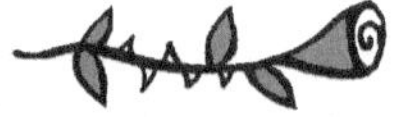

Ironically, D till recently lived in a neighbouring suburb just minutes from me.

I discovered this after I moved here several years ago when, driving past, I saw him thumping furiously along the footpath, hands in pockets and head full of musings, just as he had always done. Without thinking, I pulled over, leapt out of the car and gave him a friendly hug, which I noticed he returned somewhat gingerly.

My self-doubt was still too entrenched to presume that he may have been uncomfortable because of any lingering attraction. I felt old and frazzled and uneasy in my new solitude. Besides, I had read several articles on the famous off-Broadway/hot-in-Europe playwright and knew he was happily married with a brood of children. But his reaction told me that it was unlikely that we could be friends, even after thirty years.

We live in a fairly small community so I often saw him thereafter, which seemed to unsettle him, for despite his theatre training, he put in totally unconvincing performances each time I approached, feigning sudden, intense interest in the nearest shop window or searching wildly in his pocket for that thing that wasn't there in the first place.

I made a kind of naughty sport of approaching him anyway with a cheery 'Hi' just to let him know I was onto the game. Of course he reacted with surprise: 'Oh! Hi!' and would follow with a brief exchange of meaningless commentaries, usually on the time-worn topic of weather, before both of us would be on our way. These current random meetings were so different to all those torturous accidental encounters that dogged me in the time after he had left my side.

Just when I had begun to mercifully forget the exact shape of his face or the sound his boots had made on my doorstep or the way that he bent his head to the side in concentration, he would step off a tram as I went to embark, or enter a café I was just leaving or appear in the same queue for a movie, often with R and on each of these encounters I felt the wound in my heart burst its stitches and I would have to start the long and painful process of healing it all over again.

Fate again throws D across my path just as this book is approved when we arrive at the doctor's surgery at the same time. I tell him about the book and he congratulates me and I ask, in my impetuous way, whether we could perhaps get together to compare notes on our 'hysterical youth'.

'Yes, we all had one of those,' he says.

'I mean, the *theatre* days,' I add, hastily, to make it all sound practical and unthreatening.

He scribbles his phone number on a business card. 'Sure. Give me a call,' he says.

Months pass and I decide to call. His wife answers the phone and informs me that he is overseas. I tell her that I would like to invite them to my forthcoming exhibition and that D was going to help me with a book I'm writing but this all sounds suddenly terribly false and I am hit by just how preposterous a notion it is to have this meeting at all.

How does this woman see me? What does she know of me? Do I present a threat in some way? Has he spoken of me and if so, in what terms? Would they reflect the same love and loss and longing as I am about to express in this book?

I tell myself this is research, that we are all grown-ups and well past all that business but I find myself facing down my hidden motives. What do I really want to know?

I realise that the question 'Why?' still hangs there after thirty years.

I check myself to see if it still matters and somehow it does and I know then that I won't arrange that meeting for the simple fact that I might still want to ask that question and I am afraid that this time, he might actually answer it.

Why was it still important to know? How would that inform my life? How could it possibly change anything? What if I heard an answer that pleased me? What if I heard the worst of myself?

So I will invest the story with my own Dreamtime, as it has become and leave him to his own and, as writers, we will take risks and embellish and omit and invent our own take on the Truth and we will only ever know one story and we will only ever see one side: our own.

What do I remember? Not a lot, when I think of it. My memories of us together are now no more than dreamy vignettes, snatched moments – his silhouette pixelated by frosted glass that makes him just a breathless step away – coming in, leaving; it is all the same, the fever of anticipation of his touch and longing in the absence of that touch.

We are connected by an invisible thread that stretches across the city and it pulls him here and takes him there and always there is this sense of waiting, waiting, for the next moment. I remember his brow, the broad, high, rockface of it and the hedge of thick, red-tinged waves above. A feeling, a swoon, an energy, a charge. But that time was all so short, really, in the scheme of things – a few months, perhaps even a year, that's all – not much to warrant half a lifetime of longing, if one is sensible about it. But what has sense got to do with these matters?

It was time enough for him to march into my life and carve a tattooed line around the contours of my heart, a template of his form and his being that others could never quite fill.

'Why?' I finally asked him that morning in 1982 after my farewell party, when Fate again cruelly sent him my way one last time; days before I was to fly across the world, perhaps never to return.

'Why?' I asked, as he rose at pre-dawn as he had always done, to go home.

That last 'Why?' was a greater question; not only about those small leavings but the bigger leaving, the whole of it, the loving and the leaving, and then the comings together and even more partings.

'Why?' I asked, as he buttoned his shirt in the shadows; as he stepped into his RM Williams, the boots that made that distinctive sturdy, impatient footfall I had listened so hungrily for so often in the past. I could not see his face. He paused for a moment. He knew what I asked: the depth and breadth of it.

'I don't know,' he said.

But oh, I remember the hurt. How could I not? The shock and dismay as he disappeared from my life as completely as he had seized my heart.

And I can only blame myself. I blame myself. I have always blamed myself.

'Why?'

There is the answer. It is because I blamed myself.

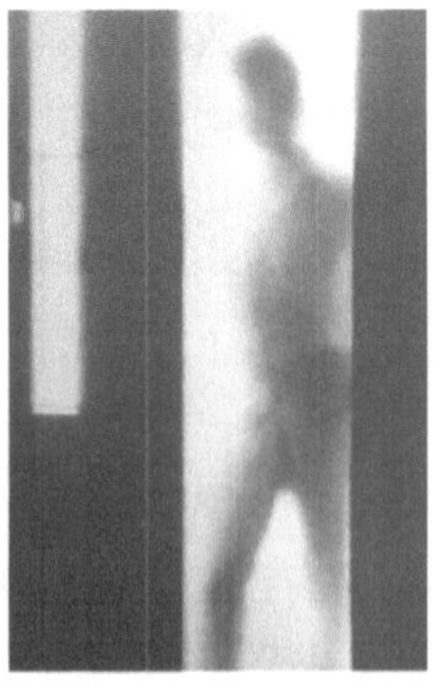

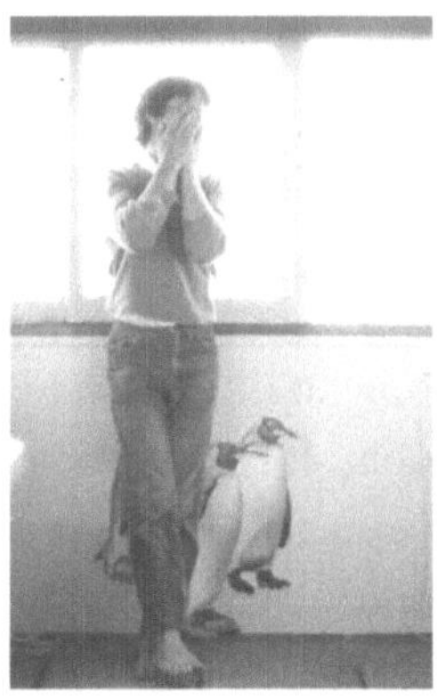

Don moves into Mr M's old room and after the insanity of that time and the self-torturing ordeal of the months after losing D, he is a calming and intriguing presence.

Calming for his order and quiet pace through life, a counterpoint to my fretful urgency; intriguing because he defies scrutiny and in doing so, attracts it. I cannot read his mind as easily as I might wish to; something that has me at once frustrated and spellbound. He is a closed and private unit, a little removed, though he is cool rather than cold.

I find myself wanting to be that kind of person: self-contained and calmly focused, but I feel like a frantic puppy around Don, fussing and tampering with peace, while he dons it as easily as his name.

'We miss the hysteria,' he writes to me in London, a year later.

And I think, 'Is that how I am known?' and then, 'Yes, probably.'

Don is a gifted painter with a larrikin streak, who cheekily managed to have published travel stories of places he had never actually visited. Another incongruity was that he also worked part-time as an armed security guard. He spends long hours in his room in those first days and emerges to reveal a neat, yet eccentric den decorated with collectable bird cards from Tynee Tips tea packets, a piano accordian parked kitschly in the corner, a rubber plant and a cane blind. He has wallpapered the room with his own sketches and a curious blend of bad-taste postcards from op shops, sent by strangers to strangers.

One day, I come home to find delicious music soaring down the hall from Don's room. It is so glorious, I am stopped in my tracks and I close my eyes to absorb the swell and dive of it as it takes me to vast moors raked by wind and a lowering sky propelling pitiless cold clouds across those plains.

'What was *that*?' I gasp.

'None other than the esteemed Ralph,' says Don. 'Picked it up at the Salvos.'

'Who?'

'The Salvos. Salvation Army. Do good works in the community.'

'Yeah, righto, Don Boy, thanks for that.'

Chuckling, as usual, at his own joke, Don hands me the record cover. Ralph Vaughn Williams, 'Theme from Thomas Tallis'. I was right, it was the moors; Heathcliff and Cathy and all that.

'Play it again,' I beg. 'Please, play it again.'

And he does, twice more, for me.

On the flip side, he plays 'The Lark Ascending', which casts me onto yet another equally sublime plane, the music pared down to the most tender trails of violin, looping and sweeping on the air currents, effortless and free and poignant as all get out.

Music was my telepathic transporter, my astral travelling machine, taking me far away into unique and foreign realms which yet felt somehow like home, eliciting something half-remembered, longed-for and just out of reach.

Tchaikovsky's Piano Concerto No. 1, at the age of 14, which arrived as a bonus album along with Jim Nabors, Andy Williams and *Sing-Along with Mitch* in my mother's first order from the World Record Club. The titanic, thundering piano, hectic chords, the climactic, dizzying thrusts of the keys and then the sweet collapse into the childlike tenderness of the second movement took me to a place of dreams belied by our humble home, the sawmill, the footy ground and the local pub.

And with D, it had been Ravel's *Ma mère l'oye* – the story within the music of the ballet crossing nations of emotion, culminating yet again in the soaring pathos of a single violin as we lay on the couch-grass lawn, sipping port like grown-ups and gazing up at the stars, dreaming our mutual dreams.

But soon it would be something less profound that would move me – 'Downunder' by Men at Work would be Mike's and my song.

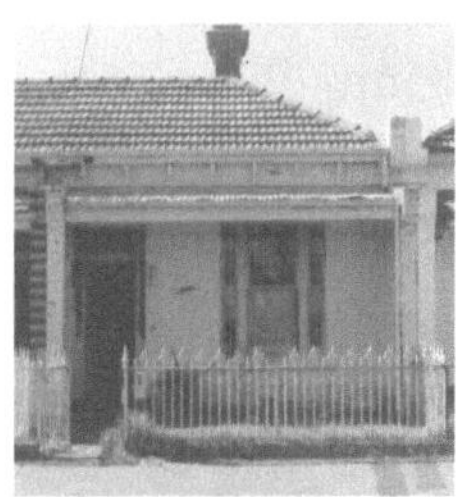

Mike and I met during a stint of bar work for a function at the Light Car Club of Victoria and ended up flirting outrageously and dancing around the bar between customers.

Mike had another part-time job which was helping him finance a six-stopover trip from his homeland of New Zealand to his final destination of London. He invited me to lunch a few days later and it was arranged that I first meet him at his workplace in St Kilda. His workplace happened to be a sex shop. I had never actually darkened the door of a sex shop before and, truth be told, beneath my liberal views lurked a shy, almost prudish side, which was asserting itself with an attack of nerves as I crossed the threshold of this strange new world.

Apparently, being surrounded by dildos and stick mags on a first date was unexceptional for Mike, who demonstrated the machinations of some of the more creepy devices with all the unabashed enthusiasm of a good sales clerk who might have instead been extolling the virtues of a K-Tel Veg-O-Matic or, the hottest new invention, the CD player.

I struggled to maintain an outward expression of world-weary ennui but inwardly, I was feeling just a touch of panic about my new suitor, as a bizarre and slightly sinister battery-operated thumb and forefinger apparatus gyrated lasciviously across the counter-top towards me along with various other jiggling dismembered body parts, which, given their forensic quality, to me resembled something out of an episode of *Cop Shop* and about the furthest thing from titillation that you could get.

It seemed that Mike's early career prospects had also uncannily involved attending to the intimacies of others' anatomy for, when mercifully soon after all the gadgets had been put away and we were seated in a café, he told me that his uncle had landed him a job during school break in a sanitary goods factory; he had spent his teenage summers packaging tampons.

However, in real life, he was a psychiatric nurse and hoped to secure a position in a hospital in London when he had settled there.

This somewhat startling beginning to our strange romance may well have served as a warning but at the time it didn't. After all, I reasoned, a job is a job and the eighties was the decade of decadent, in-your-face excess – Gordon Gekko, Madonna, AIDS.

There was something a little 'daffy' about Michael at first. He seemed to lack the finesse of others I knew and this was heightened by his duffucult Kiwi eccent but as I came to know Michael better, I found that I was warming to him more and more. So much so, in fact, that by the time he was ready to depart for India on the next leg of his journey, we had fallen in love and I had decided to travel all the way to England in six months' time to join him.

Initially, I was only marginally in love with Mike. I had not known him long enough to accurately gauge whether he was the man for me. It was inevitable that, in time, his fussy, sometimes ninnyish ways and that mincing accent would drive me to distraction but it was this and more that would ultimately seal my fate. Yet again, I had talked myself into an idea of love, so terrified was I of a life alone. Yet again, I was haunting the postman, desperate for a letter from foreign shores.

In order to make the trip, I would have to work as I had never worked before, as my savings were meagre to say the least. I commenced a regimen that would have deterred even the most able-bodied, working three jobs, six days a week, day and night and, on Sundays, catching up with household tasks and shopping.

Once again I was working with an old friend, Brian, at a photo lab – this time as a courier to the various franchises around the city. I also worked weekends at a nightclub in the city, where the crowds banked in waves at the bar had me running till the small hours.

Several nights a week, I also worked as a waitress at the failing restaurant at the Light Car Club of Victoria, under the management of the ageing and increasingly intoxicated Mollie.

As the restaurant grew ever emptier, I witnessed with horror Mollie's attempts to compensate by extending the shelf life of her remaining stock by nefarious means: overcooking a steak to disguise a green tinge on the meat, using weeks-old oil and weevily flour and serving frozen desserts well beyond their use-by date.

The final straw came one climactic night when I served a lonely table of four brave souls who sat marooned in the otherwise empty restaurant. They had chosen a seafood cocktail for entrée but when I returned to collect the dishes, I found the group staring at each other in icy silence, the food hardly touched.

'May I see the manager, immediately, please,' one man said, coldly.

I returned to the table with Mollie as, silently, the man pointed to his companion's dish. There, languishing in a pink bath of Thousand Island Dressing, lay a cigarette butt, with a lipstick stain on the filter the exact shade of Mollie's *Rose du Jour.*

There was also trouble brewing at the photo lab. Only weeks before my departure, several staff, including myself, were summoned to the manager's office and informed that our services were no longer required. We were to collect our severance pay, including holiday pay, the following week. When the money did not materialise, I spoke up and demanded that we be paid.

'Listen you,' the manager snarled, 'there has been a theft of $16,000 worth of my camera equipment and *you* are the prime suspect!' I later discovered that I was not the only 'suspect'; the entire company was soon dissolved and the owner/manager was later arrested for fraud. However, this was little compensation for the fact that the money I had worked myself into complete exhaustion for was gone forever and my savings were now severely compromised.

As my departure neared, I packed up my home of the last seven years – one of the longest of my tenancies – the home that held the memories of my days with D and my burgeoning hopes of being an artist. Once again, I was leaving all I knew in the hope of finding my place in someone else's heart.

I moved in for the last six weeks with a group of friends, including Don, who lived in Oak Grove, in the heart of East St Kilda, surrounded by Jewish synagogues and the exotically ringletted and bearded neighbours who frequented them. One housemate, Annie, a sculptor, had created a magnificent sculpture of a naked woman, who now stood proudly astride with hands on hips in the front garden, facing the street. Within days, a steady procession of young Jewish boys on bicycles had formed out on the street, tittering as they ogled the forbidden nudity.

One day soon after, Annie opened the front door to find a posse of elders from the synagogue assembled on the doorstep. They requested that the sculpture be removed. Annie refused but compromised by turning its back to the street.

It amused Don to collect unusual people and we would often come home to find all manner of strange characters populating the house, including an odd, unkempt creature who would sit in total silence throughout the shared meal of Don's famously tasteless lentil loaf, only to erupt from the table without warning and disappear without a word, leaving the assembly baffled in his wake.

It was our Sunday night ritual to pour into Don's bedroom to watch *Countdown* and *Star Trek* on an enormous black and white television Don had found in a junk shop, the size of which we had never before seen; it even had one of the first remote controls we had ever encountered.

The parties at Oak Grove were legendary and it is difficult to imagine how the ageing floorboards of the upper story were able to sustain the weight of over one hundred people dancing their hearts out to The Pretenders, Roxy Music, Talking Heads and The Stranglers.

The night before my departure for London, Don and I went out to share our last pub meal at the Grosvenor, followed by a final game of Galaxion before returning home to Oak Grove. I stood leaning against the doorway of his room as he played his guitar and sang a Loudon Wainwright song: *Soon this weary winter will be gone but don't be fooled, it won't be gone for good.*

The melancholy strains of the song, my standing in these last hours with my old friend in the creaking house filled my heart with the poignancy of goodbye juxtaposed with the edgy anticipation of the adventure that was so soon to unfold.

In the grey pre-dawn of the morning of my departure my door cracked open as Don appeared to wake me from a few scraps of tousled/excited/fearful sleep before he headed off to work.

He bent and kissed me on the cheek.

'Bon Voyage, Bev Girl,' he said.

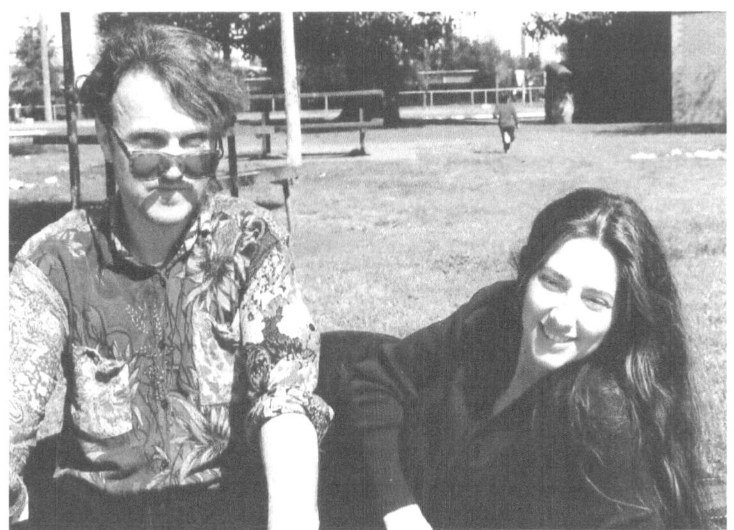

A few of us had begun to wonder a little about Don in those days at Oak Grove. Beautiful women came and went but never stayed for long.

I befriended one of them, Michelle, a small, sparky girl with wide blue eyes. We became dance partners at the Oak Grove parties, launching ourselves with complete abandon into the music, lost in the trance of it, defying fatigue and the usual limitations of our bodies till sometimes a circle of onlookers would form around us to witness this eurythmy.

'We're starting to think you might be in the closet, Don,' I said, after Michelle had also been dispatched.

'I love them all, these beautiful girls,' he said 'but they're not *The One*. It has to be *The One*.'

Years later he would finally find her, *The One*, Jacinta. I had never seen him so expressive, so demonstrative as he was with her.

Baby Henry was born in 1996 and for his arrival, I hastily painted an egg cup, but had not sealed the paint properly and when Jacinta cleaned it, the paint washed away. This was to be eerily prophetic. Don found his wee Henry still and cold in his cot on New Year's Eve, only three months later.

I placed flowers on the tiny coffin, alongside the remnants of his short life: red baby shoes, a 'Bananas in Pyjamas' toy and two baptismal candles. I was a little embarrassed by this floral token, having just engaged in a small, whispered tiff with my then partner, who had been assigned to buy a bouquet en route and had arrived, typically late, with a flaccid bunch of service station carnations – the flower that says 'afterthought' if ever there was one.

As I walked back to my pew, Jacinta suddenly rose from her seat and fell into my arms. For a fleeting moment I was taken by surprise – I was a little stunned, yet deeply touched, that out of all these loving friends, she had chosen me.

Don, his face impenetrable and stony with grief, led the sad procession from the church, holding the tiny white box in his arms.

We laid Henry to rest with other babies on a small hill in a bushland children's cemetery. Somehow, in this setting, the sorrow lifted a little. The surrounding graves made light of death, with their playful mementos – toys and angels and even a small Santa and wind chimes playfully tinkling from the branches above. There was nothing grim here; only innocence and trust.

A year later, Don and Jacinta held one of their frequent barbecues at which were many of the old faces from our time at Oak Grove. The assembled chatted, cooked sausages and drank beer just as we had always done, when suddenly Jacinta and Don emerged in wedding clothes and thus they were married, Don's mum aghast to be caught out in shorts with her hair not done, but it was perfect.

There was a day, when their brood was now four boys, that they visited. We sat on the deck, just chatting and easy on this beautiful early summer afternoon.

Don reached over to stroke Jacinta's cheek. 'You are so beautiful, darling,' he said to her.

The unabashed intimacy of this spontaneous declaration touched me somehow. It was as if it had suddenly struck him as a sweet remembered surprise, seeing her there on that golden day.

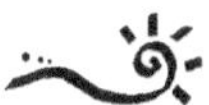

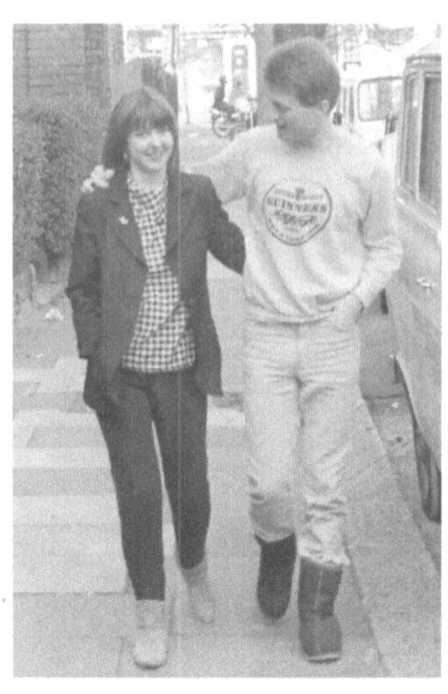

On 9 May 1982, I stepped from the plane in London. Michael was there to meet me, bearing a dozen red roses. After five long months, our reunion was all that I had hoped for; romantic and joyful. We spent a first blissful night at a beautiful little period-style bed and breakfast and the next day explored the familiar landmarks of London – Piccadilly Circus, Trafalgar Square and The Tower of London – after which Mike took me to the hotel where he had been working as a barman.

Mike had arranged with the manager for me to stay in the upstairs accommodation, which he shared with two of the other bar staff for a small rent, while he worked the last weeks prior to our planned trip around Europe.

However, two weeks later, a new 'guvner' took over the pub and immediately ordered me from the property, insisting on staff only. I spent the next few nights of exile in the cheapest hostel I could find, sharing with two elderly ladies, one of whom snored at seismic levels throughout the night, while back at the pub Mike was desperately trying to negotiate for me to stay in the apartment.

Finally, it was agreed that I could stay but on one peculiar non-negotiable condition – I was to be invisible; unseen and unheard. The scantest sighting, the slightest sound and Mike and I would be out. Thus, I spent the next month like a ghost in an attic, creeping silently on tiptoe in my own version of Anne Frank and dashing to the exit like a fugitive under dark of night when Mike and I could finally go out together. This was *not* what I had in mind for my trip of a lifetime and my romantic reunion.

I appeared to be tougher than I was but this 'toughness' was mostly apparent through a rebellious and impetuous streak. In truth, I felt like a child inside and, seeing others as being in charge, I would too readily, then resentfully, acquiesce, only to sulk or act out about it later.

It was easy for others to wield authority over me. I might silently rebel in passive-aggressive ways or seethe about 'injustices' for days, wearing myself out in the process, yet I could not bring myself to speak up directly, as I knew I would be betrayed by my trip-wire emotions.

I would complain endlessly to those sympathetic to my complaints but seldom directly to the wrongdoer, unless it was in a final fiery tantrum when I could take no more, with invariably calamitous results.

I felt good or bad depending on how the world impacted upon me, hoping to stumble upon joy in the process. I blamed external circumstances for these feelings, as if they were beyond my control and I found myself reacting to situations that were imposed on me, rather than firmly steering my own course, or even knowing, with any clarity, what that course might be.

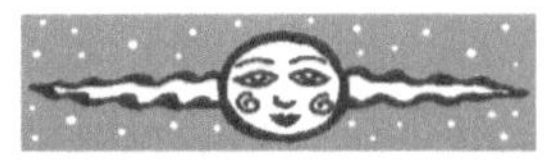

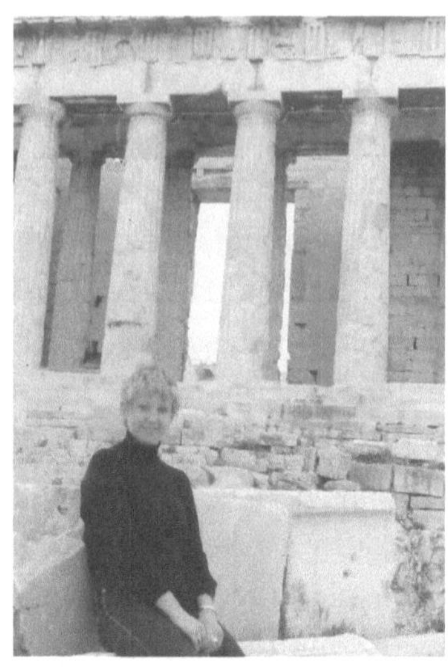

When we finally commenced our trip around Europe, Mike's and my incompatibility came roaring to the surface. We mostly fought our way through Greece, Turkey, Yugoslavia, Bulgaria, Switzerland, Italy and France. Interludes of peace and togetherness were islands of tranquillity upon which we found ourselves beached, more by accident than design.

I was controlling, while Mike was belligerently contrary, so we would often find ourselves lugging our backpacks through some picturesque village street, brawling like two angry tortoises about whether we should have turned left or right or whether or not it was smart to have packed butter on a 35 degree day.

Despite Mike's and my volatility as travelling companions, those weeks remain a precious memory, imbued with the colour, culture and curiosities that only travel can bring. I felt truly alive while exploring the new tastes, sounds, smells and sensations of these exotic locations. Travel satisfied my desire for adventure, expansion and variety in new and intoxicating ways. Every day brought with it a different spectacle or curiosity and generated a wanderlust which remains with me to this day.

Miraculously, Mike and I eventually made our way back to London still intact as a couple and set up in a cheap bed-sit in Kilburn. The building was so close to the train line that the entire room rattled and shook in concert with the rail timetable and the express seemed to be synchronised to pass at the exact time that it could best drown out the climax in a riveting drama on television.

It was not long after that, without my knowledge, that Mike applied for and was accepted for a nursing post in the far north at a county psychiatric hospital, which would mean that he would be living on-site and, depending on his timetable, be in London only on occasional weekends.

As I had already started work at a photo lab nearby, I could not join him, nor did I have the funds to extricate myself from the situation after the expenses of our European tour. I was to find myself completely alone in a city of strangers. It seemed to me to be incredibly callous of Mike to do this when I had travelled thousands of miles so that we could be together. Nonetheless, despite my tears and pleadings, he took the train north a week later.

I moved alone into another smaller and cheaper room in the building, in a bed-sit the size of a large cupboard, trying to calm myself against a quietly escalating panic at this turn of events.

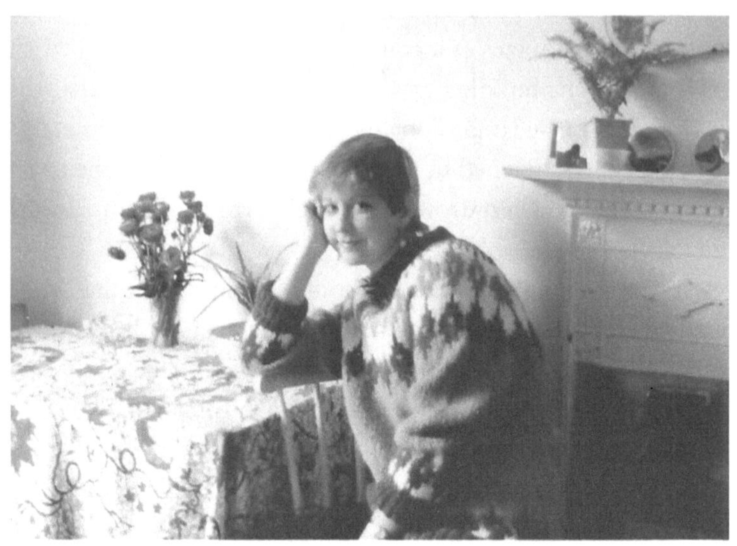

I was stymied by an extreme difficulty in deriving pleasure from solitary expeditions as others might; the idea of lone ventures seemed only to exacerbate my homesickness and loneliness, rather than soothe it. The prospect of tackling this vast and foreign city on my own terrified me and I was seized by a paralysis of overwhelm; caught between an agoraphobia of sorts and the claustrophobic, yet reassuringly familiar confines of the tiny room.

I was often to experience this strange 'paralysis' when stressed by new situations. I would desperately want to move, to get up, go out, do *something*, *anything*, but instead remain rooted to the spot for hours on end.

I invariably felt relief once I had committed to action, which broke the spell, but reaching that first impetus could take all my will and it was sometimes hours before I could break through the wall of anticipatory anxiety. At those times my thoughts would crowd in and jostle for position in a barrier of fears and remonstrations: 'What will I do? What *can* I do? Where would I go? What if I go and I feel even more alone? I'm stuck, I'm stuck here, all on my own. What's the point anyway? It's all useless. You're useless.' On and on and on.

I was trapped by my own helplessness and worse still, I was helpless to find a solution that did not rest on Mike.

After weeks of this, I finally could bear it no longer. I called Mike with an ultimatum. Either he returned to London within a month or he need not return at all. To my great relief, my bluff worked. Little did he know that I would have had no idea how to follow through had he declined.

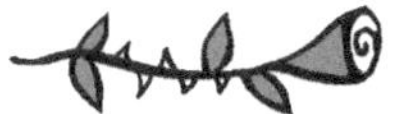

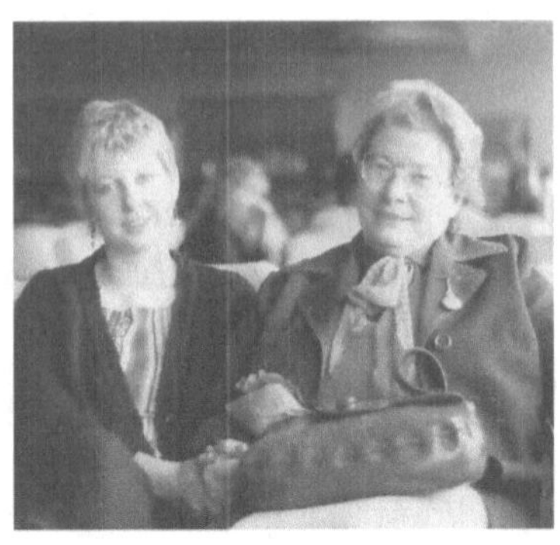

Wednesday 6 April 1983

The echo of a long-distance phone call. A pause, a faraway beep, my brother's voice, subdued. Bad news. The harbinger of disaster, my brother. Echoes of a night long ago, when he stood shadowy in my doorway. 'Bev, it's Dad. He's gone.'

Again, my senses shut down and close me off from his words 'Bad news. Mum. Heart attack. Intensive care.' A few tears squeeze my voice to some meaningless response. 'Stay by the phone.' Aisie says. 'All we can do is wait.'

Wait? For what? Until it is too late? Until I hear, 'Bev, it's Mum. She's gone'?

Time slumps past, sluggishly stretching the hours of this immeasurable day. My luggage, haphazardly packed and awkwardly arranged, stands in waiting at my door. Give me the word. Let me come. Let me go to her. In the evening, the word finally comes. It is just a matter of time. She will die.

There is silence and frustration in the next hours as I try to arrange a flight home. The night is dotted with memories, imaginings and the creeping blows of reality. It is not until the next evening that I board the plane, trembling in the face of the unknown waiting at the end of my journey. And hers.

Friday 8 April 1983

Four hours to go. This night seems never-ending. Thoughts blur as I try to commit them to the waiting page. My hand is reluctant to render them immortal but this humble page is the sole witness to a turning point in my history: irrevocable and pre-ordained.

Around me, in the darkness, voices wind through the engine's drone. Occasionally, an oasis of light picks out a wakeful passenger and there is the efficient, quiet swish of a passing attendant, the faint clink of ice against glass.

I fear that fatigue will betray me and under its burden I will not be strong enough; that I will revert to a child and quake in grief. Who is really the child this night?

If I have that chance to speak, to grasp your hand, my palm humid in your own, what do I say to you? My tears may only make you fearful. Are you afraid?

You are the image of all women, all woman to me. How you haunt me sometimes, still, with your force of love. I make no decision in my life without mentally seeking your approval; such is your power over me.

I sense the end of more than your own biography. I sense the end of tradition, of family, of home. My heart is most leaden with that which I never gave you – children who would fight for your ample lap, folded to your breast, bathed in love.

My life feels like a series of lurches, while you waited to stroke my brow when I fell …

I sense that it is not yet over. During the night, I felt her leave me. It was finished. But strangely, I now sense that she has returned and that she is waiting for me.

My sister-in-law is waiting at the airport with two friends who will take us from Tullamarine to Frankston – over an hour's drive away. Melbourne, my home, made foreign by time and jetlag, rushes past my tired eyes in smudged impressions of vivid sunshine, wide avenues and lumbering trams.

A nurse meets us at the ward and warns us to prepare ourselves for a shock. I stare at the bland white pleats of the curtain that shields her bed. Beyond lies the moment I could never be ready for; not really.

Her eyes are sharp and strange from drugs, yet with a clarity that sees through me as if I were transparent. There are no lies to be told, no impotent reassurances to be offered as a balm. There is only the razor-sharp fact of this impossible moment.

We kiss around tubes and catheters and drips – a Judas kiss, for it is now only by the charity of machines that she lives.

If only my hands would not tremble so.

Around me the presence of my family slowly seeps into my consciousness. For a moment, there had only been her and me, locked as surely as when I had lain in her womb. Her life mine. Her death mine.

But surely this is not a dying woman? This woman does not lie there frail and distant. This woman is being dragged away, kicking. Why this urgency, why this hurry for her soul? Why must so much of my life be spent without her? Why? I begin to cry.

We leave, then, my sister-in-law and I, to walk, to brace ourselves, to smoke the first of countless cigarettes, to summon strength to return.

'I can stand it Eileen, as long as she's not afraid. If she's frightened, I don't know what I will do.'

As if a premonition, these words sear me as my mother turns to me, her eyes wide with fear, 'Help me, Bev, *help me*!' and with this, she places the full burden of her death upon me.

I can't take the weight of this; I have nothing to offer. How can one so full of doubt and fears offer hope? 'Don't be afraid,' is all I can think of to say. It is an order, a plea, a scrambling for crumbs of comfort.

She has been grasping my brother's and my hands, but now she suddenly drops them as if they are electrified and stares past us to the empty space between.

'No!' she announces, to thin air. 'I will *not* come with you!' She is snapping her arm away as if someone has hold of her elbow. She starts to tremble and moan slightly, taking panicky gulps of air and, in a flurry of white, nurses rush to increase her medication. We are grateful that they ask us to leave and lurch from the room, our fingers scraping through our hair.

I am faced with my own faint faith. I have questioned too much to turn back now, having long ago surrendered any idea of a Heaven, or even a Hell, for that matter; yet I have no sense of a substitute, for Nothingness seems equally fantastic.

And there had been someone or something unseen in that room that I could not explain.

Finally, we are summoned back to her bedside. She is peaceful now, like a sleeping child, my child. I stroke her fine, sparse hair and hold her hand, now sadly adorned with chipped nail polish and her second wedding ring.

She sighs, a mighty sigh that releases all the labours of this life and then she is gone. The nurse turns off the last machine. I kiss her frozen brow. Goodbye, goodbye.

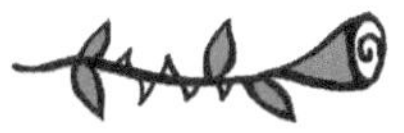

In those first days, my mother's death both humbled and unified our family. With a new bond forged in adversity, we supported each other in our troughs and peaks.

Together, we sorted her gay and feminine clothing, which lay in a mad heap of coloured wisps upon the bed: chiffons, silks, flowery cottons, black silk pyjamas (faintly provocative, hinting at unknown intimacies and private dreams), hand-knits and crocheted vests, made by her own hand.

The house itself did not strike me down as I had dreaded. Her portrait, the art study that I myself had taken as a wedding gift to her and her second husband, Keith, five years before, smiled down from the wall without menace. But I only faintly regarded it, fearful of the solemn truth slowly pervading my senses: she is truly gone.

Later, I left the others and walked to the back door overlooking the garden. My tears came gently, echoing the rain that now drizzled soundlessly but doggedly beyond as I regarded her own humble artistry – it had grown so – loved and tended it had coursed its tangled way to new dimensions.

The velvety roses beaded with rain, the sweet smell of rich, fecund earth, the matrix of a leaf against the sky; this was where her spirit lingered; this was her sweet legacy of toil and nurture. I felt her there in all that grew around me, felt her touch on every stem, felt her call from the whispering trees – I am here, always; I am here.

And so it was that one day soon after, my stepfather and I gathered these same blooms for her burial sheaf, our quiet ceremony in the winds, a tear for every flower cut and taken and our love poured into each remaining wound so that it would grow again next season and on, for our remembering.

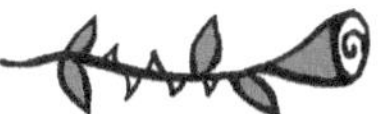

I had one month in Melbourne before I was to return to London – and of course, to Michael.

Till now, we had loved in a way that tousled and tore at us most of the time, to the point where we were no longer able to clearly discern just what it was that kept us together, yet were unwilling to part for the same reason. Then, as if a healing force, this crisis came to show us once again how much we really did care and how much love remained between us. I missed him, but this time, it was without the hunger of the year before, for paradoxically, through my loss, I had found my feet.

In the days after my mother's death, a calmness had draped itself over me; a state foreign to me and, knowing my turbulent nature, inevitably temporary, but it brought with it new strength, a sense of purpose and a yearning to give and live in the moment.

For once in my entire life I had come to like myself; to like the woman that I had become.

The first friend I visited was Java*, who lived with his partner, Ewan*, in the top apartment of an historic, crumbling mansion which had been a *grande dame* of Melbourne in the 1880s.

They had transformed their living room into a carnival welcome, draping it with electric blue streamers from which they'd cut out the words *We love you Bev*, all the more poignant for the fact that they had failed to leave a bottom border and the words had twisted and convulsed into an abstract calligraphy.

We ate in customary elegance, sipping wine from fluted glasses and talked as if I had been there only the day before in the grand room where, just over a year earlier, we had celebrated my Halloween birthday in style, with a 'Night of Romance' theme and twenty guests in evening wear.

I returned the following day to my brother's, to catch Jess, who was visiting from Broadford for a few days. Jess, who had been widowed a few years before, no longer lived at 'Glendora', which now sits like an old maid in the midst of a housing estate that sprawls in an urban rash across the original farmland.

Jess's presence reawakened cherished memories of 'Glendora' – visits to watch *Rawhide* or *Combat* on the tellie on a Friday night, with the ginger-coloured dogs chasing our car up the dirt track, barking out the news of our arrival; the men drinking beer and the women, Marsala and Coke; the scary, constantly hissing cistern of the outdoor toilet; the marble fireplace, where pine-cones spat and crackled in winter; huge floral arrangements of red berries and grasses on the mantle; the stained glass window above the never-used front door with the name 'Glendora' read backwards; brown blinds glooming the rooms against fierce mid-summer; the smell of floor polish in the hallway; the forensic parade of preserves in the still and silent pantry. 'Glendora' is now a folly, corralled by cul-de-sacs and brick-paved walkways.

Some years ago, an Allen's sweets factory was built across the road from my first home, standing where I always thought the Black Stump stood; the black stump of 'Beyond the …' fame, which was really just a stunted lightning-struck tree-trunk in an empty paddock.

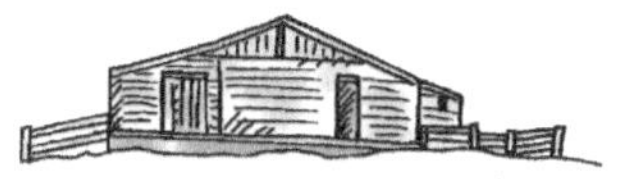

Brian had taken the day off to welcome me when I arrived to stay with him and Allen, after the funeral. We sat in the garden and talked for hours.

When Allen came home they took me out to dinner at our favourite French restaurant in Richmond, Les Halles, and I ordered my favourite: steak au poivre.

It was strange to be in proximity to the photo lab just up the hill, given all the nastiness that had occurred there, before my departure.

In 1977, after my return from New Zealand, I had found work at another photo lab, in South Melbourne, which processed high-quality prints for professional photographers. My job was as a 'spotter'. This entailed retouching blemishes on the prints with a fine brush and inks, correcting skin tones with a coloured paste and cotton wool and spray-lacquering the final prints.

I worked under the direction of Brian, who was assigned the more complex retouching and restoration and he was a master of the art. Brian was also the first gay person I had gotten to know on an intimate level. He had recently met Allen, his doppelgänger, really, since they were born on the same day in the same year. As both were Virgo, their terrace in Middle Park was a showcase of order and taste and their sense of fashion was always refined and in vogue.

This friendship was to span several decades and continues to this day. It would last through my four years abroad, the death of my mother, Brian's brain tumour and the untimely and tragic death of Allen in 1998.

Allen simply disappeared one day after he had left for a bike ride. Brian finally found him in a coma as a 'John Doe' in the ICU of a major hospital the next day. He died within the following week, never having recovered consciousness.

I wrote a dedication for Allen, which I read through heavy tears at his funeral:

My friend is gone. My friend of 20 years is gone, so soon, so suddenly; I don't know why.

Perhaps it is not mine to know ...

Two years earlier, Brian had been diagnosed with a brain tumour; it was discovered after a seizure in his sleep so severe that he had dislocated his shoulder to the extent that it required surgery.

At the time, I lived near the hospital and when I visited him, he was reeling from the news of the tumour – which was inoperable – and in considerable pain from the shoulder injury but was putting off taking painkillers until bedtime. Uncomfortable with displays of emotion, he was putting on a brave face but it was clear that he was in considerable distress.

After a while, I left him and Allen and returned home, but within the hour, I was struck by the strongest feeling that I should return. I found Brian alone, standing by the window in tears.

I had only recently completed an initiation to Level II of Reiki, a form of energy healing and I quietly suggested that I try this to at least calm Brian and help him rest a little. He agreed and seemed to be more peaceful afterwards, so I went home.

When I visited the next day, he and Allen were amazed. The bruising in his shoulder had surfaced within half an hour and the pain had completely subsided. Brian was then hooked, but knowing of his tendency to repress emotions, I warned him 'You get what you need, but it may not be what you want.'

As predicted, his grief and rage came boiling up in a later session and it frightened him off. However, amazingly, miraculously, the tumour disappeared.

Brian and Allen were my other family. We shared everything and they nurtured and supported me throughout the years. Brian has loyally stuck to a promise elicited from him by my mother years ago to 'Look after Bev'.

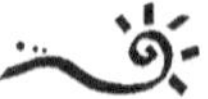

Over the first days after losing my mother, I was spoiled and pampered by my hosts, finding myself surrounded by luxuries which would have found me feeling rather smug under happier circumstances. I slept in Allen's room, which was reminiscent of the Arabian nights. Indian cloths bloomed from the ceiling above my bed; lattice-work metal lampshades patterned my walls at night; I padded barefoot on thick white shag pile and slept in a sea of shell-pink sheets.

At my disposal was everything that opened and shut, whizzed and whirred, sang and spoke but I was content to simply gaze out at the beautiful garden with its delicate ferns and sculptural succulents and jasmine winding along the fence above the small pond where goldfish flickered and flashed.

Eventually, it was time to move on. Somehow, I sensed there was a moment when I would become intrusive, so orderly was this tasteful and refined world.

So, on to Oak Grove.

I was sitting in the autumn sun, faintly amused by the total contrast of the surroundings I now found myself in, with Annie's controversial naked woman sculpture – still with her back turned discreetly to the street – among the straggly eucalypts and untended garden. On the walls behind me, the plaster cracked and the paint peeled, but I was comfortable and at home with this bohemian shabbiness.

Eventually, Annie returned, laden with shopping which she tossed down in her rush to throw her arms around me. We talked tirelessly and breathlessly, punctuating our conversation with beers, drunk straight from stubbies. I told her about London life and my travels around Europe and she caught me up on the Melbourne scene and her sculptures, describing a fountainhead she was making for a friend's country property, modelled on his face, with water spouting from the mouth. Yet again, I found myself amazed that such a strong spirit should be tucked into such a tiny person.

We had settled immediately into the role of bosom buddies as well as housemates before I left for England, sharing a common earthiness and practicality mixed with the temperament and psyche of artists at heart. We put down our shared no-nonsense, tell-it-like-it-is attitude to the fact that we were both country girls.

On discussing this one night after Annie had returned from her part-time job cleaning toilets, we decided that the quality we shared was absolute and unembellished honesty, a trait that was not universally popular but also one that was not easy to rein in. If someone were to ask Annie what she did for a living she would, without apology, tell them that she cleaned dunnies. So would I.

Sadly and ironically, it was Annie's grounded nature and belief that she was bulletproof that would lead her, in years to come, to think that she could master and control a taste of heroin now and then. She was wrong.

The last I saw of her in the heroin years was over dinner, for which she arrived an hour late, pinned and heavy-lidded. I could barely contain my anger at the priority that the drug had been given over our time together. Famished, I complained to the waiter when we were kept waiting a further half hour for our order.

'Don't pick on him! It's not his fault!' she said.

Annie, defender of the underdog, my beautiful, sensible friend, was soon to be lost to me.

Monday 23 May 2011

I had just written about Annie when incredibly, she appears out of the blue, as if conjured by my musings, when I happen to stop at a supermarket I have never visited before. Her fiery mane is now cropped; otherwise, she is still very much Annie.

We head outside and sit on a park bench and talk at a rate of knots for a while before I have to leave.

'You look well,' I say.

'I'm still on methadone, if that's what you mean,' she says.

Even so, I am excited to see her and we exchange numbers so that we can arrange a proper catch-up.

As she enters her number into my mobile phone, she warns: 'I'm pretty slack at getting in touch' and for once, I actually hear what I am being told and heed the potential for disappointment that I am being shown.

A week later, my mobile is stolen, and with it go Annie's details.

She hasn't called.

But my time at Oak Grove in 1983 was spent quietly whiling away the days in her company. From Annie I derived a great sense of determination and my own energy grew in the presence of her indefatigable spirit. She made earrings for me, bought me books, took me shopping, discussed ideas and art. Together, we tore around the city in her station wagon, her blaze of fiery hair barely higher than the steering wheel.

A new conviction was growing in me that when I returned to London I must do London in a better way; with a greater sense of adventure and creativity. I'd rested on my laurels, arrested by timidity and complacency for too long. Somehow, over this time, I had discovered the magic ingredient of being content with myself. The jokes I exchanged with others were funny without nervous effort, the conversation flowed easily in whichever direction I aimed it. It was an intoxicating, heady feeling of freedom; freedom from the shackles of a faltering self-image.

Gradually, I caught up with all the old faces – Tony, as zen and unreadable as ever; Steve, installed in my old home, which was now tatty and unrecognisable under the pile of papers, dirty cups and cat dander engulfing the rooms; Peter, charming and intrepid as always, just back from a trek in the Himalayas and destined to live permanently in Cambodia in coming years; Michelle, still a tram conductor, still planning her life and driving my old Renault.

They gathered to bid me farewell once more on a Thursday night at the Espy pub, overlooking the needles of far-off lights on the foreshore. I felt a great love for these people who had clustered around me, offering gifts and tokens and openness and a sympathetic ear; people I had grown around and from and to and with over the years.

I returned to my family for the last days before my second departure. Here, at least I was not compelled to talk, which was a relief after days of catching up. At dusk, the family visited my mother's grave. I had come to say a twin goodbye; to her and once more, to my homeland. The evening was cold, with the gathering gloom and chill wind speaking of the fast-approaching winter. An eternal flame from the oil refinery danced on the foreshore, frenzied now by the breeze.

It had been a month since we had laid Mum here. All the bright blooms had perished to the earth and the soil of her grave had settled. There remained only the shiny ribbons of dead bouquets flickering in the fading of the day.

The last days spent with my family had yielded fruitful bonding, along with niggling frustrations. Money reared its ugly head. The tiny amount that had been left to us only just paid the sum that I had borrowed to get home, as there had been no offer of assistance. My brother bought a new fridge with his share.

The tender sentiments of our reunion in sorrow had given way to our old dismissive manner of relating. Some good had been accomplished but perhaps, after all, we were too diverse in our attitudes to hope for something deeper than the fact of our shared bloodline. All I knew was that home was no longer as defined by my family as it had once been.

Keith came to collect me for our final day together. We spoke little, preferring to attend to small matters that needed our attention. I sorted things that had been in storage and Keith sat turning the bowls that he'd been making from Australian wood.

Our grief was palpable this day. We both knew that this was no longer a home, but a house. I looked at this big, gentle man and wondered how he would bear his days when life meant so very little any more. He was reduced in size, no longer the strong protective partner, suddenly older and sad. As we reversed out of the driveway, he suddenly stopped the car and raced out through the garden, returning with a single, perfect wine-red rose which he placed into my hand: the last rose of summer.

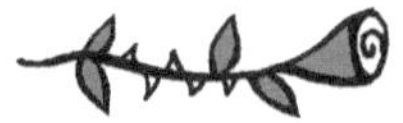

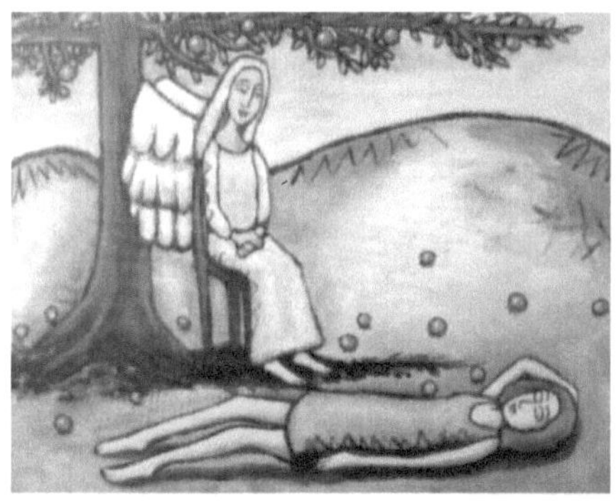

The tormented nature of my mother's last hour lingered with me as I flew back to my life in London.

If her spirit lived on, I wondered, would her fear tether her in some way? Would her disembodied consciousness wander in some eternal dusk, snagged in a nether-world between the physical, which she had clung to, and the non-physical, which she resisted?

Her words of comfort about death in my childhood: 'It's not as scary when you get older', had become lies with her last frantic breaths, and her terror in that final hour had unsettled me greatly.

Witnessing first-hand Mum's distress had given rise to many questions – most notably why a person of considerable faith such as my mother would feel so terrified in that final hour.

Surely, I reasoned, if one had faith in a God who was believed to be a loving protector and saviour, why would someone who had lived a good life face death with such *panic*? Wasn't death the ultimate reunion, the great 'coming home'? Was this just lack of faith or also a lie?

In the days following Mum's death, the image of her frightened eyes, her clutching at my sleeve, her alarmed pleas for my help replayed again and again in my mind. Worst of all, her need for comfort in words that stemmed from faith had found me mute.

I had turned my back on faith in the only form I knew it – small-town Methodist faith, which at the time meant little more to me than a nice dress and matching hat, singing hymns with Mum and sharing a polite handshake with the minister at the end of the service, while my father remained at home in charge of the roast. The sermon itself made such little impact that I cannot recall being moved in any way; that is, until one particular Tuesday in 1967 at Broadford High School when Religious Instruction was conducted by a Salvation Army captain instead of our usual clergyman.

'This is it!' he declared. 'This is the end of the world!'

A shudder ran through me.

'This conflict is prophesied in the Bible and it has come to pass!' he went on, referring to the current Six Day War in the Middle East.

Though there have since been many such skirmishes, these were the days of the Cuban Crisis and the Cold War and the threat of nuclear annihilation was constantly hanging over our heads as this particular conflict escalated frighteningly and seemed poised to be the tipping point for world peace.

Fuelled by religious zeal, the captain went on to describe the unspeakable horrors that would soon unfold – war on an unimaginable scale, demons, plague, pestilence and suffering beyond comprehension. I was sick with fear as he backed up his predictions with quotes from Revelations, a part of the Bible that I had, till this point, been mainly spared; a miracle in itself, given my annual exposure to Jehovah's Witness relatives from New South Wales, who arrived in convoy with fellow worshippers for the annual convention at the Melbourne Showgrounds.

For the next four days after Religious Instruction, I hardly ate or slept – and when I did sleep, I was assaulted by terrible nightmares about the horrors that lay ahead. I even approached the headmistress, a Catholic, and asked to be excused from the following week's session but she refused, stating, 'If it's God's will …' which only served to verify the captain's forecast and send me into fresh terror.

When the hostilities ended a few days later, the only ones more relieved than I would have been the countrymen and women of that region of the Middle East.

This incident was to have a powerful impact on the way I saw religion and God, long after the crisis had passed. I no longer felt comfort in religion and was confused by this notion of a capricious and vengeful God. I could not reconcile the idea of a loving God with one who would condemn his own children to eternal damnation, under *any* circumstances. I did not like being thought of as a sinner and resented the notion that I was in some way guilty for the 'crime' of showing up on the planet in the first place.

I also became increasingly dissatisfied that so many of my questions had not been answered satisfactorily by religion and found little comfort in the messages, which to me smacked of medieval superstition based mainly on fear and guilt. But without the anchor of faith, I was cast adrift in life without any form of navigation. I needed *something* – a guide on how to live, which I would find later through many different teachers and in many different forms.

Ultimately, I would come to the conclusion that there could only be one possible expression of a God in any form that made sense: an unconditional, detached love which left us to live as we saw fit; free to choose to emulate this love and find peace, or not.

It was early morning when my plane landed back in London after the long flight from Australia. By now a veteran of the long haul, I knew it was best to postpone sleep till nightfall at my destination, in order to ease jetlag. Though exhausted, I opted to simply rest and allow my body clock to sort itself out.

The day drifted past the window in small, passing vignettes of daily life on a London street. I lay on the bed watching the leaves dance in small flutters and flurries against the glass, meditating in the fuzzy fog of sleep deprivation. For once, I did not have the energy to do anything except lie there and I found it was pleasant to just *be*, embracing the inertia of an unstructured day. I gazed around the bed-sit in a dreamy peace, perceiving the room and its contents through a soft-focus, faraway fuzz until my eyes fell upon the chair where my mother was now sitting.

A small smile crossed her lips as she regarded my look of surprise.

'What are you doing here?' I asked, though I didn't actually speak these words aloud for somehow it seemed unnecessary to do so.

My question was twofold: what was my mother doing here, in *life* but also, what was she doing here, in *London*, so far from home?

Her smile took on a wry and knowing edge. 'It's not that far, really,' she replied.

Recalling her deathbed terror, I asked, 'Well, are you *all right*? I mean, are you okay now? What's it like?'

'I'm getting used to it.' It was the perfect answer.

I momentarily closed my eyes, savouring the sweet sense of relief and completion that washed over me, knowing she was at peace. When I opened them again, she was gone.

A month after my return to London, Mike and I decided to spend a week on the Greek Island of Seriphos, the magical place we had loved so much on our travels a year before. This was to be a week of healing for me and a chance to renew the bond between us, but instead I found that as each day passed, Mike seemed to become strangely closed and distant and took to disappearing for day-long walks around the island.

The days merged into each other, blended by the sun, the sea and the soft, sleek nights.

Sometimes I sat with Julie in her thatched bar by the beach and we draped our bare, brown limbs in the sun and I listened to her speak, in musical Greek, to the children, dogs and simple people of the island.

Michael was nowhere around. He had gone walking through the village or exploring the island. Every day he disappeared alone, sometimes for hours.

He visited Hora alone; climbed the sheer path in the pitiless noonday sun, returning in the evening in a ridiculous straw hat and with sunburned arms.

I felt no joy as he came over the dunes; only a sense of the displacement that had now loomed between us.

The next day I climbed to where the stream had run the year before.

I wanted to lie among the small frogs in the cool, clear rock-pools, overhung with flowers. This is where we had come a year before to bathe each morning and greet the day. We had stood naked and happy like small children under the seamless sky, pouring water from basins over our heads, laughing and shivering as it trickled over our skin.

Now it was dry. There were no flowers. Cracks were beginning to show.

We walked back from the village in silence that night. 'Let's finish,' was all he said.

I lay awake long into the night under the stars as he slept his guiltless sleep.

Excerpt from 'Goodbye Seriphos'

Bev Aisbett 1984

We limped back to London. Mike half-heartedly looked for accommodation but seemed in no particular hurry to move out. Night after night, he disappeared, often not returning till dawn. One night, while searching for some papers I had misplaced, I found a pile of magazines hidden in the back of a cupboard. They were gay magazines, with lurid images of muscular men in aggressively sexual poses.

I sat up till dawn waiting for him to return, the magazines laid out in silent accusation on the table in front of me. He admitted it: he had been cruising; even while I was grieving my mother in Australia, he had been out clubbing with strange men. I could not bring my mind to fully imagine what sordidness these anonymous trysts may have entailed.

He promised to move out the following weekend, so I stayed with friends on the other side of the city, bracing myself for my return to an empty bed-sit. Instead, when I opened the door I found Mike, feet up, blithely watching television. A few boxes were strewn around the room in a dismal commencement of packing and in them, I saw many of my own items: books, music and, in particular, most of the photos of our travels.

I walked straight past him and slammed open the door to the kitchen. He followed me and I turned sharply.

'Why are you doing this to me? Isn't it hard enough?'

He stood there silently; coldly unrepentant. Hurt and anger pulsed through me. I grabbed him by the front of his shirt and repeated, shouting:

'WHY ARE YOU DOING THIS TO ME?!'

I felt a hot sting across my cheek and automatically raised my hand to soothe it. We stood, staring at each other for some time, both of us shocked at how sordid it had become between us. Without a word, he packed the rest of his things and was gone within an hour. I sat in the wake of his departure, the slap still faintly pulsing on my skin, and I swore that never again would a man do that to me.

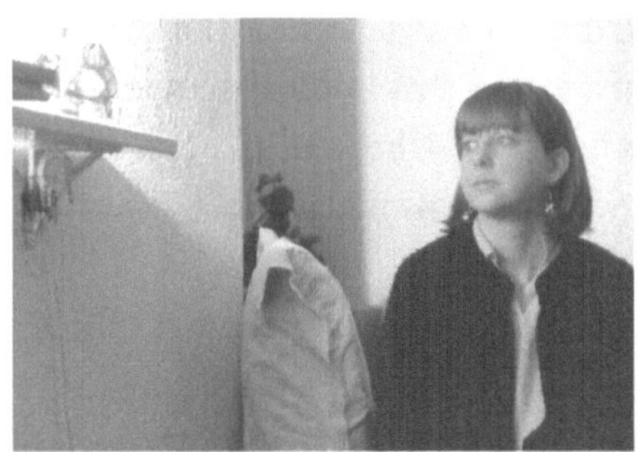

There is nothing in this world more desperately, gut-wrenchingly desolate than sitting alone in a bed-sit in a city thousands of kilometres from home – an orphan in every sense of the word – on a freezing London winter night, with no coins for the meter. At least it was for electricity. Had it been gas, it might have been a different story.

I wanted to go home but couldn't; I hadn't the money to do so. Besides, with the passing of my mother, 'home' was now a compromised notion.

Eventually, after weeks of dismal solitary existence, I spotted an advertisement for a shared household in Shepherds Bush. Once more, having a 'family' saved my sanity. I turned

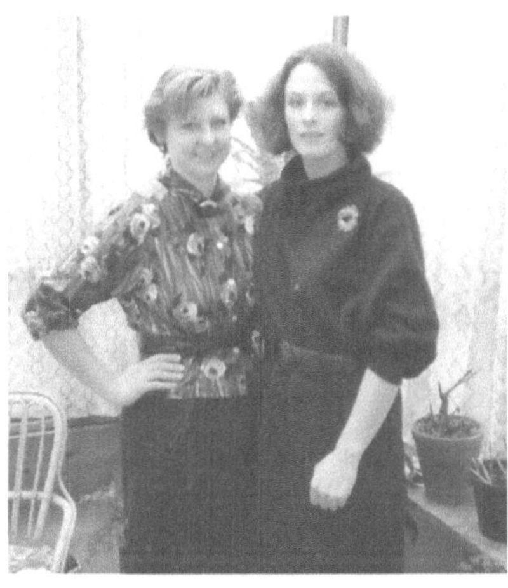

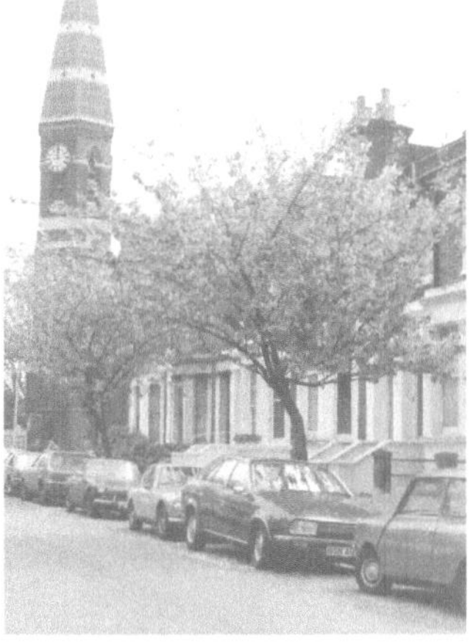

on all my larrikin Aussie charm at the interview to win over the other housemates: Pru, a Sloane type who was a graphic designer, another Mike who was a lawyer and Lynne, a feisty Liverpudlian with a sing-song accent that was so strong it was almost indecipherable.

I lived in Shepherds Bush for the next three years. During this time, London finally opened its doors to me. I joined a women's group (feminism was high in those days) and became firm friends with Judy (who is now a psychologist) and have remained so over all these years and all this distance.

My circle of friends expanded and I was finally lifted out of the gloom that had stalked me for so long. I left the Fleet Street news agency where I had worked for a year as an assistant to the Picture Editor and moved to LBC Radio (London Broadcasting Corporation) as assistant to John, the news editor, who became Judy's partner for a while.

The fact that I was a two-finger typist had somehow been omitted in the interview and I was aghast when I discovered that a major part of my job involved directly typing out stories dictated by the reporters by phone, which were then to be read at the hourly news bulletin. As usual, I refused to admit defeat and managed to get around this by feigning deafness while my fingers tried to catch up, but my typos were so frequent, I pitied the poor newsreader who had to negotiate his way through these reports live on air.

Eventually, I met Heath*, an actor who had secured some theatre work and a few small walk-on parts for film and television. We had been seeing each other for a few months when he told me that he had landed a gig in Hong Kong and would be away for six weeks. I felt a knife-thrust of the old, familiar fear that accompanied an inner hunch that something bad was again heading my way.

London 10 April 1984

Dear Java,

... Heath's trip was evil timing. Things were so new between us; too new for solid trust but we both felt sure of our feelings as we parted. He wrote often and warmly but the trip was a series of disasters, which ended with the group being split into two hostile camps, with the result that Heath and Martin, who were once the best of friends, now no longer speak to each other. The other casualty was me.*

It takes some understanding; the when and how and why of it are still a mystery to me.

The day he returned, he ran all the way from the station to see me. I was so excited and I had even set about rearranging my room to make it bright and welcoming. When he arrived, he looked tired and beaten; nonetheless we were happy.

The next day, like a cloud, he was gone. Somehow, inexplicably, while we slept, his heart and with it, his love, had drifted away from me.

It was only a tiny shift at first then I felt it more strongly until it was undeniable that something had changed. We tried to recreate the heady days before his departure but something had happened to Heath on those far shores; something dark and profound had shaken him to the core.

He went away for ten days. I waited for his call, so utterly frustrated by the shroud of mystery that hung over his silence and this second disappearance so soon after the first. I went through a catalogue of emotions: concern, sadness, anger, but I had nothing to pin them to.

He finally made contact and came to see me. The person who stood on my doorstep was a ghost; he had literally faded away; he was pale and gaunt and had black rings under his eyes.

He told me he knew little of what he was experiencing, only that his feelings towards me had changed, even though he wished it was otherwise. He was still not able to pinpoint the source of this but clearly, something had happened in Hong Kong well beyond the arguments and pressures of the tour.

Two months on, I am none the wiser. Sometimes, it feels like a heavy sadness on my shoulders: that I had a glimpse of something fine that was cruelly snatched away without explanation but I swear, no more will love bring me to my knees. I can no longer die a little death each time it goes. I must believe that ultimately, it will find its way to me when I really and truly believe that I am worthy of it and with each new strength that I gain in these challenges, hopefully that day draws closer.

I still see Heath when it doesn't hurt too much, for fundamentally, there is still a love between us, though now of a different and imprecise form. Perhaps, in time, we will find a form of that love that is free of the tension that now exists, when we can settle for that which it has become, instead of yearning for what was and perhaps, in time, he will share his secret with me.

It was months before Heath finally revealed what had occurred in Hong Kong. He had been raped by a man.

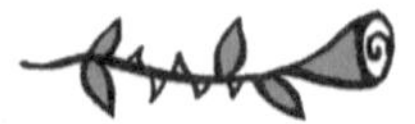

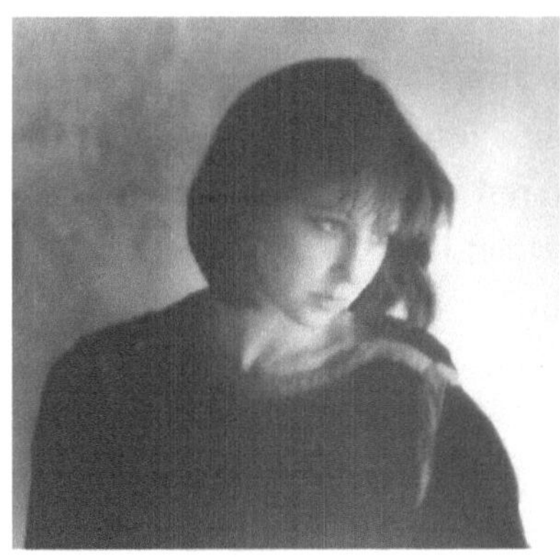

I am like the lake
Reposed to the eye,
Gentle to the Dreamer,
A Mirror to the Fearful Leaper
And looming, breathless and consuming
'To the Swimmer out of his depth', *Water Woman*
Bev Aisbett 1980

Water: I am all water; all currents and rips and damp, subterranean caves.

Scorpio with Pisces Ascendant (both water signs); Water Dragon in Chinese Astrology.

Some days I drift, some days I carve through seas with heroic knife-like thrusts, some days I float on my back and see only a seamless dome of glorious sky and some days, I can only just keep my head above water.

Like the captain of an unreliable ship, I try to negotiate the waves that threaten to engulf me. Sometimes all that there is left to do is simply hang on.

Eventually I will come to know that drowning in order to resurface is a cumbersome and unnecessary process. Diving into the troughs may be more intriguing than swimming in the shallows but the view from the bottom is of a vast and engulfing wall which, from that perspective, I can only deem insurmountable.

Instead, I must learn to ride *with* the waves, like a surfer, surrendering all resistance to the treacherous rips and powerful undertow and when I sink I must cease fighting and float up towards the light.

I was born on Halloween: All Hallows Eve; originally a Celtic tradition which heralds the onset of the Northern winter. The ancient Romans celebrated it as *Feralia*, a day intended to bring rest and peace to the dead.

Though it hasn't really taken off here with its Americanised (read: *commercialised*) themes, there is a still a certain ghoulish charm associated with a night when the dead rise to dance upon the Earth once more.

And this is the Scorpio journey: to explore the dark and the dreadful and retrieve from the abyss the secrets of life. The emblems of Scorpio speak of powerful extremes: the scorpion itself, feared for its ferocity but which, according to myth, stings itself to death when ringed by fire; the Phoenix, destroyed but rising again and again from the ashes; and the brave Eagle, who soars above all Earthly concerns, at last calm and confident in its power. Death and Rebirth is the Scorpio way, which is at the heart of Halloween.

Hence I am drawn to the deepest mysteries, the mystical arts, the metaphysical, the spiritual, the vortex, the quantum sciences, religion and philosophy; seeking, always seeking to find the answers to myself.

Astrologically, mine is a difficult combination, I discover, especially with that miserable rising Pisces making me too sensitive and prone to self-pity and a moon in Aries creating volatile emotions.

Characteristics:
In the positive – loyal, caring, observant, indomitable.
In the negative – self-effacing, irritable, resentful, confronting.

Numerologically, I am 22/4: a Master Number, and with this comes master challenges.
In the positive – a leader and teacher.
In the negative – serious, restrained, blocked.

The Enneagram says I am a Personality Type Four, the Artist/Romantic.

It is this that describes my complex path most clearly. I see from this that which confounds me and also that which drives my need to create. Researching the Enneagram profiles, I find that: fours are highly creative and usually artists of some kind but are also drawn to explore the secrets of the psyche. A Four as a therapist will usually be involved in deeply transformative work.

Fours experience feelings on an off-the-scale level, with abandonment as a major ongoing theme stemming from childhood and played out throughout life – there was once perfect love, but it was withdrawn or lost and there is the fear that the same will happen again. Fours tend to deal with this sense of abandonment through either depression or hyperactivity or by swinging between the two.

Feelings of loss are internalised by a Four into a sense of personal lack; even if successful, a Four will still tend toward feelings of unworthiness, shame and even self-hatred.

Transformation is possible when the Four focuses on what has been found, rather than lost and on gratitude for all that is right, even if that seems the smallest of blessings at the time.

While these things do not *define* me nor limit my free will, they do help me to clarify a personal objective for my time on Earth, provide some explanation for my trials and a way to identify and better understand the strengths and weaknesses I encounter in myself and others.

I need this road map for myself, even if it is superstitious, for I am often puzzled by my own nature. It is as if I am plugged into an alien circuitry through which my emotional codes are governed by a cryptic logic, the workings of which I cannot fully comprehend. Sometimes it feels as though I invent emotions not yet dreamed of – strange states of sensitivity, subtle unsettlements that alight upon me with vexatious unpredictability.

Each day is launched by these emotional experiments as I wake to discover what mood has attached itself in those moments of surfacing to consciousness. From there I either corral perturbation into something more accommodating of the everyday world or, on rare and blissful occasions, bathe in the splendour of an effortless communion with the equilibrium of the day.

I am dazzled and intrigued by the gypsy band of moods that move in and camp in my psyche each night. It has been my greatest challenge to embrace this unpredictable aspect of my nature. At my best, these forces are harnessed into passion, enthusiasm and inspiration; at worst, I am bogged by the weight of some distracting pull towards a darker place; at the very least, I must reach for acceptance of the fact of this strange inner alchemy.

My quest is to come home to myself and find a welcome there.

August 2010

I am halfway through researching the journals and it is hurting me.

Reading about my former self is like picturing a character in a novel and I am confounded by this poor woman's inability to find lasting peace and happiness and the way that luck kept pulling the rug from under her. No wonder she often felt that the Universe had it in for her somehow.

I feel for her – she tries so hard, yet is in constant rebound: a human skittle, standing up, being knocked down, standing up, being knocked down; living life like some endurance test.

I wish that I could have written a happier life for her, where things were not so complicated and hurtful from the start. I wish I could have given her confidence and clear direction earlier in her life and spared her such unnecessary pain and confusion. I hope I can give her a happy ending …

This protracted winter continues to chill: arctic winds blasting me with hail as I brave the park on the foreshore for my dog-walking duty. I feel like this day: blustery and confused, grey and sad. Perhaps writing this is too much for me, after all.

I am crying now – I can't help it – with great, ropey sobs like I once did so often. Its intensity and foreignness is at least a reminder that I'm comparatively free of this gut-wrenching stuff nowadays. Used to bawl at the drop of a hat, me. Now it takes the drop of a bomb.

There are times when I'm just plain over life; just tired of it, as now: tired of the fight, tired of trying; trudging on, day after bloody day towards some invisible carrot on a stick. I need to talk to someone; I'm not coping very well but it is always difficult to know with whom to share my darkness; it's usually too much for others: perhaps they are simply a little afraid of it, or because of my damn independent streak, they think I can cope.

Kyle* comes to mind: a dog-walking friend, with whom, over the years, a trust has developed; yet our encounters are spaced far enough apart that intimacy is not greatly risked by disclosure. Kyle will not be afraid, I know. He comes immediately and while our dogs frolic and gambol, impervious to the freezing wind in the grim, wintry dusk, Kyle puts a hand on mine as I shiver and weep.

'If I was writing my life story, I'd be feeling pretty much the same at this point,' he says, 'but this is so very important for you to do for yourself, now.'

He's right: this is no quant memoir; this is a healing journey to my very core. Why did I keep all those journals? Did I somehow know that this day would come?

'It's going to be painful,' he says, 'but keep walking, right through the centre till you come out the other side. You can do this. You must do this.'

Must. Should. Have to. Those now-forbidden words.

But he's right. I must.

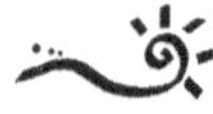

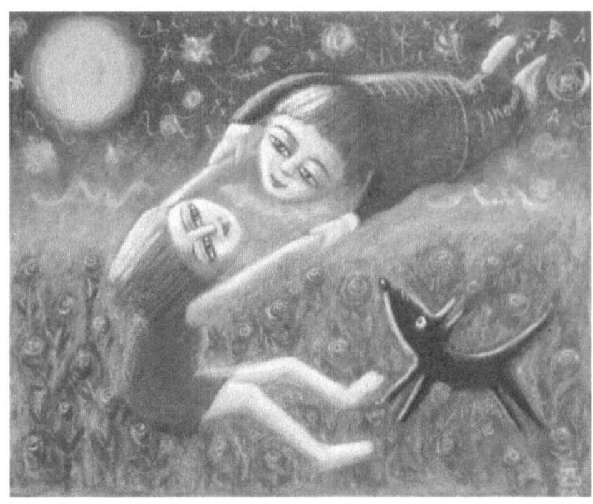

My brother writes to me in England, in a letter of black poetry and thinly veiled hints of suicide. His marriage is falling apart, and he with it. I carefully construct a letter in reply, knowing its importance; wanting to reach over the span of the world to some part of him that will step up to the challenge.

There is something about my brother's need for love which pushes away the very thing he craves. A man who, like my mother, had sentiments at odds with the harsher realities of life, he nonetheless swung wildly between extremes fostered by parents at both ends of the spectrum – a sentimental romantic one minute, then intractably pragmatic the next.

Though diminutive in stature, my father was tough and wiry. He had been a bantam weight wrestler and was not afraid of anyone. 'Iron Man', as Aisie called him, recalling an incident he had witnessed during his teenage years when my father was a tow-truck driver and often first on the scene of an accident. On this occasion my father was trying to free a man trapped in his car but his efforts were continually hampered by a passerby – a 'rubberneck' who seemed to be transfixed by the proceedings and refused to obey my father's demands that he leave. Aisie looked on in horror as my father retrieved a tyre lever from the truck, strode over to the man and struck him across the shins.

My father could not abide 'sissies' and Aisie, floundering in the dreamy pools of his gentle Piscean nature, was always to be found wanting in my father's eyes.

Sunday 7 July 1985

Dear Aisie,

Last week I came across an interview with Shirley MacLaine, the actress …

She spoke of having studied many views, both Eastern and Western, to arrive at her own personal philosophy … She wrote: 'You get back what you give out. If you give out anger, you get back anger. If you give out negativity, you get that back too. There are no victims.'

I found myself thinking a great deal about these words in the following days; in particular, the comment 'There are no victims', which seemed to be harsh words for someone suffering …

… And yet, it kept striking me that there was an undeniable, even though painful, truth in that statement.

When I look back on my own life, I see a pattern. The greater my sense of self-worth, the more comfortable I am with myself, just as I am, the greater is my success with people, and with the world.

In truth, this was really only a recent acquisition, especially in my search for love.

My own painful truth was that I needed to suffer. Why?

I found there was only one answer: because, quite simply, I believed that that was all I deserved.

In a way, suffering brought its own perverse rewards, though it would have been impossible for me to admit or see that at the time.

When I was struggling, people noticed me, and negative attention was better than none at all. It made me special and unique to be the victim of Fate's cruel twists. Blaming fate and circumstances, bad timing and other people also absolved me of responsibility for my own choices.

It was far easier to fail than succeed … Why bother? I would only stuff it up again, lose, have my heart broken one more time …

Oh boy. See the games we play? These sad, dangerous, crippling games.

How to stop this? How to say 'I don't want to play anymore?'… Perhaps it is that simple: to really, truly not want to play anymore; to not want to suffer anymore …

… Have faith in yourself. This is possibly the toughest challenge of all. Have you noticed how it is ten times easier to forgive failings, weaknesses, even downright shittiness in others, than it is for us to forgive ourselves?

Yet, we are in the end, all that we have; our own best friend or our own worst enemy, our jailer or torturer. If your best friend was suffering, was lost, was afraid, would you kick him in the face? Keep him up all night with horror stories? Tell him he's a flop? Or would you put your arm around him, help him to his feet, offer him comfort and hope and be a friend? That's what you must do for yourself.

… If you don't like your life, change it. Take back the reins. Steer yourself … 'How can I? … I have responsibilities. People rely on me!' …

How reliable are you now, with your true feelings locked up inside; all those unrealised dreams and hopes and ideas screwing you up?

… There may be some losses; we are given no guarantees – but have faith in those who love you and

trust that love. You are not chained by anything *except yourself and your fear. Deep down, you know what you must do …*

… Find out how others who think differently feel. Listen, really listen and consider. A lot of people were very sure about their ideas and truly believed them until they experienced otherwise …

What is out there is not a guarantee of happiness. What is out there is every bit as challenging and in some ways, more but what is to be gained is a life lived without blinkers on and a quiet pride in yourself for being true to your heart.

Imagine a tree, deeply rooted in the earth, warmed by the sun, cooled by the rain, reaching for the sky. It yields to the storms, but with ease. It knows its foundations are strong. It offers shade and protection. Be that proud, living thing.

One of my favourite quotes is from The Prophet *by Khalil Gibran, which describes love as being a threshing ground – while love can raise you, it can also cause you pain. It says that we can choose to step away from love and, in doing so, avoid pain, but that would mean we would also sacrifice our true potential for joy.*

… Happiness, peace, beauty are still there but first you must find these things in yourself *…*

Find them. Grow. Ask someone how, if you need to. Take back that most precious thing: your life. Here is one person who has faith in you.

My love and thoughts are with you.

Your sister.

A week later there was a reply from Aisie.

Tuesday 10 September 1986

> *Boy, you sure know how to see through all bull-dust and hit right at the guts of a problem! Once again, you have been spot on with your summing up of the situation and your advice to get out there and go for it was very timely indeed. You're right, and I am.*

In his parochial vernacular, he was saying that he had found hope again and with this, I felt a closeness between us that I had not known before in our adult years. The miles that separated us both geographically and emotionally were swallowed up by our disclosure; we now shared the bond of family in the truest sense – brother and sister, flesh and blood.

But come Christmas Day I received news that he had again been contemplating suicide and was behaving so erratically that the family decided that he was in serious need of help; an executive decision was made whereby he was dispatched to a mental institution for three days – a place he hardly belonged.

Clearly, it was time for me to go home.

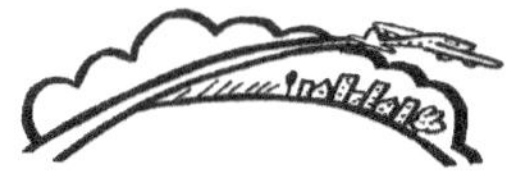

Arriving at Tullamarine Airport, I stumbled from the plane that had taken me from the gloom of a London winter to the dazzling heat of Melbourne in midsummer.

Having purchased the cheapest possible flight home from a dodgy 'bucket shop' travel agent, my trip had involved a fourteen-hour stopover where I was trapped in Hong Kong airport which had sent me to the edge of insanity.

In a matter of weeks, I had packed up my four years of London, leaving hardly a trace in that grey, impersonal metropolis, save for dear friends like Judy, who ran along the platform next to my train to Heathrow, just like in the movies, waving goodbye and dabbing her eyes with a hankie as if I was heading to war.

And on my arrival I thought perhaps I was.

I was jet-lagged and exhausted but as I watched Aisie walk towards me, he seemed even more so. He looked one hundred years old and a boy of ten, all at once.

Driving too fast with a white-knuckled grip on the steering wheel, he equally rushed through the events of recent weeks: the pills, the ambulance, the institution, the 'Big Crash' as he called it. I couldn't help but notice that he seemed almost proud in the relating of his tale of disaster, as if this had been some kind of grand adventure that had cracked open the shell of his anaesthetized life.

Melbourne flicked past and three years on, it seemed pleasant enough, but perhaps not enough for keeps.

Aisie had become slightly scary in his desperation. There was still so much for him to know yet his resistance was a fortress against anyone making significant inroads that might lead to progress. He was crying out for the help that he was simultaneously batting away. His face unsettled me – tight, hollow-cheeked, overly alert; his eyes a bit wild.

The kids were now grown and pleasantly parochial; lacking sharp edges, they instead seemed to have adopted the same resigned pragmatism as their mother in response to the high theatre of Aisie's undoing.

I felt suspended and disconnected, as if I had stumbled onto a movie set, instead of the reality of the next chapter of my own life.

Wednesday 8 January 1986

> *This is heavy weather. Aisie is like a caged animal. There is an awful tension around him and he needs an exhausting amount of reassurance and attention that I can't totally give.*
>
> *He is desperate for answers and comfort yet cannot claim either, for no matter what I offer, he seems to be deaf to my attempts.*
>
> *This morning, in the kitchen, he began to cry and held me to him stiffly and said, 'I love you, Sis,' for the first time.*
>
> *And I said, 'I love you, too,' because it would have been too cruel not to.*

But in truth, I didn't entirely love him then, not there in the kitchen, with things all tangled and so emotionally loaded. This was not my brother but a stranger, begging me for an intimacy we had never really established. This was as clumsy as our youthful wrestling; touching, yet not touching.

He is saying, 'I want my wife and family back,' but the whole family knows that there is an element of untruth in this; yet he remains terrified of the truth, which is that he does not really want these things, at least not as they are. It seems that he must live the lie and die inside or live the truth and die to all that has defined him.

What he cannot admit is that it is not this reality that he wants, but the Wife, the Mother, the Homemaker, the Lover, the Romantic Dream. That which he fears most is living alone or, more accurately, loneliness, which is understandable but the longer he squashes down that which he knows is right and true for himself alone, the more the fear festers and grows.

And Eileen is equally inaccessible, coping in her own way by scudding airily over the top of her frustration; the anger muted, watered down and unspoken. By contrast, Aisie is all words – he assails me with words, as if enough words will provide a solution. He wants me to give him the precious secret and cannot see how much it rests within him. 'I'm trying,' he insists but I know he's not. He doesn't even know how to begin. What he really wants is rescue and there is none – at least none that will do him any good, since rescue seldom does anyone good.

At night, I hear the screen door slide and I know he will be sitting in the darkness of the garden, searching the great wheel of stars for answers, his dark shape a cracked monolith lit by the back and forth fireflies of one cigarette after another. I want to be able to go to him, to sit with him and be his kith and kin but somehow, I cannot. Instead, I lie there listening, knowing that, in the end, he will have to sit alone, resenting, till at last he can sit alone in peace.

God it's such a mess! I am reluctant to play counsellor, as if I could! Instead, I opt for a safe distance by acting only as a sounding board, giving noncommittal responses, because I sense that it is far too treacherous to do otherwise. Aisie expects me to be on his side and, in truth, this is not a given.

It is killing me because I am wanting to scream at him, 'Wrong, Wrong, Wrong!' but I simply can't. It is obvious to me that he is not ready to embrace the self-accountable concepts that might set him free. He is caught up in self-pity; blaming others, or Fate, for his circumstances. Or blaming himself, which is worse.

Try as I might to feel otherwise, I find myself disappointed in him; in my big brother – who I had always admired – not so much for this vulnerability but for his attachment to it.

On so many levels, he is a man of high intelligence and refined ways but so often he betrays this by shutting down into stubborn denial, with all attention focused on his suffering.

In time, Aisie finally gave up his futile attempts to mend his marriage; after many months he was recovered enough to pack up twenty-five years and move out of the family home and temporarily into a caravan park. Being alone did not suit him any more than it did me but his new neighbours were at least company; even though 'dinkum', hard-living types who might have stepped from the pages of Banjo Paterson, they were aligned with Aisie's 'everyman' streak.

'Besides,' old Joe or Bert or Bazza or one of them might have said, 'it'll be only a matter of time before a nice lookin' bloke like you meets some new sheila.'

As if he hadn't already.

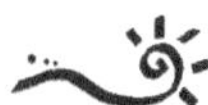

I had returned to Australia in a state of flux. To my mind, I was now without a country. After London and Europe, Australia appeared dull and unsophisticated to me. Watching the news had me shaking my head in dismay as the carefully groomed newsreader opened his mouth and poured forth pure nasal strine.

We watched a lot of news that day – 31 January 1986 – as the *Challenger* spacecraft plunged to Earth in repeated replay against the backdrop of horrified gasps of the parents of the ill-fated Christa McAuliffe.

Most of all, I no longer had a sense of home and family. With my mother now gone and my brother a tortured wreck, I truly felt like the orphan that I was. It was not long before I retreated to the city, feeling like a traitor but unable to take any more of Aisie's troubles for now.

I camped at friends' places, including Oak Grove, replacing my brother's gloom by recounting tales of my adventures, but much had changed, of course: I had changed.

I caught up with Annie and spent a self-conscious night with her in my London New Romantic bob and puffy-sleeved shirt among the punk-edged, grungy black uniform of the patrons of the Espy pub. I was rootless and confused; neither here nor there and while I toyed with the idea of returning to London, I was unsure whether that was my first choice or my last hope.

During this uncertain phase, I happened upon a tiny caretaker's cottage which suited the need for cheap and temporary accommodation while I thought things through. Besides, it was quirky enough to reignite my bohemian streak. The dimensions were Lilliputian. The entire cottage would have fitted into my current bedroom. The shower was crammed in next to the stove, so, if I wished, I could have been grilling a chop with one hand and shampooing with the other. A hunting foray to the local op shop furnished the room with a sagging fold-out bed, which was really just a piece of foam bent in half with a nauseating orange floral cover from the high 70s.

The addition of a card table and some folding chairs meant that I could entertain two guests at a time, though it was a squeeze and if anyone should try to sit on my 'sofa' they would soon sink slowly towards the corner. I made a sign out of a piece of wood and christened the cottage *The Lady Wanda Horsblott Home for Wayward Gnomes.*

Continuing the temporary theme, I signed on for temp work and as a result, for the first time in my life, experienced the joys of working for the Australian Government. This was the heyday of the Public Service – the last party on taxpayer's money – and it was an eye-opener after the restrictions of the private sector and its limited budget.

The fact that it was my first day was as good an excuse as any for lunch (as were birthdays, funerals, winning a game of golf, getting a haircut or breaking wind). After an hour and a half of uninterrupted drinking, I was becoming somewhat concerned about returning to my desk but my boss was gaily ordering another round for the team and raising his glass to the assembled, so it seemed rude not to join in.

And so I became initiated to the ritual of the Extended Friday Lunch. Midday would herald an exodus to the pub and the one or two employees with a conscience were cast adrift among a sea of empty desks to hold up the country singlehandedly, while we paid homage to the Aussie larrikin spirit at the bar.

One of the regulars was Harry*. (I always called him by his surname. It amused me that someone could have two christian names as their handle.) Harry was a good man, with a retirement fund and fondness for a red. In fact, he had quite an advanced cellar in the crawl space under his mother's house and had accumulated some precious vintages over the years. He studied wine, was enraptured by wine and waxed lyrical about peppery tones, strawberry highlights and musky after-tones, so it was with horror that on one occasion he visited his cellar to discover that there had been a snail plague and that a favoured snail delicacy was wine labels .

Harry was beside himself. There was no telling a Chateau Plonko at $5.95 from a Grange at $100 a pop. By day's end, he had spread enough snail bait to cause the extinction of an entire species.

Though kind and amusing, this was not the type of man I had ever envisioned spending my life with. But I was tired. I had taken a hammering. I had lost my zeal for the challenge of more exotic men. I had given up the dream of my intellectual writer/artist/film-maker and our home in the country with big windows framing bucolic scenes, our desks abutted and the two of us reading poetry by firelight.

I had given up on the hope of a wild and passionate love affair that would sweep me up to the same place that I had shared with D. Those days were gone.

I was at a play with Harry soon after we slid comfortably but unspectacularly into coupledom when D appeared at the same show with his new love. Perhaps it was his future wife; I don't know. What I do recall is the torture of sitting a few rows behind them, agonising over my secret ambivalence towards my new partner, while before me the silhouette of my true love touched heads with his companion and lovingly draped his arm around her shoulders.

Who can explain the strange chemistry that ignites a great love? All I know is that my days with D were a rapture of ardour and expeditions into my spirit unlike any I had ever known. Perhaps it was just that we were young and eager for life; perhaps it was the times – the transitional phase from the expansive and innocent freedom of the 70s to the edgy creativity of the early 80s – that swept us along, but whatever it was, D awakened the hidden dreams of a country girl to reveal not only her most secret core but also the artist hidden within.

It may have been the feelings that he created, rather than D himself that I missed most, the possibilities for my own life that he showed me that never came to be with another. The dream of another life, an artist's life; of heart over head; of unpredictable exotic exchanges, volcanic arguments and torrid reconciliations; a life of surprises and passion, shared introspection, scribbled musings on a scarred tabletop, ramshackle towers of dog-eared books, wildflowers in jam jars, walls congested with art, bohemian rooms filled with morning light, the outlines of lovemaking sculpted into concertinaed sheets, the phone ringing, an aria playing, a cat picking its way along the neighbour's fence and a poem written for me taped to the bedroom mirror that said 'I love you' in a thousand different ways.

And, of course, never a dull moment.

Instead there was the known, steady path and while it served to soothe the burden of so many past accumulated shocks, it did not thrill me because it was known; free of nasty surprises. There was comfort and ease but no fire. I missed the fire. Lord, how I missed the fire.

But Harry offered continuity, grounding and security, something I had rarely known with a man. I could rely on him; I didn't have to second-guess him and for once, I knew where I was, instead of feeling fretful and self-conscious as I had done with more complex men. Harry was good to me and he encouraged me.

So what if my heart was always a little elsewhere? He gave me a home, a known, a place that was for me and so I locked away my ardour and my passion and settled for fondness instead and made that do for the next six years.

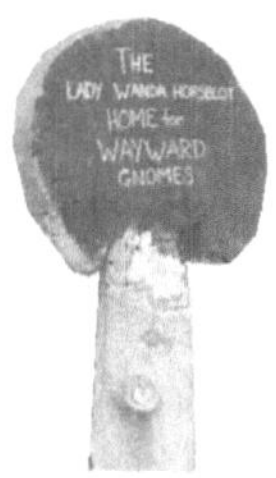

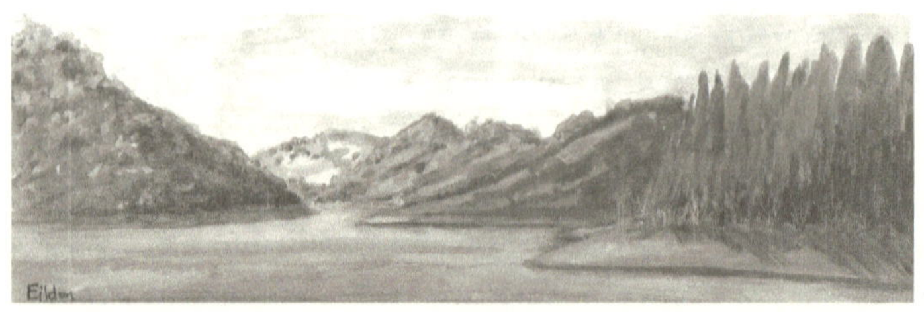

Friday 16 January 1987

> *It is the first night of another glorious summer holiday at Eildon.*
>
> *As usual, I go through my strange insomniac ritual of a first night anywhere; wide awake and going crazy because I am wide awake, while the rest of the house dreams away but I am so happy to be here again.*

We had arrived around midday to the spectacular stretch of lake: blue-green and so enticing on this shimmering hot day that I wanted to plunge in at first sight. 'This is the closest thing to Paradise,' I declared and Harry nodded.

I leapt from the car, threw on my bathers, dashed to the pontoon and dived in. The water was, in every sense, delicious – warm, silky, clean and clear. It was intoxicating and I was in such a frame of mind that I enjoyed everything and everyone, even the yob streak in some of the men, even airy Jen* and difficult, intense Cheryl*.

> *The day was spent in a sweet narcosis; floating on the pontoon, an indulgent lunch on board, visits to the houseboat owned by Tom's cousins and beautiful satiny swims in the bottomless lake. There was a sense of rejoicing in simply being alive; a celebration of sumptuous freedom and the golden glory of endless summer at our disposal.*

At day's end, we chugged back on the pontoon to home base, happy and sunburnt, Cheryl steering on Tom's knee with Harry skiing behind in a lazy way in order to conserve his strength for the long ride back. He was almost forgotten there as he trailed behind like a tethered dinghy, part of the boat and part of the water.

This return trip was almost spiritual. I leaned back, draping myself along the seat, lost in the roar of the boat. The pastel colours of evening: soft yellow, gold and pewter grey, had tinted the surrounding hills a misty mauve reflected in the darkening water beneath us.

Overhead, a hodgepodge of varied cloud forms, banked in high tiers, vaulted into the sky like buttresses in a cathedral.

The lower stratum created long, soft shadows on the upper clouds, caused by the low sun – a phenomenon I had not recalled seeing before, and one that created a feeling of awe in me of how high, how wide, how deep was the life that surrounded me. I felt my soul leap up and dance on all this glorious air and space. This wonderful, magical place!

The boat sliced through the inky water, which appeared thick and oily as if viscous to the touch, solid and slippery and as we carved a swathe above, all below returned to secrecy again in the coming night as if sealed off by a skin like that on hot milk.

Summer was my season and water my element, so Eildon was a perfect combination. We visited Eildon often, both in summer and in winter, as guests of Tom*, a friend of Harry's with whom he played squash every Thursday for years. Tom's wealthy parents owned the timber holiday house that sat at the end of a vertiginous dirt track, overlooking the man-made lake which stretched for miles in curved inlets banked by the Australian bush, which was thick with rosellas, cockatoos, possums, wombats and kangaroos.

In the evenings, we sat on the deck to watch the spectacle of sunsets paling over violet hills and the denuded dead trees which clawed at the water like grey skeletons rising from the ruins of the old town of Bonnie Doon; long drowned on the floor of the lake. Below, kangaroos emerged to drink, their arrival heralded by sharp reports of cracking twigs and fallen branches as they thudded through the eucalypts on powerful legs to the water's edge.

A barbecue would follow, comprised of steaks of monstrous proportions and salads made by the women, if Cheryl would allow them unsupervised access to 'her' kitchen, of course.

Cheryl, Tom's girlfriend and later wife, was one of the few people I knew who made me feel that I was comparatively low maintenance. It was inevitable, at some stage during the holidays, that Cheryl would erupt from the table in tears during a game of Trivial Pursuit or Monopoly, with Tom obediently following her to the bedroom to comfort her.

Other guests were usually Tom's relatives or sporting buddies. The conversation left me unchallenged in the main, with the women discussing babies and household concerns and the men, footy teams and drunken masculine adventures, but I was content enough to relax my overworked mind for these precious days in return for the splendour of Nature that was my real host on these trips.

In her arms, I wandered in contentment along the banks of the water, listening to the shufflings and stirrings of invisible fauna hidden in the undergrowth and savouring the fragrant eucalyptus tang as I rubbed the green-grey discs of gum leaves between my fingers. I swam for hours at a time, weightless in the water, marvelling at how far down into its saltless depths I plunged when I dived and feeling a tiny, exhilarating frisson of fear at the muddy secrets of the buried town that would reveal itself one last time in the drought of the year 2000.

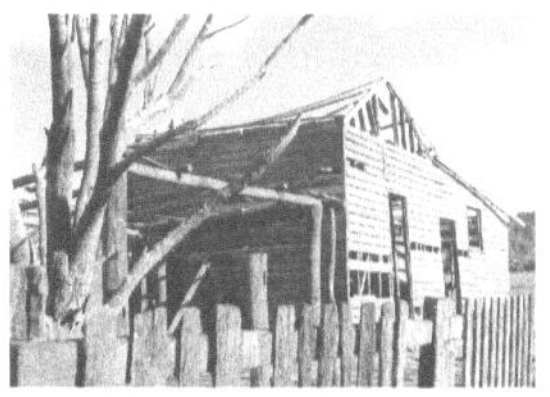

Wednesday 13 January 1988

My brother is in a relationship with a woman called Libby and as a result, seems to have undergone something of a metamorphosis. Two years ago, an anguished man; he now seems to be spreading his wings. Consequently, our relationship has developed into more that of equals, rather than siblings. I suppose I can count this as something of a shared triumph.*

However, I say all this with some reservation. He is still very self-absorbed and surprisingly naive for a man giving 50 a nudge.

I'm frustrated that he still wants to be rescued by the female equivalent of a knight in shining armour. Until he is prepared to make decisions without a prop, he will not be totally free – but there is little I can do about that.

I'm happy for him but I also fear for him. He has a tendency to plunge headlong into things, holding nothing back and leaving himself with little as a result.

I suppose it is lack of experience in these matters that precludes reasonable caution on his part but there is an ever-present whiff of desperation behind his best intentions.

He has already persuaded Libby to meet me and I feel this is rushing the meet-the-family thing, but I guess if she has agreed, then it must be okay.

I find it slightly strange that Libby is only a year older than me. Though there was the gap of twelve years between my parents, it's still something that takes a little to get my head around. After all, this is my big brother.

I sincerely hope that this thing with Libby works out, I really do.

It was the evening of my dinner with Aisie and Libby. To my surprise, I found myself feeling quite nervous. It appeared to be the same for her because conversation limped along well into dessert. I felt tremendous pressure to be the wonderful sister that Aisie had spruiked me to be. Though only a year separated our ages, Libby had a more 'grown-up' quality to her that contrasted to my slightly scruffy and bohemian style as well as Aisie's rough-around-the-edges parochial streak.

Libby drove a BMW and was dressed in an understated little green number with a smattering of tasteful jewellery. She knew how to order in French, while Aisie asked what fettuccine was. He drank beer as Libby delicately sipped champagne and talked about travelling around Europe, while Aisie declared that if he won TattsLotto he would buy a caravan park on the coast of New South Wales. It seemed a strange match.

The whole time, he gazed adoringly at Libby whenever she spoke and he now seemed to have adopted views that were foreign to his own. Despite his enthusiasm, I also sensed that this was not all that he had hoped for; that she, too, was keeping him at a distance.

When we came back to our place for coffee, Aisie cornered me as soon as Libby had gone to the toilet. 'Well?' He was almost panting. 'That's one very special lady,' he said. I was finding it a little difficult to agree with the same level of enthusiasm, but this was a kneejerk reaction in the face of such expectant zeal.

'Yes, well, she is quite nice,' I said. 'But not to be rushed, I'd say,' I added as a caution. What I really wanted to say was: 'For Christ's sake, back off a bit!' Instead, I offered a diluted version. 'You do rush it a bit. Give it some space.' Of course I knew that this would be ignored, which is the way of most advice, when I think of it.

Mercifully, Libby returned soon after, so I was given a break from this inquisition. However, the evening rounded out well, and they stayed until after midnight.

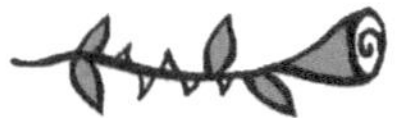

Several weeks on, an old friend was visiting when the phone rang: Libby.

Saturday 27 February 1988

'Has Aisie arrived yet?'

'No, why?'

'He may be upset and I thought I should warn you.'

'What's happened?' I asked.

'I'll let him tell you,' she said. 'Just tell him – one more hurdle,' she added mysteriously, then proceeded to invite Harry and me to lunch the following week for Aisie's birthday.

I was puzzled.

We didn't have long to wait for all to be revealed. Aisie arrived ten minutes later, his face clouded and fierce. Harry hustled our guest and his shopping trolley out the door.

I sat my brother down and handed him a beer.

'What's going on?' I asked.

Apparently, Libby's ten-year-old daughter wanted Aisie out. As a result, Libby wanted time to discuss the matter with her, and from that make a decision about the future of the relationship with Aisie. Clearly and reasonably, to my mind, her daughter came first.

Naturally enough, Aisie was concerned. It could mean the end of a beautiful relationship but his response was bordering on hysterical. Despite all my and Harry's efforts to placate him, he was inconsolable. On and on and on it went, with Aisie flopping about in his misery like a landed fish.

'Should I ring her?' he asked.

'It might not hurt but you have to decide if you really need to,' I replied.

Of course, he rang. She reassured him that she still felt strongly for him and instructed him to ring tomorrow, after she had spoken to her child. Eventually, he mooched off to an appointment. We decided not to go out. It had been a long day.

Predictably, my brother was up with the lark, poking his head around the door asking if we wanted a cuppa, which translated as: 'I want company', so dutifully, we got up. Over breakfast, Aisie was at it again. 'I don't know what to think. It's not knowing that's so hard. I can't handle waiting.' With anyone else, I might have been listening; but I had already heard this twenty times the day before, and I would hear it again, all day this day, hundreds of times.

We decided to go shopping, grateful for the distraction and Aisie went off to the St Kilda Esplanade to find a birthday gift for a friend. By the time we rendezvoused at the car Aisie was jumping out of his skin. He had tried to call Libby from a phone box, only to find that the line was engaged.

We returned home, and Aisie began to call Libby every five minutes, feverishly punching in the numbers, only to find that the phone was constantly busy. He was beside himself. I managed to talk him into going on a run with Harry (and received a glare from Harry in return), which got him out of the house for a peaceful half-hour but as soon as he returned, the routine started all over again.

Eventually and to our great relief, he finally reached Libby later in the afternoon. Harry and I held our breath, only to find that she hadn't yet discussed the subject with her daughter and Aisie was required to wait even longer. I don't know who was more disappointed.

And so it went on, hour after hour. 'Her voice was strange/ she was different./I don't know what to do/it's not knowing that's so hard/I can't stand it.'

In the evening Harry made good his escape to his mother's for his usual Sunday night visit and left me to it, traitor that he was, though it was probably fair revenge for my earlier ploy. I tried every diversionary tactic I could think of but nothing worked.

Mercifully, the phone rang and I practically dived upon it and prattled for over an hour on every subject I could think of to my bemused friend on the other end. After the call, I then proposed dinner and retreated to the kitchen, which provided an excuse to send my brother to the shop for a 'missing ingredient' (which I already had in ample supply) and after dinner, I told him I wanted to watch a program on television.

The second the credits rolled, he was off again.

'Look!' I said. 'I simply cannot think of anything else to say to you! I'm at the end of my tether!'

'Well,' he replied indignantly, completely missing the point, 'I am at the end of *my* tether!'

Eventually, the long night was over, and Aisie trailed out to the car, but it was still another twenty minutes before he finally got in and drove away. I sagged inside the house and reached for a stiff scotch. I have seldom been so relieved to see someone go.

'God,' I said to the ceiling, 'do us all a favour and make this one work out, will you?!'

Friday 4 March 1988

Aisie rang this evening to casually declare that he and Libby were still an item. After the hysterics of the previous week, it seemed that the whole issue with Libby's kid had simply petered out. I couldn't believe it. I also wanted to kill him.

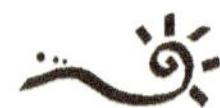

Watching Libby at Aisie's birthday lunch two days later, I again found myself intrigued by her and Aisie's partnership. She seemed just a little aloof and there was something slightly scratchy around the edges that pushed its way through in her manner, like the way she couldn't seem to resist having little digs at Aisie.

I found it interesting that, once again, Aisie had chosen a woman who was in the main undemonstrative; a strong-willed woman who seemed unable or unwilling to meet his needs for affection and appreciation. This was far from the romantic heroine he may have visualised in his dreams.

Monday 20 June 1988

Aisie has moved in with Libby.

He appears to have changed quite a lot; better in some ways, equally irritating in others. He is becoming quite cultured, of all things and he is now terribly formal and polite. He even had a dig at me today for sounding strine! I don't know which Aisie I prefer.

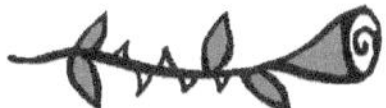

By 1990, Harry and I had bought a small cottage in inner city Richmond and I had been working for three years at the Royal Victorian Institute for the Blind (RVIB), a labyrinthine Victorian mansion set in the splendid sweeping gardens of the era. I had an unusual job, creating tactile interpretations of diagrams and illustrations from textbooks to assist visually impaired students with their studies.

All manner of materials were used to make these diagrams: string, sandpaper, plastic, buttons, wire, fabric; in fact, anything that might give a tactile sense of the visual item. Once completed, the diagrams were labelled in Braille and placed in a press under a plasticised sheet which, when heated, produced a raised impression of the original diagram.

Despite the creative aspect of this job and the opportunity it afforded to do good works, the work was sporadic and limited in terms of career advancement and I still had higher aspirations.

Though I struggled mightily to find self-worth in relationships, I had developed a certain 'can-do' attitude regarding career objectives, which had driven me since the early 80s. I simply ignored my lack of broader education and the fact that there were no letters after my name. I set the goal high and then found a way to reach it; usually by winging it.

Thus, I once convinced a TAFE administration that I was qualified to teach writing with one published poem to my name and acting workshops to a professional troupe with only community productions under my belt. Through these creative gambles, I found myself mixing with artists, writers and musicians and I was like a sponge; soaking up an exotic, bohemian world which stretched my imagination and fostered a unique and alternative take on life.

Each achievement brought the prospect of ever more varied possibilities, which queued to burst forth from within like rare plants that had finally seen sunshine after years in shadow.

But the real driving force behind my endless and ensuing productivity was not only the liberation of my latent gifts but also the sense that if only I could do more, be more – better, wiser, prettier, stronger, happier, funnier, sassier, more successful – I would be loved. And yet it would seem that I had not, nor could ever, do enough.

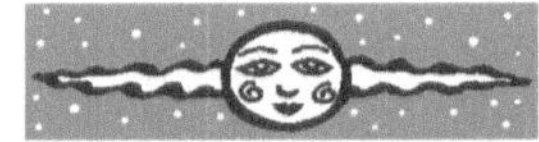

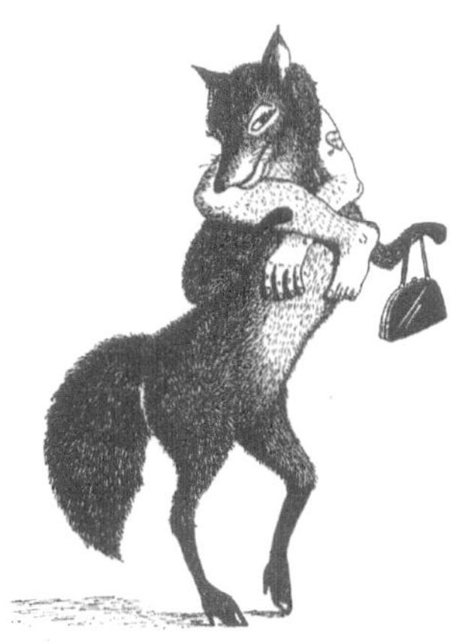

In my free time, I resurrected *Animal Revenge*, a cartoon series I had created in London for an animal welfare fundraiser, which had received an enthusiastic response and sold out on the night. I developed further panels, completing a final set of fifteen cartoons. This was laborious work as, without a light-box or computer, I drew freehand in pen and ink. If there were any mistakes that were beyond the wonders of liquid paper, it meant starting the drawing again from scratch.

Next, I worked up the courage to subject the cartoons to the scrutiny of an editor, in the hope that they might actually be published. Taking a 'sickie', I made an appointment at the then Melbourne *Herald* (now *Herald-Sun*). Folio under my arm, and with an outward composure which belied the quaking within, I showed the cartoons to several editors. Their comments were favourable but none were willing to publish them.

Dejected, I turned to leave when Jo Wiles, the editor of the Sunday magazine supplement, approached me as I was about to exit. 'Aren't you going to show me?' she asked.

She quickly inspected the cartoons. 'Can you leave these with me? We'll start running them next week.'

I walked – no, I *floated* – out of the *Herald* offices that day with a pending contract for *Animal Revenge* to appear weekly in the magazine.

Emboldened by my success, I then approached Bruce Guthrie, the editor of the *Sunday Age*, and landed a gig as illustrator for Terry Lane's weekly column. I was on my way.

After illustrating for the *Age* for several weeks, I was distressed to find that one Friday, my illustration brief for the coming Sunday's column did not arrive, nor did it come for the next few weeks. I began to fret. Attempts to get past Bruce's secretary to speak to him personally were futile and messages left asking him to call gained no response. There was the same roadblock when I tried to contact the deputy editor, who had commissioned my third drawing.

I could see my big break evaporating after only a few weeks. So important was the *Age* gig to me that I had sat up till the early hours doing my debut illustration; a highly detailed pen and ink drawing of the Earth covered in urban sprawl. After hours of painstaking and detailed drawing which went well into the night, in my exhaustion I knocked over a cup of coffee – and as a result, the drawing was unsalvageable. I sat up till dawn doing another version from scratch, in order to meet the Saturday noon deadline.

Now it seemed that the small window of opportunity had shut as quickly as it had opened.

Mulling over my dilemma, I suddenly hit on an idea to send the editors a comic strip 'letter' describing my predicament, which I hoped would grab their attention.

One panel depicted the 'Little Girl from Broadford' floating ecstatically out of the *Age* offices, having been accepted for the job, another showed the previous illustrations with the favourable responses of the editors captured in speech balloons and I drew myself sitting up all night with the phone chained around my neck, waiting for the call that did not come. In the final panel, I drew my hand attempting to draft a written letter to the editors:

'Dear Shi ...' one letter began, with the rest of the word crossed out. 'You bunch of ars ...' was next, also crossed out: 'Listen, you bas ...' Then finally: 'Bruce: I am still ready for the "stable".'

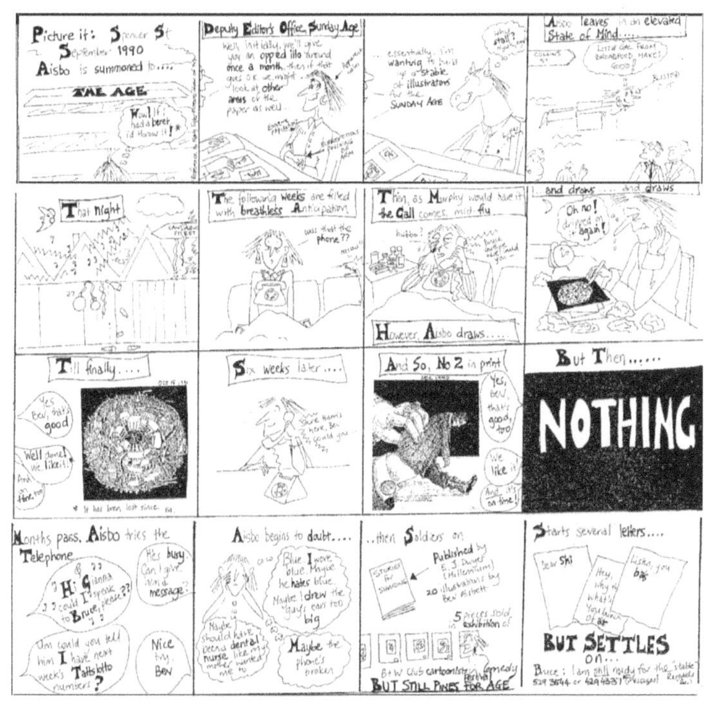

Within days, I received a reply from Bruce Guthrie: 'Dear Whatsername, we haven't forgotten you; honest!'

The briefs immediately resumed and kept coming for many months thereafter.

Two further regular comic strips followed at this time – *Sarah Slakk: Woman of Robust Appetites* in *New Woman* magazine and

The Fletchers, in *New Weekly*, along with illustration work for major publishers, government and corporate publications.

I also began tinkering with an idea for a series of illustrations using the theme of puns about cats and sent off an unsolicited batch of pen-and-ink drawings to publishers HarperCollins, then known as Angus & Robertson.

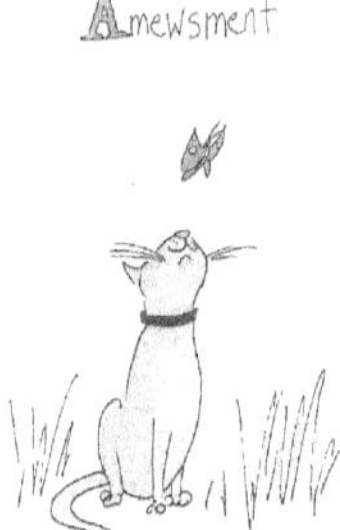

To my amazement and delight, the manuscript was immediately accepted and my first book, *Purrsonalities: Life with Your Cat* was born.

With a resume now including the *Herald*, a book about to go into print and a regular gig at the prestigious *Age*, I felt I was qualified to join the cartoon elite, the Black and White Artists' Club of Australia, known by the acronym ABWAC. Members included such cartoon luminaries as *Herald* cartoonists Jeff Hook and Bill Green (WEG) and the *Age*'s John Spooner and Leigh Hobbs, along with many artists who had enjoyed their heyday in *Punch* and *Australasian Post* in the 50s and 60s.

Buoyed by my growing success, I also decided to take the plunge and pursue a full-time career as a cartoonist and illustrator and quit my job at the RVIB, thus taking a giant leap into the unknown with no safety net; a fact I was regularly reminded of by comments from all quarters.

'You're quitting to be a *cartoonist*? How many of those do you see making a full-time living? Gee, I wish you luck with that!' and so on.

My initial optimism was wobbling. What was I thinking? What if I failed?

In 1991, I set up office with a fellow cartoonist, John Allison.

By this time, I had extended my clientele to include several spots in *The Bulletin* and *Woman's Day* and regular cartoons in periodicals such as *Education Quarterly* and *Health Issues*. Even so, the work was unnervingly sporadic and payment at times unpredictable, which sometimes meant weeks on end with no set income.

I also started to notice that the ideas, which had flowed so easily when I was a wage-earner, were now buried beneath a fretful layer of self-doubt. I became convinced that my recent successes were one-offs; that I had simply been lucky and my colleagues' warnings of failure by may yet be proven right.

Wednesday 6 November 1991

It is one of those awful sulking days, the sky dense and low and looming over the city. It wants to cry, but can't quite and meanwhile borders on a fever with the effort.

I, too, find that at the end of a quite an active day that I am strangely wanting and unsatisfied, as I have been often of late, as if this career dream is not enough.

A strange dread hangs over me, as if this will all evaporate or snuff out, and I'll be left empty-handed.

Things that should be just so exciting somehow aren't. I finally had word from my publishers and my second book, Muttmobiles, *is accepted. The contract is in front of me and they are offering me a healthy advance. My God, this is big, but I am as flat as a tack. Why?*

Tonight, driving home, there are two kids on bikes without helmets swerving all over the road. I shake my head at them and they swerve right at me and I say, 'Do you want to die young?'

'Fuck you!' they say, giving me the finger, and I feel awful – horrible little shits – a rage rises in me and I momentarily want to run them down. I drive into my street hoping they haven't seen me stop outside my house with my trusting little cat waiting for me – I have visions of a horrible malice, and I cringe.

What the fuck is wrong with me? Get a grip! I am in the middle of a wonderful adventure, and I'm undone by some stupid kids! I can't figure out why I feel so edgy of late.

Is this just a bad dream? If it is, please, please let me wake up! How did I get here? How did it come to this? What did I do wrong?

I'm panting, pounding along the footpath as fast and hard as I can, somewhere in the suburban streets of Sydney. I don't know where I am, I don't know where I'm going; it doesn't matter. I will walk in this weird, half-run for hours if need be; I just have get out of here.

I must look the way I feel: frenzied, wild-eyed, out of control; some crazy person talking to herself. With each step, I'm chanting a kind of mantra: 'I'm OK, I'll be all right', but I'm hardly convinced. I feel far, far, far from OK. I am so fucking scared!

Sheer terror is propelling me along this street and the next one and the next. The fear is breathtaking, all pervasive, yet there is no-one following me, there is no assailant, no imminent disaster, no physical threat, but there is also no escape, for I am running from myself.

My mind has turned upon me. I have become my own enemy.

The calm, banal aspects of suburban life around me are somehow charged with a new, sinister edge. The colours of this morning seem somehow unbearably shrill; there is no warmth in them, no comfort. My heart is rioting in my chest, beating so hard, I feel as if it will crash through my rib cage at any moment.

'I'm OK, I'll be all right', over and over, until at last, after an hour or more, mercifully, the intensity eases. I sag into the doorway of an abandoned shop and weep with relief.

It was supposed to be a pleasant trip to Sydney. Instead, I had detoured down an entirely different and sinister path. I had begun a journey into hell. I had stumbled into the pit of crippling anxiety. What I was experiencing on that suburban street was a panic attack, in all its awesome ferocity. I instinctively knew that my life would never be the same again.

I not only knew it – I was terrified by the undeniable, irreversible fact of it.

11 November 1991, Remembrance Day

> *I remember, too well, 16 years ago, feeling much as I do now. I've had a living hell in Sydney. I wanted to curl up and die.*

It was a combination of things; a subtle but insistent tingling of unease had begun to gnaw at me ever since I left the Institute and the safety and security of a regular wage, known tasks and predictable tomorrows. The insecurity of going it alone and with it, new isolation and a question as to whether I was really good enough to succeed – all these things had built up and my new-found confidence and optimism were suddenly very shaky indeed.

Friday, the night before the flight to Sydney, and my attendance, as a now-registered member of ABWAC, at the prestigious Stanley Awards for cartooning and illustration, saw me still awake at 2 a.m. in some undefined lather that defied all attempts to sleep and as a result, three hours sleep had to suffice for the flight to Sydney, the dinner and on to at least 1 a.m. Somehow, I got through the event, though I was lacklustre and strained and far from enjoying the experience. I felt like an intruder there among Australia's finest; invisible, a nobody.

John, my office-mate, and I were two of only four Victorians at the function and the locals at our table were not exactly exuding welcome. Sydney scooped all the awards and an hour into the evening, all I wanted to do was go home to my bed at Harry's elderly aunts' place – Fon and Babe or 'The Silver Girls' as I fondly called them.

At last I left, sharing a taxi with a fairly drunk individual who happened to be heading in the same direction and feeling somehow disappointed and unsatisfied but with what exactly I wasn't clear. Though I was sleep-deprived from the previous night's internal dramas, I was in no better state this night; compounded, of course, by my irritating inability to quickly acclimatise to foreign surroundings. It was 3 a.m. before I fell asleep. Three hours later, I was again awake. The same, strange background agitation was still there and it was gaining momentum.

I decided to attend the ABWAC annual general meeting at the State Library at noon. By the time I had negotiated a vast and alien Sydney, found a bus and raced through the downtown area (by this stage, running extremely late) I was feeling close to hysteria.

I sat in the meeting willing myself not to run screaming from the room.

Something terrible and distantly familiar was reasserting itself – the sensations were undeniable; I was in the middle of a hideous and overwhelming panic attack – a horror I thought

I had left behind in the 70s, along with kaftans and bongs and love-beads.

I sat there driving my fingernails into my arm in a desperate attempt to control the feelings of sheer terror that were raging through me. It was a repeat of all those years ago, 1975, when I had also visited Sydney, in a bizarre coincidence, and if you're feeling vulnerable, Sydney can eat you alive. But unlike 1975, I thought I'd worked through all of this. I remembered saying at the time, 'I will never feel that fear again' – and yet here it was, overwhelming me, spiralling out of control, making me feel like I wanted to die, wishing I was someone else, somewhere else, and wanting to run: but where?

Then, as suddenly as it had appeared, the fear magically lifted away, almost as if a spell had released me. I found myself totally calm, though a little stunned. I turned my attention to the meeting with the gusto of a prisoner given a reprieve. No-one around me knew that I'd been writhing in my own private agony a few moments before. Suddenly I was asking questions and being a part of it all and I thought, 'Thank God, thank God that's over!'

But no. Of course it was not going to be as simple as that.

When the assembled moved to a restaurant, the anxiety rolled over me again in a series of sickening waves. As the bright and witty exchanges of my colleagues flew back and forth, I sat grimly staring at the food I could hardly eat, mustering a grotesquely skewed smile in response to any wayward banter that happened to come in my direction.

Eventually, John and his friend Bob and I headed off towards the Opera House.

As we walked through the gardens en route, the bizarre and jagged tangle of a dragon's blood tree caught my eye. It seemed to symbolise the way I was feeling inside – a visual version of that awful hot/cold sword of fear coursing through me and I could only think 'Why? Why is this happening again – I beat this, I am strong, but dear God, get me out of here; anywhere but in this place, this time, and this feeling!'

I kept freezing on the spot. John, unaccustomed to this strangeness, sought for a gesture of comfort by holding my hand. Bob was kind, but rather dismayed and I was at once embarrassed but utterly petrified. Then, as mysteriously as before, the fear suddenly lifted and I felt calm and foolish, only to find that, minutes later, it came roaring back again.

I rang Harry back home in Melbourne from the Opera House – poor guy, I was totally freaking out, then I rang again to say I was okay, and then again to say I wasn't and then I was, and so on all the foul and hideous day.

The three of us walked for miles, stopping now and then to order me a stiff scotch – trying anything to anaesthetise the shredding fear, but to no avail; the alcohol just emphasised my exhaustion – and around 6 p.m. I put my companions out of their misery and took a taxi home to the Silver Girls. Only Babe was home – at 80 she was remarkable, very sharp and perceptive. She was very kind and could see that I was in turmoil but could offer nothing that might comfort me.

Eventually, I rang Harry again, and this time he was better prepared. By now, I was uncharacteristically humble and willing to do what anyone suggested and the sound of his voice was especially quieting. Babe was relieved to finally have something helpful to offer and gave me a sleeping pill, as Harry had suggested.

And I could see why they were called 'Mother's Little Helpers', because, almost magically I found myself feeling calm and peaceful and mercifully able to sleep at last at 8.30 p.m. I had finally ended Day One in Hell.

As my eyes opened to the day early on Sunday morning, my heart sank as I discovered that this was to be Day Number Two.

The fear had reassembled itself as the drug wore off and I was again jumping out of my skin.

I rose and in desperation, rang Lifeline, hoping to find a kind soul who would understand and hopefully offer a helpful solution. Instead, I found a counsellor who, to my astonishment, confessed he knew nothing about anxiety but suggested that a nice chat might cheer me up. It didn't.

As the morning wore on, I rang Harry again and once more he came to my rescue. This time, he suggested that I do something very physical, so I went for a walk. I strode out until I was pounding along the street, saying out loud, 'I can win, I am strong, I will not let this thing beat me, I am okay,' and so on, walking faster and faster and reciting these bumper sticker slogans over and over like a mantra for close to an hour.

Yet again, as suddenly and mysteriously as it had come, the anxiety lifted in a beautiful release and I collapsed into the doorway of a vacant shop and wept sweet tears of relief. Though on shaky ground, I had somehow burst through the worst of that savage fear and in doing so, I found faint hope that the whole event may have been a fleeting episode.

Suddenly, it was just Sunday and it was just Sydney and I was just on the street and I was just going to have a nice lunch with my niece Michelle and meet her new boyfriend, Mark. I returned to Babe and Fon's in triumph.

'I'm all right!' I declared.

Mark and Michelle came for me at noon. I didn't want to think. I didn't want this thing to get a chance to get hold of me again, so I talked and talked and talked, cramming the space with words, words, words; sealing any little crack where fear might sneak through and I joked about my terrible Saturday, sending it and myself up as if it was a foolish thing, a triviality and wasn't I a silly old duffer for getting so worked up over nothing?

I was not entirely convincing – either to myself or them, as Michelle seemed to be regarding me with some concern but said nothing at the time, though the next day she would call me in Melbourne: 'Are you all right?'

We had lunch at the same place in The Rocks where I'd been the day before. As we walked through the bright carnival of crowds at Circular Quay to a market outside the Opera House, I was struck by the contrast of the ordinariness of this scene to the surreal horror of that poor quivering wretch who had walked there just the day before. I shuddered inside. It was still so close; I could still feel the edges of it.

That evening, with wan relief, I boarded the plane for my return trip to Melbourne. But I would find that home was no longer a sanctuary. I disembarked from the plane with extra baggage in the form of a monster. IT had been wakened from his sixteen-year slumber and he was terrible indeed.

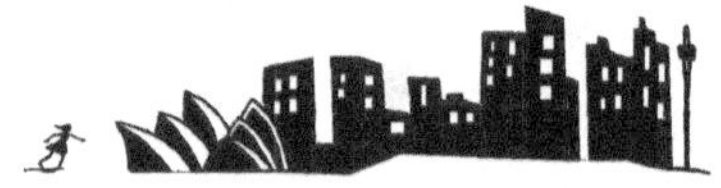

Sunday 24 November 1991

Strange days indeed. I rang my brother, seeking a kind word and maybe some point of focus. Surprisingly, he came up with the goods as he had once done years ago when he sent Jan my way.

Sometimes naming the devil sends it away, and he pointed out just how much it was drummed into us by our parents never to take a risk, ever – and this reminded me of my parents' disappointment when I announced that I was going to follow my heart and leave dental nursing to study photography and their lack of enthusiasm for my new and exciting creative ventures, such as writing and theatre.

No matter that I had achieved some degree of success in these areas; they still seemed somehow disappointed in me for having strayed from the 'norm'. My play had been performed to excellent reviews, I was one of the 'Carringbush Writers'** and had several short stories in print, but they seemed unimpressed by these things.*

No wonder this was now so hard for me. I was taking a survival risk every single day and it didn't sit naturally.

These things resonated but I feel there is more to this than practicalities.

I have discovered that it is possible to experience life as vapid and empty. This is quite frightening in itself. Things like small talk, getting dressed up, buying things or going

---

* *Fourplay* – co-written, produced and directed with Sue McClements and Suzanne Kersten, with cast including the above along with Glenn Filbin and later Simon Fisher. First performed at the Festival of Australian Student Theatre (FAST) 1980 then after at various venues and accepted by La Mama Theatre.

** Writers group established by Frank Hardy (*Power Without Glory*) 1981 for new and emerging writers.

out to dinner now seem pointless and futile. But what then is left to replace the comforting, ordinary things that define our lives?

Today I had been more depressed than anxious and, in a way this was a blessing because experiencing a permanent state of panic is so totally exhausting and all-consuming, it is almost too much to bear. With this brief, though gloomy respite, I plunged myself into work, snatching at the moments of freedom from the snarl of confusion that anxiety brings.

Tuesday 26 November 1991

I am still hurting on a deep level, and I wonder about that wound, where it comes from, what it means and most of all how to heal it once and for all. It has resisted a great number of bandaids over time, and still weeps at the slightest nudge.

I suppose it is a credit to me that I have functioned as well as I have, considering how close by that vulnerability has always been. No wonder it has all bubbled up into full-on anxiety, given the pressures I have placed upon myself.

But the question remains as to what happened to make me feel that I was so small and bad and tainted and unclever despite all evidence to the contrary?

I don't know the answer but during a relaxation session, which conjured sweet images of streams and forests and a woman (me?) trailing a lazy hand in the water, so smooth, soothed and cool, there remained a sense of foreboding, an unnamed dark spot, a pulse of fear and a deep, deep grief that could not be named.

This thing hangs over me in a dark, impenetrable cloud and my greatest fear right now is that having known this, it will be impossible to un-know it: to return to all I once knew of life, only weeks (or an eternity) ago. I am so grey and unhappy, so crippled at the moment. I want this to be just a distant, old, faded, bad dream but I have now seen something and having seen it, I know that my world can never look the same again. There is no turning back and for now, I am blinded to anything beyond this obstacle.

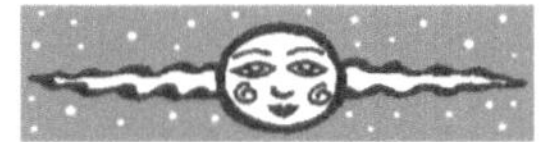

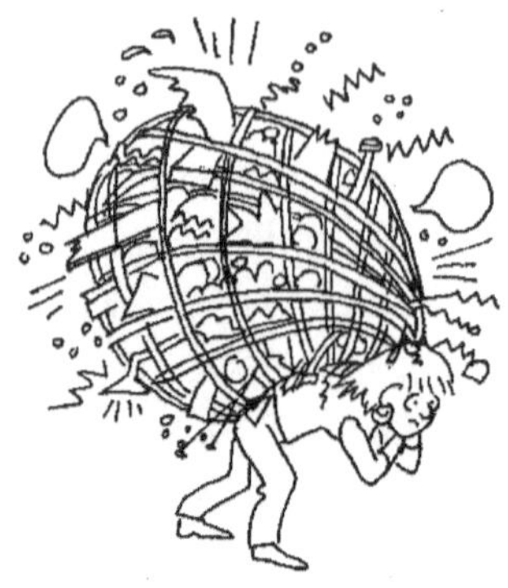

Saturday 7 December 1991

What an alien and terrible world I am inhabiting at this time; a twilight world of tortures and torments that taunt me and tease me and give me no peace.

One weekend during this period, we were invited to join a party of friends at a beach house at Wilsons Promontory. Under normal circumstances this would have been wonderful but these were not normal circumstances. I was the abnormal circumstance.

I spent the days in a haunted internal exile, swamped, confounded and betrayed by a feeling of being apart and difficult and different to those around me, whose gay and blithe engagement with life was like a foreign language to me now. I had become marooned on a distant land and could find no way of crossing the vast and desolate sea that had cast me there.

On the rainy Saturday, the group hung around the house for hours. Empty, unstructured time had become an agony to me, as it left me alone with my thoughts and my thoughts were spears and lances and weapons of mass destruction.

I was desperate for sleep. Yet again, I had roamed the house on the echoing, endless Friday night, a miserable insomniac phantom, willing the mercy of dawn and taunted by the sounds of effortless slumber emanating from the other rooms. Eventually, when the weather lifted, the others left to play or watch tennis and I stayed behind to rest as best I could. But rest would not come. Instead of sleep came a steady and sad procession of Gothic ideas and images.

In my mind I could see the long, empty canvas of beach and the blue promontory in the distance, hazy in the steel of overcast light and gathering sea mist and I wanted so desperately to just walk off down that beach, away, away, diminishing then disappearing forever, as in the final frames of a movie. I lay there planning the note that would beg them not to look for me but asking instead for them to just accept that I had departed physically in the way that I had now departed mentally, emotionally and spiritually, from this life.

I meant no harm, nor to cause pain but this, my own pain, was something I felt I could no longer carry – this sack of broken glass and splintered wood and gravel and shards of steel and bone, this sack of grotesqueries that I now dragged clattering and clanging behind my every step, the festering carcass of sadness and fear that pulled me down – and others with it.

I lay on that bed for hours in a strangely ecstatic, exquisite sense of futility and this absolute romance, this final solution, this dream/nightmare answer was the only answer, wanting, wanting to vault from the bed and scratch that note and walk away … and then I heard the car tyres on gravel and laughter and the bright clatter of footsteps entering the house and I returned instead to the true nightmare that was the reality of living another day like this.

Sunday 15 December 1991

We went to a garden festival to support friends who'd won an award and included in this were the paintings I had done on their garden walls, which my friends declared were the winning factor.

I recalled the agony that went into creating those paintings and how their execution was so excruciatingly compromised by the din of fear that was coursing through me at the time; how I forced myself to plough through the dense static of my vicious thoughts and a racing pulse, willing my hand to render gentle images of wood sprites and nature spirits which were so tenderly contrasting to the raging war within.

At the event I was sluggish and uncommunicative. I could think of little to say and couldn't raise the energy to connect mind to mouth; I walked around in my own airless chamber, cut off from the happiness and life of the carnival around me.

I feel in those moments as if the whole world is happy except me, that nothing can touch me, move me or excite me, as if I have been amputated from the simple pleasure of being alive.

Yet I am aware of how much like a diva, how indulgent this mooching around may appear to others, which only adds to my already burgeoning self-loathing. I am slightly crippled as if I am functioning without a limb or as if I have a debilitating wound. It would be helpful if I did, in a way. At least the evidence of my suffering would then be visible and perhaps more acceptable.

Later, I call a friend whose husband is a psychologist and she asks him to speak to me. I detect a slight sigh in his voice. Fair enough, I suppose. He probably sees it as work on his day off but he does give some helpful advice such as seeing this as a sort of physiological tendency, similar to that of someone prone to migraines, and therefore in the context of an 'episode' rather than an all-consuming condition.

He explains that the aim is to surrender fighting and resistance and stop thinking in terms of a permanent state and suggests that I try to take on only one thought at a time and place a limit on how much time I spend on that thought and deal with the issue completely before moving on to the next.

I tell him that I'm most grateful for these insights and for his time and I make a personal note to myself to stop pestering others so much.

Despite my best efforts to apply my friend's husband's advice, I still found myself in a terrible state and in being so, I felt that I had let myself and others down. I strafed myself with absolutes: Should! Must! Have to! about not yet having mastered this thing.

Compounding this was the additional problem that I felt that I couldn't now call on anyone that I knew for help; that I had already overdone this with those kind enough to support me and that others would simply not understand.

I am sure that Libby now sees me as Aisie's neurotic and over-reactive Drama Queen of a sister, someone not to take seriously; something, to my shame, that I am now proving to be.

And even Harry, who loves me, surely must be harbouring serious concerns about my sanity, yet I cannot be who I want to be for him and now he must be suffering too, because of me.

> *How do I change the very core of my being? How do I become other than who and how and what I am? And indeed, who and how and what am I? Right now: a cringing, sad, fearful and lost creature. I weep as I write this; great, gut-wrenching sobs. All feels lost to me now. I can't even remember what feeling 'normal' was like anymore.*

I missed people, or rather, I missed being *of* people, being one of them: normal, ordinary, just living and breathing without a second thought. I missed life, or more accurately, I missed the feeling of being alive as a right, or even a blessing, rather than a punishment.

One night, I drew a picture of that fear; the monster living within me. It was organic, emanating from a centrepoint in my solar plexus – the *Seat of the Soul*, as it is known – with arms that wrapped around me like an evil octopus; electrified arms with spikes, the better to hold me to it.

> *Sometimes I even go to crazy places in my mind and imagine it is the product of some ancient curse or that it is actually an undetected alien implant or that I am plagued by some strange and as yet undiscovered illness that will condemn me to this ongoing torture for the rest of my life.*

The lack of sleep was overwhelming. I averaged only four hours sleep each night for weeks on end. I was in a loop, for any attempt to rest was thwarted by wild palpitations and even wilder thoughts, and so I skidded along the surface of sleep, unable to dive deeply into its precious sea of oblivion and healing rest. I woke each day startled by a hammering heart and seized by a breathless rush that set me upright in a fearful spasm to begin my next twenty hours in hellish wakefulness.

Attempts to rest during the day were equally fruitless, taunted as I was by an otherworldly and alienating quality to the light leaking into the room from the day outside and the familiar objects that surrounded me – once so ordinary and comforting – were now inexplicably sinister, and as I lay down and tried to surrender to the sleep that I longed for, my heart again raged so strongly that I was virtually lifted off the bed.

Thursday 18 December 1991

This anxiety is crippling me and sabotaging any chance of success that is within reach.

I suspect I am suffering most from a lack of confidence in my own ability to perform when I have to but this is all bullshit, really, because I can and I have and I do – I just have to convince myself of this and must do so soon.

Meanwhile, I am not enjoying much at all; least of all my daily appearances at the office where I just sit and freak out about sitting and freaking out. However, when I happen to forget myself for a while I'm okay.

Soon, I hope, I pray this phase will be just a distant memory; a blip on the screen and little more, but for now it continues; there is ice in my veins and a constantly panicked, pounding heart. I tell myself continually that this is foolish, out of proportion but somehow the truth of this eludes me.

Deep down I don't believe that I'm a crazy person but I certainly seem to be behaving like one!

Each morning, with sickening regularity, I am awakened by a chorus of doubts and fears about my skills, my talents, my ability to make a living, about isolation and boredom and even my worth as a person.

How I long to snap out of this! I do not fully understand the source of this mess; it is deeper than reason; complex and treacherous.

It is beyond my comprehension how a little self-doubt could have the force to blow my world apart.

Harry, who disappears daily for long jogs to compensate for a voracious appetite for pasta and wine, urges me to do the same, or similar, or as much as I can manage, with the idea that this will purge me of the anxiety that is coursing through me like a runaway steed. After days of his prompting, I finally give in; more to shut him up than anything else, being (a) unconvinced of the efficacy of this and (b) having a natural aversion to exercise, a legacy of having been a chubby kid who was self-conscious about her body.

So, it is with considerable resistance that soon after, I am furiously thumping around the oval, chanting my breathless mantra 'I'mOKI'mOKI'mOK', which actually translates to 'WishIwasOKWishIwasOKWishIwasOK'.

I can hear my heart slamming in my ears and wonder whether the poor, exhausted organ can bear any further acceleration than it already endures with the anxiety. The drumming of my feet sounds far away – in fact, my whole body feels alien to me, as if I am just a head on a stick, lugging this body around like a sack, this head full of shrieking horrors and imaginings that I know are bloody stupid but which rant on mercilessly regardless. It is as if I am channelling Stephen King on crack.

And the ordinary world of trees and houses and dog-walkers flickers by in an eerie freakshow as I rotate as if on a parkland whirligig, tethered to a central fulcrum of fear. No matter how fiercely I stomp around this oval, no matter how hard I pound, my mind remains stubbornly tuned to Radio Doomsday. I simply cannot connect with the day and make it ordinary. After four laps, I give up and slouch home.

'How did you go?' Harry asks expectantly as I return, flustered and unkempt but there is no need for me to answer. It is obvious that I feel every bit as crazy as when I left; only now I am sweaty as well.

An hour later I churn through traffic to the office, cursing at the small offences, real and imagined, of other drivers; blaming them for my inability to be a normal human being. It is easier to be angry than afraid. Anger spits the fear outwards, which mercifully directs the arrows away from me.

At the desk, the same paralysis that has cocooned me in ice every day since this horror story began, once more immobilises me.

I am like an engine revved too high but I press on with all my courage, knowing that I must, knowing that this is the only way through; trying to get my derailed thinking back on the right track.

But there are times when I find it hard to catch hold of those zigzagging negative thoughts before they run off the rails.

Old, bad habits resurface – labelling, defeatism, self-loathing – yet I can't quite get to the root and pull them out before they take hold. These weeds are so entrenched, they cling to their foundation with a fiercely dogged tenacity that cannot be budged without Herculean effort.

Before me, an arctic plain of blank paper awaits my genius. I stare blankly at this white plateau and I do not have a single thing to offer it; not one idea, pen stroke or image comes to mind. I cannot work. I simply cannot begin and from this the fear unfurls in a concertina of terrors dictated by IT.

You're kidding yourself
You're crap at this
You were just lucky before
How are you ever going to get this done when you have no ideas?
This is all a mistake
You're no-one
You're nobody
You'll fail

At the other desk, John seems breezily inventive; calmly scratching out his quaint cartoon figures with their characteristic fat bellies and long legs, combined with effortlessly witty captions for truckie magazines and road safety posters; filling entire pages with ideas.

Another hour passes in this lockdown. I want to, I can't; I have to, I can't; I will, I can't; as I try to clear the way for an overriding internal directive that will firmly, forcefully take the whole bloody matter in hand, stop all this fucking dithering about and make an order for an immediate detour in the brain away from all this crap to where the ideas are stored and for the hand to bloody well just pick up that friggin' pen and get on with the show, thank you very much, if you don't mind!

Eventually, somehow I sneak up on myself and at last the internal circuits of nerves and synapses remember how to pick up the pen and do this and the ideas department cracks open its doors for a moment and I make one stroke and then another and at last, thank God Almighty, the spell is broken and, thank God Almighty, it's only 11 a.m. today and not 2 p.m. like the other day.

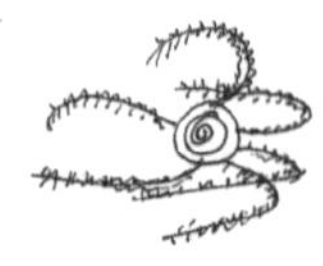

Sunday 22 December 1991

A session with my psychologist. Amazingly, she wants to use a lie detector of all things! Apparently it digs up buried subliminal issues.

She has me imagine a bucket into which I am to throw all of this heavy stuff and then label the bucket with the name of each item as it goes in.

At first, the obvious concerns pop up; the usual suspects: fear, insecurity, sadness and so on and then a thought flickers briefly through my mind that at first I don't really notice because it seems irrelevant.

Even so, that infernal machine picks up on it in a flash with a mountain peak suddenly spiking onto the graph.

'Wow, what's that one?' asks my therapist.

The word is 'Desire'.

I had no idea at the time just how relevant that would turn out to be.

I ask her, 'Do you normally see people as frightened as me?'

'No,' she replies, 'they're usually in Melbourne Clinic, drugged to the eyeballs. In fact, you are one of the most frightened people I've ever seen. But you are also one of the strongest.'

It was obvious that I had only two options: to give in and go completely mad or to fight back.

Christmas was coming. How would I survive it? Bloody Christmas, with all those expectations of gaiety and goodwill.

The psychologist had suggested I obtain a copy of a book by Dr Claire Weekes – *Self Help for Your Nerves*. Though I found it somewhat quaint with its 1962 formality, nonetheless, in the following days this book became my salvation.

Dr Weekes' words conveyed messages that I could relate to and which brought relief: I had classic symptoms, I wasn't alone, there was a way out of this. She described the sensations I was feeling – palpitations, trembling, an inability to focus, dissociation and that sharp, icy dagger of panic and fear – IT, as I had come to name this thing.

Yet how would I fight this? IT seemed almost like a living being. IT was like an entity that seemed to operate beyond my control. I felt possessed and IT was the demon that had invaded me.

Dr Weekes' words gave me the first tools to begin the process of exorcism by showing me a common-sense and practical way of dealing with an irrational force. According to Dr Weekes, there is the awakening shock: in my case, this appeared to be my leaving secure employment and the ensuing insecurities about my worth. The mind/body fears this fear and so a state of high alert is established, in case the fear should return. At the same time this creates a hyper-vigilance whereby the sufferer interprets even minor stresses as potential threats.

To counteract this pattern of 'fear of fear' one must fear it less and let the 'tiger' come, without resistance, thus neutralising it by offering less reaction. In time, its ferocity will gradually subside because it will have nothing to grab onto.

I tried this out the following day, when I was woken in the early hours with my heart racing as usual. This time, instead of responding with my usual additional disappointment and frustration, I stilled myself as much as I could and allowed the fearful feelings to come while repeating: 'Accept, accept' and found that it was much easier to ride it (or IT) out this way.

Dr Weekes' advice was enough to give me new hope and the rudimentary tools that I so desperately needed to at least make a beginning, where once there had seemed no hope of an ending.

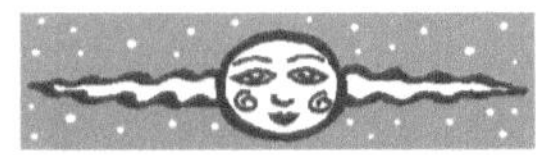

Friday 10 January 1992

It's over. All the terror, tremors, palpitations and weirdness is over. Just like that. I'm not sure how, but I have my life back again! I feel as though I've been on a round trip to hell and survived.

Right now, it is even hard to imagine that feeling.

I saw a new psychologist today who happened to be standing in for the person to whom I had been recommended at Melbourne Clinic.

The session was unremarkable, in a way, for there were no penetrating processes, nor profound insights but perhaps that was the most important factor.

He simply told me I was reacting to stress; that I had probably been under stress for quite some time, that I would be over this soon and there was no need to go digging out old pain – I could do that for the next 20 years and get nowhere – and most of this arose from low self-esteem and that's *what I needed to work on; simply that.*

Within an hour, the symptoms that had raged and lurched and shredded me to bits for months, suddenly subsided to something minor and manageable.

It seemed incredible that all that anguish could have been caused by something as simple as stress.

Yet here I was; my old self again.

When I came home, calm and easy, Harry declared, 'It's so good to have my girl back!'

I couldn't argue with that.

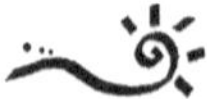

Saturday 8 February 1992

> *It is very hard for me to write this. I thought that I had bottomed out; that I had experienced the worst of the anxiety and, more importantly and more tragically, I thought it was over.*

In rebound, the anxiety was unbearable, as if, in its short dormancy, its fury had redoubled in vengeance for my being foolish enough to think that I had conquered it so easily. As before, I was back to a meagre four hours sleep to see me through another day of punishing fear.

I struggled to make the smallest and most insignificant decision. The agony over a simple task like getting dressed was the equivalent of climbing Everest. I had to will myself to complete the most mundane duties, from cleaning my teeth to making toast for breakfast. Upon leaving the relative sanctuary of my home, the complexity of the outside world loomed large and threateningly as I tried to negotiate the daily machinations of getting to work.

Harry thought that a helpful move would be for me to try out for a government training scheme to assist those who wanted to start a small business, which would also provide financial support while I became more established. All well and good for someone who had a full night's sleep behind them and whose heart was not threatening to smash its way out of their chest.

The three-day intensive was a horror for someone with anxiety: we were set tasks and tests at an alarming rate; spreadsheets, business plans, budgets, costings and the grand finale – a stand-up presentation whereby we were asked to deliver a convincingly passionate testimony to the worthiness of our planned enterprise.

The 'reward' for completing this was seven days at my beloved Eildon, to which Harry had already departed two days prior. I was to drive up to join him on the Friday night after the course. Peace, rest and rehabilitation awaited me among the eucalypts, overlooking the beautiful bowl of the lake where I had spent so many happy hours in what now felt like another lifetime.

I swooned out of the seminar room, utterly spent but overly revved. My nerves were screaming in a jarring soprano clamour, fuelled by scant sleep and the unyielding scrutiny of those three days.

Arriving home, I tried to pack. I couldn't. I couldn't remember *how* to pack. I lost my keys. I forgot my wallet. It was all taking too long and daylight was slipping away. I tried to remember how to get to Eildon and I couldn't. As I drove my ancient Volkswagen through peak hour traffic, my internal chaos was transforming this into a ride in Hell. Around me, all was shrill and intensified: traffic, lights, noise, my heartbeat, the white noise in my ears, till all seemed blended into a strange and sinister puzzle that I simply could not interpret.

I had been driving for over an hour and was still in the suburbs. Night was rapidly approaching and as the headlights of oncoming traffic flicked on, the blur of beams swooping out of the darkness only added to my confusion. I was breathing in short, terrified gasps, reciting the phrase that had become my mantra: 'I'll be OK, I'll be OK', panting it over and over but not believing that this would be true for me ever again in this lifetime. I had lost the thread. The ground yawned open beneath me and I was falling into its depths.

I stopped at a phone booth and called Eildon. Harry's calm and reassuring voice came on the line and I clung to it as to a life raft.

'I simply *cannot* do this! I can't get there! I have to go home, I can't *bear* this!'

He did his best, telling me there was no hurry, it didn't matter what time I got there but when I *did* get there, I would feel so much better and so on but the words were meaningless to me; I was spinning out of control. I staggered back to the car, trembled the key into the ignition and turned it. The engine clattered, gasped and completely ceased; I had seized it.

The final straw, the snapped thread, the last gasp. I hurtled out of the car into the street, so filled with fear, this nameless Gothic terror, this ridiculous mania, that I began crying aloud, 'Help me, help me, for God's sake, someone HELP ME!'

A few metres away an elderly Iranian man, who I had barely registered in passing when I was in the phone box, was walking away slowly, carrying his shopping bags. Upon hearing my cries he turned and without any hesitation or dismay, calmly placed the bags beside him, walked back towards me and gathered me in his arms, where I collapsed, weeping like the child that I had become. As I drooped against the rough cloth of his old coat, he patted and soothed and said, 'It's all right, you're my daughter; you're my daughter.'

The opening of the floodgates into weeping had released some of the iron grip of fear and when he saw that I had calmed enough, he gently guided me to the phone box yet again, where I rang Harry to come and get me, then back to the car, where I sat blindly dumbfounded and spent behind the now redundant steering wheel, while this kind man sat beside me and simply waited with me for my help to come.

Whether because of his limited command of English, or his innate acceptance, he asked few questions, instead sitting patiently in the now descended night, gazing ahead in league with me to some future and obscure horizon and now and then gently patting my hand.

We exchanged details when Harry finally arrived and as we disappeared into the night to Eildon, he resumed his slow and patient progress, shopping bags in tow, towards home and a family who were no doubt waiting in alarm.

Eildon came and went but not peacefully. I had wandered into new and sinister terrain. This was no longer a matter of a little stress or a touch of self-doubt. This was the fight of my life.

Ten days later I returned home to find a note on my front door: 'Please call Jeffe Jefari.'

I called the number and a man, surprisingly fluent in English, answered with that name. At first, I wondered if I had been duped in some way but he then explained that he shared the same name with his father.

'Please, who are you?' he asked. 'My father kept asking us to bring him to see you and we didn't know why. He was most insistent but we could not arrange this.'

'I'm just someone who was not well and he helped me. I'm very, very grateful to him. He was very kind to me. Can I ask why you wanted me to call you?'

'My father died last week,' he said.

I hung up from that phone call with a sense that something profound had taken place between we two strangers on that dark, dark night.

I have often wondered how different things might have been had it been another person, another reaction; indeed, someone from my own culture, and I have also wondered about the strange statement with which my champion chose to comfort me: 'It's all right, you're my daughter.'

In more ways than I, or he, would ever know, our meeting was fated.

The dedication in *Living with IT* reads 'To Jeffe Jefari, my Guardian Angel'.

At Eildon, I discovered that out of the ten people present, three had been through the same thing as I was going through – in fact, Karen had been through it three times. Despite my fears of revealing the extent of my problems, I found that those present were wonderful: supportive, gentle and understanding.

By now, I had surrendered my fierce resistance to medication and decided to try the anti-depressants prescribed for me the day before my departure. Although the drug seemed to initially calm me on that harrowing night, I found I could hardly put two thoughts together the next day. Immersed in a deep, uncomprehending fog, I could hardly read, or make sense of things. If this was how it was going to be, I wondered, how was I possibly going to be able to work?

After driving into town, Cheryl left me sitting on a park bench like an invalid aunt while she went to get some groceries. Somehow I had to push through the dense mist that engulfed me. I went to the newsagents and bought a pen.

On the back of the piece of cardboard bearing Jeffe Jefari's address, I began to draw a cartoon. It seemed to take forever to align my mind with my shaky hand but eventually, I finished it. Though not my finest work, it was a small triumph but the effort involved was a daunting prospect for any hopes of being able to work effectively.

Early that evening, I was quite calm. I sat on the balcony and watched stars twitch on the water for more than an hour. Then it was time to take another pill. Within two hours, the panic had risen again to an overwhelming level.

The women rallied around, collected Harry, issued us with torches and sent us on a walk. I have a blurred memory of those cones of light carving through the blackness of the bush and the background echo of the voices of the others emanating from the house. It was as if I was walking through a dream and sleep that night was the usual battlefield.

The next day Karen said, 'You go through the worst pain that anyone can imagine. If you sleep only four hours, that means twenty hours of waking horror. No-one deserves to go through that. And each night, you give yourself a pat on the back, because you've lived through another day. You got through it but you know that there's still tomorrow to deal with and the next day and the next ...'

We decided to return home early. I said goodbye to these wonderful friends. At the very least, this period had taught me about the basic goodness in people. All of them had been so kind, so caring. No-one judged me. Without their support I would not have gotten through as I did.

As we wound back through the Black Spur, I asked Harry to stop the car. I stepped out and stood there with my eyes closed and breathed in the sweet, sharp smell of the bush, which rushed up to meet me. I traced the vaulting trees with my eyes, right up to the sky, which was the colour of turquoise, and in that moment, I felt that maybe, maybe there was hope where there had been none.

I had learned about the value of friends and my own strength, neither of which was to be underestimated.

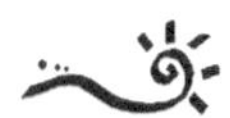

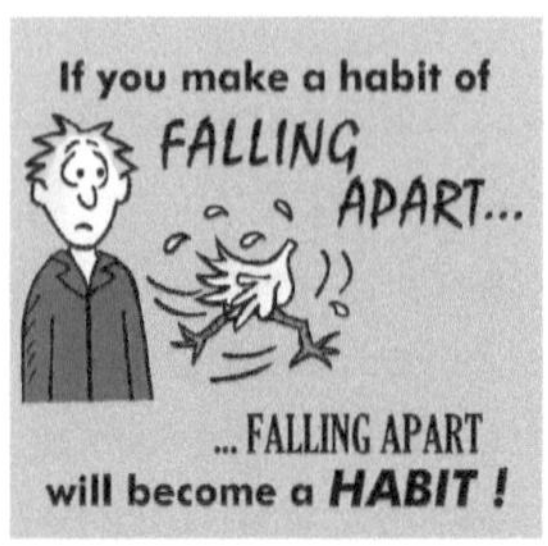

After the trauma of my trip to Eildon, it was blatantly clear that a long journey to recovery still lay ahead of me and that I would need regular and ongoing help.

Upon my return, I resumed my counselling sessions in earnest, though this time, I refused any further anti-depressant medication and instead resorted to a milder tranquilliser to take the edge off the worst of the anxiety but I was still loathe to entirely hand over my wellbeing to a drug and took less than was actually prescribed. Though this meant that I experienced more of the anxiety than I might otherwise, it was nonetheless important to me that I be the one steering my own recovery, rather than medication.

It was during this time that I was introduced to Cognitive Therapy, which had demonstrated considerable success in treating anxiety disorders by addressing the negative and self-defeating patterns of thought associated with anxiety. I immediately recognised the toxic thinking that had hounded me all of my life and how the 'inner critic' voice in my mind was one of constantly berating and undermining admonishments, terrifying predictions of a disastrous nature, even though life suggested contrary outcomes, and habitual and unhealthy attachments to hurts and slights from the past.

My language, both internal and external, was peppered with resentments, criticisms and pessimistic expectations and I began to see that it was no surprise, given years of this kind of poisonous internal propaganda, that I had ended up in the state that I was. The more I learned about the cognitive approach, the more it made sense to me and the more I monitored and modified my self-talk, the less anxious I felt by degrees.

Even so, I was keenly aware that this was no quick-fix. It would take time, patience and considerable discipline to turn around a lifetime of toxic mental and emotional habits. I was used to reacting in an extreme way. It would be a matter of re-training my mind into new and healthier responses and constantly assessing and revising my emotional default position as each new challenge and situation presented itself.

To help make sense of this, I turned to my creative skills to simplify the concepts I was learning into concise messages that would have an immediate impact whenever I found myself swerving into crisis.

I created flash cards that, along with a cartoon, displayed simple affirmations that would help keep me on track – 'This will pass', 'Give it time', 'Let it flow, let it go' – and placed them around the house. Reminders of the main messages of the cognitive approach were also included, such as 'No putdowns!', 'Be gentle on yourself' and so on. Each time I slipped into overwhelm, these simple messages reminded me to guide my thoughts back on track. Slowly, I started to improve.

At first, progress was plodding but in time I had learned to monitor my self-talk to the point where a small internal 'alarm bell' would alert me to a put-down or a negative prediction or a re-running of old miseries, which I would then re-direct into a form which was more supportive, calming or optimistic. In doing so, I was slowly but surely steering my mind into new territory by building a mental bridge that led to a healthier place, instead of the knee-jerk flight to the 'dark zone' that had become a habit; one which had only *worsened* my anxiety.

Nonetheless, I found this challenging, as, in truth, there was a certain comfort in the known, pessimistic path and it would require much ongoing focus and determination to shift the patterns of a lifetime. As the weeks passed, I became more adept at this and found that the more I *neutralised* my self-talk, the less impact anxiety had on my ability to function. Though the anxiety had not entirely subsided, I was in a far better state as a result of my efforts.

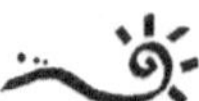

I was just beginning to find my feet when I decided to attend the ABWAC Christmas party of 1992.

Though I was still a little unsteady, this being one of my first outings where I had managed to consign IT to the back, instead of the driver's seat, I was determined to enjoy the evening. However, my first encounter of the night was with cartoon archivist Jim, or JB as he was known to me.

Jim was so dedicated to cartooning that at one point he had sought employment as an airline cleaner, in order to have access to discarded international newspapers. By this stage, Jim had filed and catalogued almost four million cartoon items in his garage and his dream was to create a public museum of cartooning, a dream that had been frustrated several times at the eleventh hour by myopic politicians – and a dream that was met with considerable disdain by his then wife.

'He may have four million cartoons,' she was once quoted in a newspaper article, 'but I have one match.'

Jim's natural passion and enthusiasm were not always matched by sensitivity to the receptivity or state of mind of the listener. I would discover in later years that one often needed a thick hide when exposed to Jim's uncensored candour and a thick hide was certainly something that was missing for me that night.

For whatever motive, Jim proceeded to tell me all the reasons why this was the worst possible time to launch into cartooning and how most cartoonists didn't really get enough work to live on at the best of times and that these were far from the best of times, what with it being Paul Keating's 'Recession we had to have'. Now on a roll, he added that there were few female cartoonists who made a go of it in this cut-throat industry and anyway, most work that was published in the major press was cheaper syndicated strips from overseas.

This little talk with JB sent me over the edge – I could hardly breathe. I thought my head was going to explode. I felt as if I was hearing him from within a deep, echoing tunnel – I could see him mouthing the words but the sounds were blurred and mingled into a faraway droning *blahblahblah* that I could no longer comprehend, yet I was rooted to the spot. My heart was beating with such fury, I feared that at any minute it would burst through my chest onto the carpet in a palpitating red mess.

Thank God for Lee Hobbs, who suddenly materialised by my side and led me away from JB, who, always most contented when delivering a sermon, was carrying on regardless. Stunned, I allowed myself to be guided to safer territory. It only occurred to me later to marvel at the way that Lee had divined my distress at such a distance among a crowd of people.

Lee told me he knew exactly what I was feeling, that he had experienced anxiety and he understood. The effect of this was instantaneous. To know that another had felt this way, that I was not alone, nor was I insane, was enough to calm me sufficiently to get through the rest of the evening, though I steered well clear of JB for a long time afterwards.

Strange that Jim would come to be a friend in coming years. It was hardly an auspicious beginning.

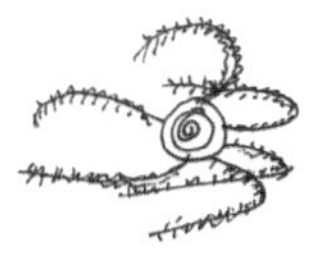

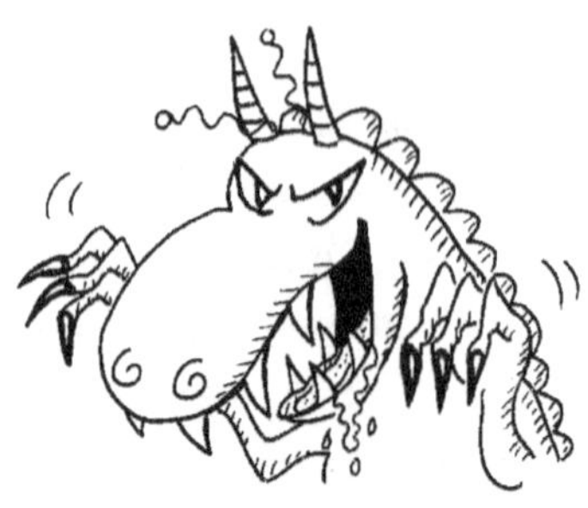

Despite, or even *because* of, these setbacks, I was slowly learning to defuse the worst of my anxiety in a wider range of situations and each test was a necessary element in building my resilience. I was 'training my brain' to respond differently to stress and it was imperative that I keep a close eye on my thinking at all times, as laxity would too easily lead to my mind meandering off-course into perilous territory out of sheer habit.

Another major factor in my progress had been the use of my cartoons to help keep things simple when I was struggling with overwhelm. In fact, the 'visual shorthand' of the flash cards, which became an essential tool for my own recovery, had been so effective it occurred to me that this approach might benefit others, too. I started to put the ideas together as a manuscript which included a cartoon character representing the 'inner critic': the internal voice of negativity which ran in league with anxiety.

I had observed that people tended to call any state of discontent *IT*, as in: 'I can't stand IT', or 'IT's ruining my life!' as if referring to an outside agent, so the name for the character was obvious; also being the name I had chosen for my own anxiety monster – IT. By creating a cartoon IT, I brought the monster down to a manageable size. My IT was now more 'naughty' than evil, more annoying than overwhelming, more troublesome than terrifying.

I had discovered a new and powerful use for cartoons. Woven with and often substituting text, the images demonstrated and deconstructed complex concepts into the simplest and most accessible terms, while the gentle humour brought light relief and a degree of detachment. The lessons I had learned regarding the importance of accepting, rather than resisting anxiety were incorporated in my chosen title: *Living with IT.*

Soon after, a publisher from HarperCollins was visiting from Sydney and we arranged to meet for dinner at a Melbourne landmark, the now historic Miettas restaurant.

I was also delivering the illustrations for *Muttmobiles*, the companion gift book for *Purrsonalities*, featuring visual gags about dogs and their owners in cars. I handed Lisa the illustrations for this book, then shyly produced the rough draft for *Living with IT* and slid it across the table to her.

'I don't know whether this is of interest,' I began but Lisa had already snatched up the manuscript and was reading it with a look of excitement.

'Are you kidding?' she said.

The rest, as they say, is history. Six months later, *Living with IT* was in print and listed in the top ten bestsellers in its first week on the shelves.

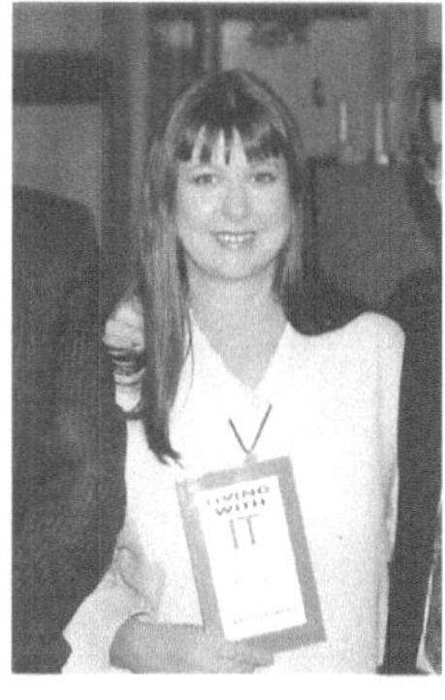

The irony did not escape me that I was back at the scene of my not-so-distant nightmare – Sydney – for the interviews for *Living with IT* and once again, I found myself scared witless, though with my debut on live television and a day full of media interviews ahead of me, this time, anxiety seemed a fairly normal response.

I tried everything to sleep the night before: warm milk, network shopping channels, meditation, warm baths, reading the telephone directory – but nothing helped. In desperation, I even woke Harry back in Melbourne with a phone call at 3 a.m. He did his best, poor man but that didn't work either.

Eventually, I hit on an idea that was to get me through on many a future occasion. I started to talk to myself in the reassuring and gentle way that one might do to soothe a frightened child. That seemed to do the trick and finally, somewhere around 5 a.m., I managed to scrape together a few hours' rest before my big day.

To my relief and despite all the agonies of the night before, I found that I sailed through the interview, especially given that it was conducted before a live audience. I managed to be fluent and focused and did quite a good job, showing little evidence of nerves. Ray Martin was a very kind and considerate host and went to some lengths to put me at ease.

Having managed to wade my way through the ensuing entire day's interviews with some aplomb, I was already feeling like a trouper by the time I was to appear the next morning on a breakfast show. Prior to going on air, the female presenter came into the make-up area where I was getting the once-over, including a hectic hairstyle typical of the early 90s that involved strange teasings, upliftments and headscarf entwinements.

I was tired but quite calm; however, my host appeared to be having something like a panic attack herself.

'Are you *okay*?' she asked, somewhat earnestly.

'Yes, I'm fine,' I said, and I was. By now, I had fifteen interviews under my belt.

'Are you *sure*?'

'Yes, really, I'm okay!' and I smiled warmly just to show her that I really was okay but clearly she remained unconvinced.

'If you find that you're not coping,' she went on, helpfully, 'just give me a signal, and I'll try to cover for you,' and with that, she laid her hand comfortingly upon my own.

I decided to go along with this. There are only so many ways you can reassure someone that you're okay without coming across as the opposite. 'Sure, no problem, thanks.'

However, by the time we were seated in the studio, she was perched rigidly on the edge of her chair. Her eyes were fixed on me in a hyper-vigilant manner as if I were some dangerous nutter who was about to have a violent meltdown on the spot and thus ruin the neatness of her lovely little breakfast show – and her future career prospects, while I was at it.

In fact, her nervousness was so infectious, I found my own calm unravelling and as a result, at one stage somewhat harmlessly stumbled over a word, at which point my host's eyes widened in alarm and she seemed so close to lunging from her chair, I thought I was going to be rugby tackled to the floor at any moment.

I smiled as benignly as possible and corrected myself and it was all smoothed out in seconds and she ever so slightly settled, though it was apparent that she was still on red alert for the rest of the interview, just in case I had a meat cleaver secreted somewhere.

It was a valuable reminder of how contagious negativity can be.

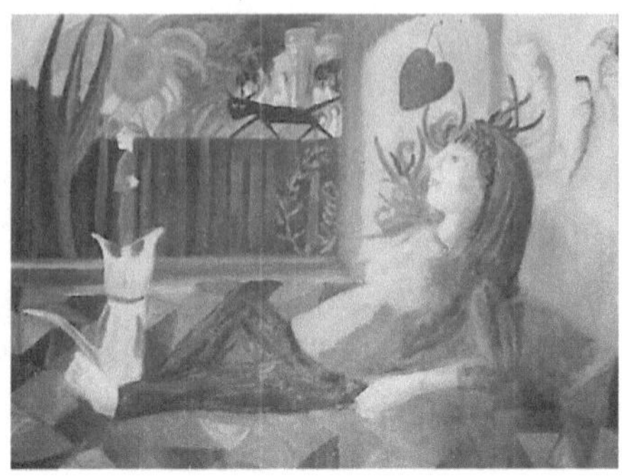

Though I had made great strides with harnessing my renegade thoughts, I still struggled with issues around my self-worth – now accompanied by a gnawing and unsettling discontent on a deeper level that was slowly but surely pushing its way to the surface.

I had kept a lid on a secret for six years. Each time it rattled its box I tightened down the lid, blocked my ears and closed my eyes but it became harder and harder to keep this secret to myself or, more accurately, *from* myself. The truth was, I did not love Harry; at least, not in a way that defined a true relationship.

The word 'Desire' that had surfaced so mysteriously in my session with the lie detector, now sat like a heavy stone in my heart. I did not desire Harry and the undeniable fact was, I never really had. I made excuses, I dodged and ducked, I invented reasons for us to connect less and less on a physical level – he snored, so I moved to the fold-out couch, I had a headache/stomach-ache/toothache, I was busy working on something – but this erosion of intimacy was also wearing me away and it must have been the same for him.

We became housemates, sharing a home but not the deepest part of ourselves. I felt myself drying up inside but was terrified to leave the safe confines of my known world and step back into the free-fall of a life alone. My guilt over this was a festering wound. I felt unworthy of him. His faithfulness and loyalty served only to illuminate my inner treachery and yet I was powerless to change the way I felt. The best I could do was bury the truth and hope that I could make it work.

More than once, my therapist had pointed out that the dynamics of Harry's and my relationship was more like parent and child than equals.

Wednesday 26 August 1992

Finally, in this last session the scales fell from my eyes. Though I had mercilessly blamed myself for my shortcomings, I had failed to see that I was not the sole contributor to my growing discontentment.

The rules for us as a couple were mostly laid out by Harry and constructed to keep Harry in his comfort zone, in the main. Though kind and supportive, Harry was a father figure in my life; a man with firm ideas, definite opinions and set rituals which were actually quite unyielding.

He saw the world in more pragmatic and clear-cut ways than I and, while his practicality was sturdy and secure, it was also restraining. The rules of moral conduct were clear: fair and clear; nonetheless absolute. If I was attracted to another, the relationship would have to end.

The dilemma I faced inevitably brought me to an impasse. While I struggled to feel the desire that I yearned for within the relationship, should that desire be awakened by another, it would mean the end of us.

The rules had been written by a society that adheres to fidelity regardless of circumstances and condemns those (as

I condemn myself) who fall short, regardless of the heart's calling.

Can I really abide by the rules at such a cost to my spirit?

But my own self-loathing overpowered the fact that Harry himself played a role in our growing alienation. To my mind, my secret longing was disloyalty.

Over a year earlier, I had succumbed to temptation one drunken night at an ABWAC meeting with a visiting cartoonist who also happened to be a married man. I was caught out through an intoxicated lack of judgement that in a way absolved me, for no-one with presence of mind would bring home a prospective lover and kiss him in her own backyard.

Harry, who had witnessed this from the bathroom window, saw my ruinous hangover the next day and let it go but I received a nasty phone call a few days later from a friend of Harry's admonishing me like an errant child for my infidelity. And like a dutiful child, I took his word for it; that I had behaved shamefully and Harry deserved better and of course, I had no right to live my life as I saw fit or answer only to myself.

But now the pressure was again building within me. Inevitably, I was tested again when I impulsively responded to the flirtations of a man in my office building but pulled back at the last moment.

Then, I was in his arms and it was so good. We came together, then suddenly pulled apart, torn by duty and guilt. One of us would move away, the other close in, on and on; this strange back and forth dance between longing and loyalty. I was breathless with the feelings that now coursed through my inner numbness. How long had these feelings lain dormant? When did they slip into slumber? It wasn't about sex, it wasn't even this particular man; it was aliveness that I craved.

Nothing had happened, yet everything had, at the same time. I remained where I was after he left for a long time, drenched in a dream-state, gazing out at the beginnings of spring that had once more revealed its glory to me. For this brief period and for the first time in months, I was free of dread. I felt calm and enchanted and the thought came to me '*This* is how I am supposed to feel!'

And, incredibly, I felt *no guilt*, relieved as I was that nothing had *really* happened except an idea; no guilt, that is, until I came home and found Harry proudly showing me some quiches he'd made to take to squash and how he'd fixed the clock I'd found at a jumble sale and arranged an extension on my car insurance, and I felt again that hard, bitter wad of badness ball up in the back of my throat, choking me for my sins.

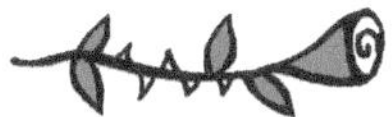

Sunday 25 October 1992

Halloween approaches and with it the trick or treat of a landmark birthday – and as this birthday approaches, I find yet again that the month of October is a difficult one for me, as if the planets crossed swords at my birth, my beleaguered birth, and they do not greet each other any more peacefully on a return visit.

All I knew of any celebrations was that Harry had organised something for me of some significance but where I would once have been excited, I found that I was actually feeling frightened instead.

But of what?

Of not doing it justice for him; of being unsettled, distracted and not joyous enough; being bewildered and uncommunicative – and so, like a snake biting its tail, I went round and round on this old, familiar, toxic loop of dread.

I knew I had to try and rise above this predictive dithering but I found it difficult to do so. Already, during the week I had been a petulant sod and a lesser man than Harry might have told me to piss off for my ingratitude.

Driven by some pedantic notion, I told him that it was important to me that my birthday be celebrated on the actual day, for this year fate had scheduled my birthday on a Saturday but Harry had chosen the previous week for his secret gala. I insisted that any other day would not feel right or true for me and whinged about this until we were on the verge of a row.

So it was, that when I saw just how much love, care, effort and thought had gone into this night, the ugly, selfish version of myself flew up behind my eyes and lodged there, infecting all my senses with its grey and ungrateful stain. And my only thought was that I was unworthy of all this love and care; that my motives were self-interest alone, and I proceeded to prove it by giving a very confused and ill-defined speech in which I even forgot to thank Harry.

I was mortified, when, after I sat down, Julia stood and announced to the gathering, 'And I think we should all drink a toast to Harry for all he has done.'

Consumed with embarrassment and shame, I again rose to my feet and tried to offer my thanks. But of course it was too late, and only served to heighten my blunder. The rest of the evening, I felt only a sick feeling of disgrace and found I could hardly speak to these wonderful friends who were all there, shining for and giving to me.

Worst of all, I could not fathom my own behaviour. Why had I been so insistent about the date? Why was I so hell-bent on squeezing all the joy out of things? Who was I *really* punishing and for what crime?

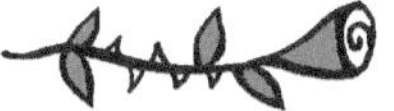

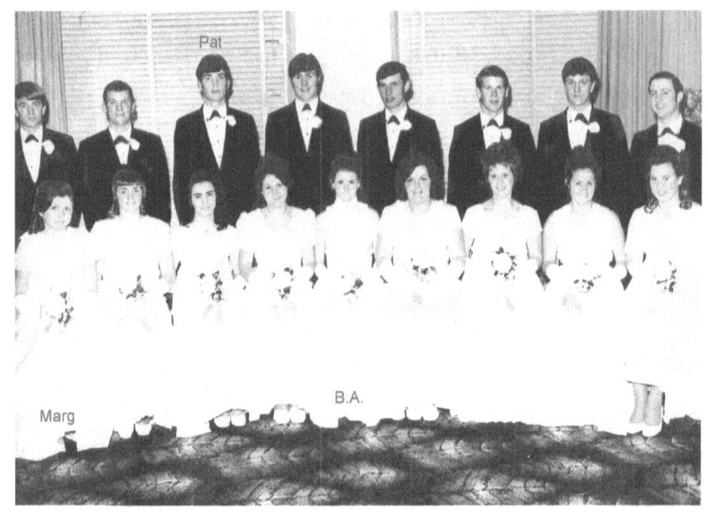

A phone call from my old school friend, Marg, was to set in train a complete turn in my history.

'It's Pat. He's had a bit of a tough time – cancer – though he's in remission now. He's cut himself off from his family and he's living like a hermit in the Dandenongs. He might appreciate a visit from an old friend. Might cheer him up.'

I imagined a dishevelled, toothless and malodorous vagrant, wasting away in a hovel, subsisting on cold baked beans and throwing dog turds at anyone who might trespass into his cloistered life but when I rang him a week later, I was pleasantly surprised by his warm and hospitable response when I asked if he would welcome a visit from me.

Patrick, the third son of the local postmaster and from a good Catholic family of eight children, had been my first love.

I was only 14 when my admirer began his relentless pursuit. Pat attended a Catholic school in Kilmore, while I went to Broadford High School, which meant that there was a period during which our holidays began and ended on different weeks. Pat hitchhiked to Broadford each day during this period in order to hijack me in the laneway which was my route home.

It was a typical teenage romance, full of the hormonal confusions and angst which define this awkward phase of not-quite-children and not-quite-adults. I was at once mortified by this boy's persistence yet longed to see him waiting there when the school day ended. For several days I employed diversionary tactics to confound my would-be suitor, while I tried to figure out what to do with this pleasantly perplexing stalker. I took a wildly circuitous route home to avoid him but still he persisted. He was love-struck and so was I but my hard-to-get behaviour was less to do with coquettishness and more a by-product of insecurity and shyness.

Finally, I succumbed to the temptation to walk past where he waited and allowed him the prize he so cherished – a quick peck on the cheek – after which I ran all the way home, certain that my mother would detect some evidence of my lasciviousness but, to my great relief, I was greeted in the usual manner. When school resumed, Pat was forced to rely on one of the Kilmore locals who attended my school to act as a go-between.

I don't know what form of bribery or threat was involved in recruiting this messenger but since the victim was a far from attractive character with unruly teeth and bad body odour, it may have been reward enough to be on the good side of the handsome and popular Pat and his cronies. It was this courier's task to hand-deliver my first love letter. He stood resignedly at the turnstiles at the local pool, jostled by the scrum of water-logged boys, reeking of chlorine, who burst from the change rooms, flicking towels, hooting and rattling through the gates.

My own cluster of girlfriends skidded to a halt in alarm when this unsavoury creature approached me. 'You Bev Aisbett?' he hissed from the corner of his mouth, as if he were the Man from U.N.C.L.E. I lasered him with a look befitting a warty toad.

'Yeah. So?'

'Got something for ya,' he said, stealthily producing from a frayed sleeve a slightly damp envelope which he pushed into my hand before disappearing into the queue for the bus.

My girlfriends clustered around me as I bore the precious cargo along the street. We resembled a multi-legged creature as they giggled and gasped over my shoulder, urging me to open the treasure, which was imprinted with the tantalising legend *S.W.A.L.K* on the reverse.

I waited till they were virtually panting with anticipation before I finally opened the envelope. My heart was racing as I unfolded the letter. 'My Darling Bev,' it began and my companions swooned with delight and envy, especially when we reached the signature, which was an embroidery of kisses.

The only social event available to us on a Saturday night in those early days was the Kilmore Dance. There we pursued our small-town romance as it wound its way through fights and reconcilations, endings and restarts, other romantic experiments and the complex unfurling of the beginnings of maturity.

While our city cousins were embracing the unfettered freedoms of the 60s and its banquet of discos, drugs and free love, we were content to Waltz or Foxtrot or Evening Three Step to the ratcheting clump and thump of an out-of-tune piano, the burp and fart of a saxophone and the swish and twiddle of the drum kit of the three-piece band of elderly citizens in tuxedos who droned their way through the musical selection of a High Tea.

My father would dutifully ferry me to the event, impatiently honking the horn in the driveway prior to departure as I completed the finishing touches to an entire day's preparations which usually included my mother's frantic last-minute attempts to complete an outfit I had designed only a week before.

At midnight the dance ended with a squawking rendition of *God Save the Queen*, and, snatching last-minute secretive kisses, we would then spill onto the street where my and other fathers were waiting to transport us home.

Eventually, progress reached our small town and a disco was launched in the newly reconstructed Broadford Town Hall and it was not long before the Kilmore Dance became a relic as our loyalties shifted without a backward glance.

One night I glimpsed the sad spectacle of one of the last Saturday nights of the Kilmore Dance. As we drove past, framed by the doorway were three forlorn couples marooned on the now abandoned dance floor, with the band stoically working their way through the repertoire with the same resignation to their inevitable fate as the musicians on the *Titanic*.

Twenty-five years later, I was steering my old Volkswagen up and along the verdant and looping route to Pat's place on the slopes of the Dandenong Ranges in driving rain so intense it threatened to sabotage the entire expedition. Small waterfalls were forming on the sides of the mountain, creating rivers in my path. The windscreen wipers toiled to clear a patch for long enough for me to see through to negotiate the bends and curves ahead of me. I strained forward, trying to decipher the road ahead through an increasing fog forming on the glass, swiping at it periodically with a sodden tissue, only to have my view obscured again a few seconds later.

I ground down to a snail's pace while I considered abandoning the whole venture but something greater than myself was willing me up that mountain and I was bound to keep going, no matter how long it took. In one sense it was reasonable that my anxiety was off the dial as I negotiated the dangerously slippery road but it had nothing to do with practicalities. This anxiety had a completely different tone.

It was behind the way that I had timed this visit to coincide with Harry's annual snow trip. It lurked in the background as I took extra care of my appearance that day, choosing (unconsciously, I insisted) an outfit that echoed times past: a cheesecloth shirt, red velvet vest and jeans. I reasoned that I was just visiting an old friend but not for a moment was my palpitating heart fooled by this. On some level I knew that this was no ordinary day and the wild and portentous weather confirmed what I deeply knew.

The road I was now taking was not the one upon which I would return.

I sat outside Pat's cabin for over twenty minutes, willing myself to broach the torrent of water strafing the car, as well as the stream of weird, other-worldly excitement that was racing through my veins. Neither the rain nor my accelerated pulse showed any sign of abating, so eventually I flung open the car door and plunged through puddles the few metres to the cabin.

The door was opened by a tall, shaven, still-handsome man, groomed and fresh in clean jeans and a carefully selected shirt.

'Hi,' I said.

'It's still you,' he said.

'Well, there's a little more of me these days,' I replied.

'And a little less of me,' he smiled. 'Come in.'

I entered a room furnished with care, the colours made richer and cosier by the soft envelope of grey outside the windows. It felt homey and soothing. Through the doorway I could see a tasteful lunch laid out in the kitchen and in the meantime, Pat offered me wine as we sat opposite each other in easy chairs.

The rain thrummed and tattooed on the tin roof, drowning out all but scraps of music that was playing softly in the background. I recognised strands of Tracey Chapman's 'Fast Car'.

Pat was saying something: his lips were moving but I did not hear a word. I was suddenly deaf to anything other than a fury of excitement, danger and once-dormant desire that was waking within me like Kali, rising like kundalini and ransacking my reason, my natural caution – like a car speeding the wrong way down a freeway.

I could hardly breathe. A hum was coursing through my cells and tunnelling my vision, muting my senses to anything but this monumental moment, this prescient present, this never-ending now. In a sweet and drunken coma, I found myself rising as if not in my will; a sleepwalker snagged and propelled by a dream from which she is helpless to wake; and I launched myself off the chair as if from a clifftop to the fated destination of his arms, his lips, his eyes, which registered a sweet surprise then closed in surrender to the strange and potent spell that had brought me back to him.

I launched myself off that chair and in doing so, simultaneously launched myself into the thin air of my future: the free-fall of my destiny.

Night had fallen by the time Pat walked me to my car. In the distance the city lights dotted the darkness with random starry sequins and soon, I would be drifting down the mountain, my headlights just another of those millions of stars in the city's constellation, returning to familiar, yet now alien, territory.

Pat leaned through the car window and kissed me one last time.

'Goodbye my first love,' he said and stroked my cheek.

We were both wise enough to know that this was not a continuance but a conclusion.

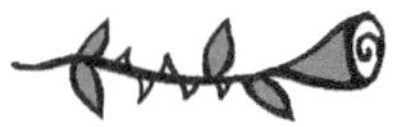

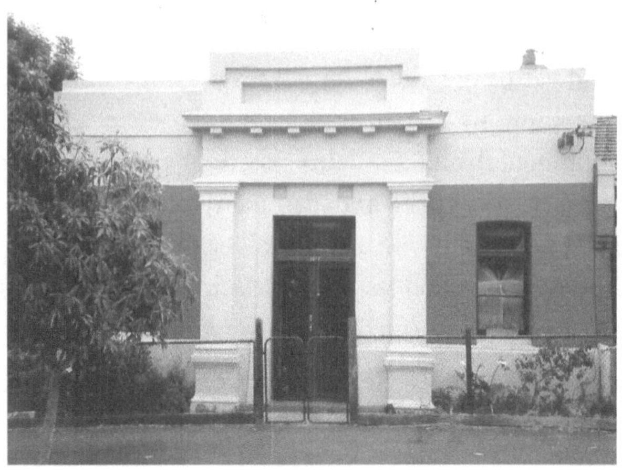

There was simply no question about it now. I could not stay with Harry.

My secret faithlessness now made physically manifest had sealed my fate, not because I would not be forgiven – I knew I would – but ironically, through a sense of loyalty that prevented me from dishonouring Harry by continuing to live a lie. I no longer belonged in this safe, contained world and, truth be known, I never had.

But in having pulled the rug out from under my own feet, there was nothing left to hold onto and – as I knew it would, but hoped it might not – once again anxiety ushered me through the door I had just opened.

Even so, there were optimistic omens as events unfolded with such casual ease and synchronicity, I was left somewhat stunned by the snappy pace at which the Universe was delivering the goods. These 'interventions', for that is what they seemed to be, served as affirmations that the terrifying and unknown path that I had now set myself upon was the only path for me, and that there was to be no turning back.

Within only a matter of days, I had found my next home;

a true artist's pad in the heart of Richmond, something that I might have only dreamed of once: quirky, unusual, a little bohemian.

The building had been a Manchester Unity meeting hall at the turn of the twentieth century, then a spiritualist church in the 1950s. The size of a small scout hall with a large, vaulted main room, it was a perfect artist's studio. A bedroom, bathroom and kitchen had been installed at the rear over the years.

But it was not only the nature of the place and its resonance with me that was provident but the way it came to be mine. It was owned by the sister of an elderly lady called Molly who had lived here into her 90s with her beloved cat, Scottie, until she had been recently moved into care, leaving Scottie behind. The new tenant, if deemed suitable, would be offered a reduction in rent if he or she would take Scottie.

Being a cat lover, and a cat owner (his name was, believe it or not, '147') that was, of course, me. I even included a copy of *Purrsonalities* in my application, which was successful, aided by an equally strange incident.

In order to view the property, I paid a deposit for the key.

While I wandered through the rooms, a couple appeared at the door and let themselves in. When I protested that I had paid for the viewing, they became aggressive. 'You mean you're not going to let us look around? You bitch!' and pushed past me inside. On returning the key, I reported the incident to the agent.

'I thought it was strange,' she said. 'They just asked for an application and when I asked if they wanted an inspection, they told me they'd seen the house from the outside. 'Right,' she said, screwing up their form, 'they're not getting it. You are.'

So, Stanley Street was mine. Little did I know then that cute, fluffy Scottie was actually Satan's handmaiden, the Cat from Hell, a fact I later discovered when I returned home to find that she had defecated from one end of the white couch to the other and 147 now cowered under my car on the street and would not enter the house without me as an escort.

It was no wonder that Scottie had been in a bad mood from Day One. I found out later that her owner had consistently fed her a daily dose of whisky in her milk and she was now drying out.

I spent days making a soothing nest for myself and placed one of Annie's sculptures in the centre of the room.

My move to Stanley Street was an honouring of my truth, but it was far from an ending or even an arrival. I had only just begun a journey into myself that would unfold, in a multitude of ways, throughout the coming years.

Christmas Day 1992

I knew it would be hard but not this hard. With my accursed disposition, not only do I have to contend with the sadness of parting and uncertainty about the future but these normal emotions are converted into the sickening swell of panic, which I must also endure.

Oh, I was so sure of myself: so smug about the good omens of this step when I threw open the doors of this house! But each day, waking to a new and alien silence, I find myself asking, 'Did I really think I could do this?'

The fears that I so valiantly consigned to history have re-emerged. They pop into my mind in small, miserable bubbles which I try unsuccessfully to push away.

I need to keep strong tabs on my moods; keeping a watch for creeping depression or niggling fears by structuring my days and keeping busy, turning my attention outwards and away from myself and reducing stress in my life, for I am vulnerable again.

Having left Harry, I realise that I am missing the point of this whole venture: being by myself and being okay with that. Leaving was my choice, and these are the consequences of that choice.

But the fact is, there is only me, and sadly I find myself so wanting.

So close is that white-knuckled madness and again, I feel unfocused and afraid, wandering aimlessly through the long, unpopulated hours, wanting them only to end.

Once more, I am stranded in a vast desert of fear, yet I am now embarrassed to ask for help. After all, I am the one who cast myself off with such bravado.

At the edge of hearing is that old and terrible calamitous cacophony of my thoughts. It is yabbering, jabbering on and on and on, with notions revolving around a central fulcrum of palpitations, jammed muscles, lethargy and an inability to commit to anything except the monstrous noise of my own renegade imagination, whirling off into new bleak terrains of loneliness and overwhelm.

Is this the cost of following my heart, my truth? Must it be so high?

Though I had entered a renewed battle with my insecurities, nonetheless I had maintained a good friendship with Harry and was pleased for him when he eventually started a new relationship with someone better suited to him. I attended their wedding three years later and have remained firm friends with them to this day. For once, there had been a parting in my life that made sense to me, even though the anxiety preceding and following it was enough suffering for any person.

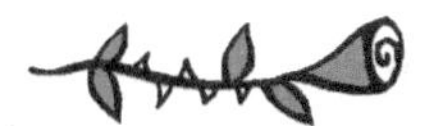

Having tackled one monster – IT – I had inadvertently created another: the idea that I now had to be infallible; this was given weight by a passing comment by a reader of *Living with IT*.

'Having written that must be terrible,' he said.

'Why is that?'

'Because now you have to be together all the time.'

I bought into this nonsense for some time; in fact, it has taken many years to stop flogging myself if I stumble upon old vulnerabilities.

While I had covered enormous distance with my anxiety at the time, I was still very much a work in progress; as indeed I will be for the rest of my life. Like many, I had initially and mistakenly believed that recovery was a matter of simply licking this thing in one fell swoop and then I would be done with it, or IT, forever.

The crushing disappointment I felt each time I found myself back in my 'dark zone' was bad enough but my damning self-condemnation for doing so was even worse. I felt like a fraud. Who was I to be telling others, with evangelical zeal, that overcoming anxiety was just a matter of thinking right when, in a crisis, it was sometimes all I could do to summon one positive thought?

In time I would learn that recovery from anxiety was not an *event*, but an ongoing process involving constant adjustments and fine-tuning with each new challenge. Through diligently making these adjustments and acknowledging the lessons to be learned from each new situation, one gains a milder perspective of that which might have earlier been perceived as 'traumatic' and eventually learns to take life's ups and downs less personally. Slowly, one masters detachment and with improved resilience, old triggers are deactivated, with the result that there are fewer circumstances which might prompt anxious reactions.

Mastering 'divine indifference', as a friend once called it, takes time and practice and is not a matter of eradicating the things that challenge – they will always exist – but of finding new and healthier responses. This requires toning of one's previously flabby 'emotional muscle' and is only achieved by actively applying the wisdom gained through life's less palatable experiences.

Of course, if I was to master this, I would need to refine the art in new and more complex arenas: undoing old knots one by one; meanwhile learning to turn *to* instead of *on* myself, in times of stress. Sometimes, in my quest to think positively, I was stretching too far, only to be frustrated to find myself still stuck which, in turn, led me to question the overall integrity of the cognitive approach.

However, this only demonstrates the kind of *all or nothing* thinking that goes with anxiety: something *always* works or it *never* does. When one is in despair, reaching for joy can be too great a leap; a state so contrastingly foreign, it remains unbelievable and therefore unattainable. Better to move up the scale in increments, aiming for anger, perhaps, to get some fire in the belly, then from anger into frustration, then from frustration into acknowledgement of progress, however small, then to hope and so on.

My biggest handicap was my pride and, of course, the ego. As writer Stuart Wilde states:

> *The ego – it constantly seeks to make itself important. It wants things for nothing. It needs attention. It wants reassurance. It needs to know. On a spiritual path, you accept that you're only ever going to see a few yards in front of you. The need to feel secure is one of the ego's bad habits. To be enlightened is to feel secure because you don't know what's coming next.*

In this case, my ego was indulging in a grandiose martyrdom common to anxiety sufferers by arriving at the somewhat arrogant conclusion that the wellbeing of the entire world rested on my shoulders. This is typical of the kind of pressure I constantly put myself under. I expected that as I was now an ambassador for recovery from anxiety, I should be in a permanent state of unflappable tranquillity.

What I had failed to give myself credit for was just how far I had come – I saw only how far there was yet to go. I had yet to embrace the fact that I may always need to factor in my vulnerability to stress; seeing this as a big deal, when, in reality, it might be as simple as acknowledging that I *was* easily stressed and that it would be better for me to live more gently.

For those prone to anxiety, a delicate balance is required and for some like myself, with a highly sensitive nature, this can entail a lifetime of vigilance. Clearly I had some knowledge but there was still much wisdom to be gained and only deeper experience along the way could bring this. Most of all, I had yet to learn to be much, much kinder to myself. I needed to give myself a break and recognise that, after all, I was only a flawed and wonderful human being, like everyone else, doing the best she could with what she knew.

The need to be seen as being in control is something I observe as strongly present in people with anxiety. The fear of one's worth being judged and found wanting is the driving force behind perfectionism and the 'Type A', high-achiever approach to life common to sufferers. In fact, I believe that the fear of others' scrutiny and feeling 'not good enough' is at the very heart of anxiety. Unhooking from an unhealthy concern about others' opinions is crucial to recovery.

Sunday 16 January 2000

> *What a ridiculous amount of time I have wasted trying to figure out how others wanted me to be! Should I be Cool? Edgy? Funny? Detached? Bold? Vulnerable? One of the boys? The girls? Generous? Assertive? Loud? Quiet?*

I'd search for clues and try to accommodate. It seldom worked, of course. There'd be a tiff or a conflict of interests and I'd say too much, or not enough, or close down into hurt, or be too sharp or, worst of all, collapse into tears and the 'real me', the one I defined as the 'difficult me', would inevitably be exposed.

The thing is I didn't really know who the *real me* was. Was she the one who fitted in and pleased or was she someone who just walked a different path and would only ever really be known and loved by a few? I had become used to gauging my worth through others and in doing so, my faith in myself was undermined by the mixed messages of those who came and stayed and those who came and went. My sensitivities were not only like antennae picking up the slightest shift around me (with my feelings following suit), they were also contagious, with my moods infecting those in a nearby radius.

I had no choice but to accept that there was no point in trying to disguise my inner weather, for it emanated from me like a force-field, but because these internal seasons were volatile, it was hard enough for *me* to keep up with, let alone for others. As hard as I tried to accommodate social mores, there was an inner rebel champing at the bit to assert herself. She popped out bluntly, forcefully, tactlessly at times – but if I apologised for her, this would only further highlight her gaffes, so I remained silent, inviting misunderstanding and creating a myth of ruthlessness and insensitivity.

In her defence, I admired her for her bravery. She wanted to help by seeking clarity; by clearing the air, by being *real.* She spoke the unspeakable, came out with things that others thought but did not say; popped pompous balloons and highlighted hypocrisy, cajoled cowards and unearthed hidden insecurities to bring them into the light – but of course, these gifts were not popular.

And while she could give it, taking it was another matter. Her fragile self-worth took a beating but though she often took it hard, she was brave enough not shy away from the message.

The 'Bitchface Incident', during my reunion visit to Paul S. was especially enlightening on several fronts. Although relatively minor in the grand scheme of things, it was nonetheless a potent reminder of the power of words to either harm or heal. I realised that no matter how lightweight or playful was any nickname I may have devised for Louise by her invitation, it would have still been a judgement of her character and a statement of my own opinion of her.

It is the adoption of others' ideas of us in childhood that can cause a lifetime of harm. We believe that we are 'stupid', 'lazy', 'bad' or 'hopeless at', for no other reason than someone told us we were those things. However, such words can only inflict a wound if we accept that the criticism is in some way true.

In the 'Bitchface Incident', I was still carrying a degree of guilt for having behaved in what I regarded as a selfish way all those years before. If I had truly absolved myself, I would have been able to simply laugh it off. So often, I see people crippled by a costly investment in someone else's opinion of them made years or even a lifetime ago and, ironically, they have ever since set out to prove their critics right. It is astonishing that it dawns on so few of us that we have the right to *disagree*! Further, we didn't have to believe the criticism in the first place!

One of the most empowering epiphanies of my journey out of anxiety was to accept myself as I was, rather than who I thought I should be. I did not have to *prove* my worth; I needed to *know* it.

'So you don't like me? That's a pity.'

And with this, I arrived at two of the deepest understandings about the nature of anxiety that I had discovered to this point: the first being that the problem is not a lack of love from others but a lack of love for *ourselves*. Secondly, I came to the question 'What is anxiety?' In other words, what are we *really* afraid of? And the answer was: annihilation, disappearing, becoming or being invisible to others, loneliness, abandonment and, at the very heart of these fears was this: 'I am afraid I will be kicked out of the tribe. For, if I am, I may not survive.'

Anxiety is thus a primitive fear, reverting to our most basic survival instincts – the impulse to flee perceived danger and the need to belong to ensure safety. This need to belong carries a heavy price. If we wish to belong, we must please, and to please, we must be accommodating and to accommodate, we must factor in all the many and varied preferences of those around us, which we can never hope to do; instead we turn agonising somersaults, trying to be this for one and that for another.

What if I turn somersaults for you and you reject me just the same?

I will blame *myself*, of course! I must be very unlovable indeed, to be rejected by you! I *am* unlovable – just look at me: I'm wrong, I'm different.

No matter how damning the outward evidence of my unacceptability, and no matter how cruel rejections felt, they came nowhere near the punishments I inflicted on myself as a result. I could see myself and my crimes and misdemeanours so clearly through the eyes of others that my defence attorney could only throw up his arms and quit before we had even begun. If they were right then I must be wrong. If I am right, they must be wrong. Case closed; no middle ground.

Others were the 'grown-ups' – nicer, clearer, calmer, more together and, above all, more easily forgiven, so it must be *my* fault if I was not shown respect or if my feelings were not being considered. Either that or they were heartless bastards, who should have been nicer to me; who should have looked after me better.

It was perhaps why I fell in love so often and so easily. I was looking to others to provide the sense of worthiness I lacked in myself. It simply did not occur to me that I had not fully considered if someone was right for *me* – if I was right for them, that was proof enough of my worth.

Nor did it occur to me that it was *I* who was choosing people who displayed selfishness from the start or were simply incompatible in myriad ways and that I was doing so out of an unconscious re-enactment that would prove the veracity of my abandonment story, again and again.

I would come to recognise that people very quickly show you who they are and you either heed this or ignore it at your peril. I would also learn that others do not change to suit you, nor should they. At last, I had helpful insights from which I could master a more detached perspective.

And finally, I would realise that not every encounter was an audition for a lifetime and that not everyone I met had the deep emotional commitment to my wellbeing that I might have hoped for, in my longing for 'family'.

But how was I to come to know all this?

The hard way of course!

It would only be through a journey involving further painful rejection that I would finally find a more loving path by ironically learning to leave others and their needs almost totally out of the equation.

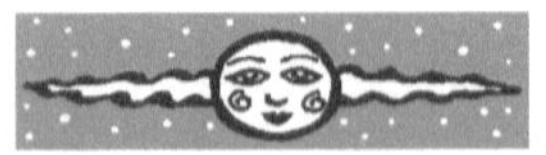

Tuesday 8 June 1993

A brief respite from the ferocious fear that has coursed through me again lately.

I can now count the days free of it on one hand but at least there are now some to count.

But each time I emerge from a downer, I find that I have a little more clarity as a result; that I come a little closer to tantalising freedom. Yet there seem to be so many hidden clues, a combination of buried things that make up this Frankensteinian creation that I can't quite rid myself of completely.

How sweet this brief peace feels! I have no concept yet of it being permanent; these are just snatches of hope along the way. Each time I dare to believe that this has ended and wonderful ordinariness returns to the day, I am snapped back to further terrors, almost redoubled by contrast, as if as a punishment for joy.

This slow and tortuous clawing back to life – how long it takes!

Last night I watched Wim Wenders' Wings of Desire, *a beautiful, magical tale in which angels hover close to us humans, listening to our thoughts and reach out now and then to correct the course of these thoughts to hope.*

How I have called out to my own imagined angels to place their hands upon me! How I long for a miracle to spur me on! Are miracles happening and I just don't see them?

I feel like a ghostly tenant wandering through the rooms of the world – half-connected, belonging neither here nor there; in some twilight zone where I know so much yet understand so little; mistaking odd impulses and sensations for something else, which always translates into fear.

My work (or lack of) is a source of additional pressure these days – I have one big project, but without it I would be destitute as all else has fallen away.

Do I really trust that I will always have enough as I have been assured? Why do I have so little faith? I want so much to trust that I am safe in the world and that there will be abundance for me if I can only believe it enough but there is so much that I have had to take on this meagre faith of mine.

I am trying to find my way but there is always this snag, this jab of disbelief that holds me to inner misery and a belief in punishment. Ironic, for one so lacking in faith, that I should invest so much in an idea of divine retribution.

But I do feel punished at times, for the 'crime' of simply being born; the challenges coming thick and fast – too thick, too fast.

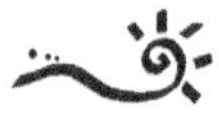

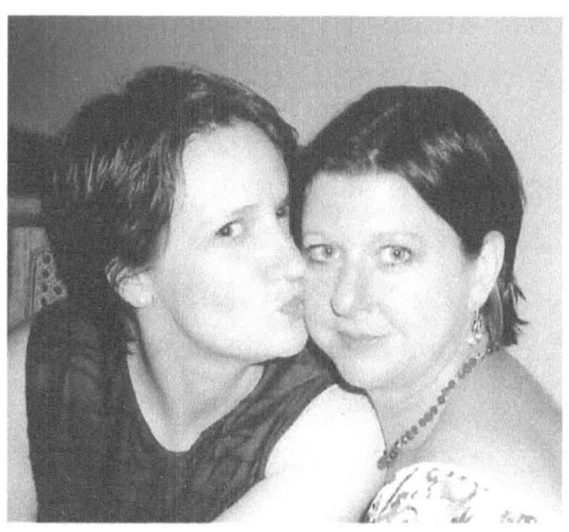

Here it comes; the evil rush, the raging pulse, the clamp on the neck, the bolt in the jaw; any minute now will come the full blast of pain – Gothic pain, pace-and-rock, weep-and-wail, beg-for-mercy pain; a pain to fear, a pain to invoke terror; exquisite pain, off-the-dial pain.

They call it cluster headache or cluster migraine but to sufferers is it known as The Suicide Headache.

Even the term 'headache' is inadequate. Think of headache and you have a minor inconvenience. 'Here, pop this painkiller and carry on with your wedding as if nothing has happened.'

This is no headache – it's a dental drill through the face, a neural fire, a ripping, tearing, searing thing that can only have come straight from Hell. It is called 'cluster' because each sufferer has his or her own strange clockwork version, based on some unfathomable circadian formula peculiar to the individual undergoing this ordeal. My version is every two or three years, for two to three months, every other day, two hours into sleep, each attack lasting up to twelve hours.

I met a fellow sufferer once who lived nearby. Her pattern was several half-hour attacks every day for six months. Neither of us knew which was worse. I guess there are no prizes in a competition for Greatest Agony Endured.

We spent one afternoon comparing notes on the sheer ferocity of this thing; sisters in suffering, our pity for each other's ordeal articulated by the exchange of exhausted tears and the holding of hands; sharing an intimate agony for which there was no adequate language.

My clusters began when I was home for my mother's death. Like any great disaster, the details remain clear and sharp in memory. Java and I were on the train, returning from the city, when I suddenly clasped my face and gasped.

'Are you all right?' I heard him say from some far-off place but I couldn't say whether I was or indeed what the sensation was; I only knew it was sinister, that it was awful, that it was scary.

That first episode was more of a test-run for the main event, really. That one was comparatively minor; easily fobbed off as a once-off, an oddity, a 'What the hell was *that*?' I would find out exactly what a hell it was, for over twenty years.

As dreadful as the anxiety had been, it paled in comparison to this diabolical physical cousin. To have suffered both in one lifetime seemed cruel beyond measure.

I was halfway through the cluster of 1993.

I had dragged myself into the office the day after an attack, in an attempt to meet the deadline of an illustration job that I had been trying to slot in between my attacks, but I was hardly in a fit state. I was pale and haggard from the nightly ordeal and it clearly showed, for my dear friend Regina recoiled when she saw me during a visit to the office that day.

'My God, Bev, you look half dead! You poor thing! That's it. I'm going to call Georgia. At least it's worth a try.'

Regina was clearly desperate to help me in any way she could because her childhood experiences with her mother had been far from idyllic, spent in eccentric households with confusingly liberal approaches to child-rearing which had led Regina to seek a relatively conservative path as an adult in order to bring some stability into her life.

Georgia had been heavily into the New Age ever since Regina was a teenager and was now a healer of sorts. As a result, Regina was somewhat disapproving of Georgia's wacky beliefs and metaphysical dabblings, so it was significant for both of us that she had suggested this course of action. I had never met Georgia before and she and I were the same age, so it was ironic that it was Regina and I who were friends, given the age gap.

Georgia, a handsome woman with a laid-back style and a passion for cigarettes, ushered me into the back garden. 'Just lie there, Darl. You'll be just fine.' I was directed to a massage table which had been set up for the session under a large and spreading tree.

I knew little of what Georgia had to offer but my exhaustion had made me pliable and non-resistant. I lay gazing up at the sky crosshatched by the branches overhead. On Georgia's direction, I closed my eyes and, sensing her presence next to me, I felt warmth emanating from her hands triggering a tingling throughout my body which grew ever stronger until it became a surging electrical flow that was almost frightening in its intensity.

Almost immediately, I found myself sinking into an altered state – at once trippy yet somehow natural – which cast me onto another plane where I was totally removed from the world, and even my body, in a zone of timelessness and profound peace. Time had completely collapsed and my body had dissolved and with this weightlessness and formlessness, all awareness had dissipated; other than of an infinite Now.

Like Alice, I had tumbled down the rabbit hole but there was no destination; only an exquisite vacancy – there was no pain, no fear, no struggle and no 'I' to have that pain, fear or struggle. There was Nothing and in Nothing, there was All.

The experience of the *I* that had plunged me into a pitiless exile through my 1970s drug epiphany had then sent me tumbling into the maw of anxiety. Now, this collapsing *I* was simply the dissolution of the ego. I was no longer separate in my uniqueness but essential to the whole.

I have no idea how long I lay there but when I eventually (and reluctantly) opened my eyes, the world seemed completely transformed. Everything I observed was now crystalline; clearer, cleaner, softer; the garden luminous and more alive than I had ever before perceived. I could feel the hum of the world; the vibrating song of life that I had been deaf to until now.

I would remain in this altered state for the next three days. I could not explain it, nor did I care to – to try to would have broken the rapture. Nothing mattered – all striving and longing had disappeared and with this, the sense of struggle that had ruled my life for so long was now replaced by a serene and unassailable detachment.

Soon enough the mutinous intrusions of the day-to-day world would dissipate and override my small taste of nirvana, but having tasted this morsel of bliss, I was hungry for more.

I gave up reading novels and ploughed through numerous books on philosophy, spirituality, alternative religions, personal development and the New Age; I was fascinated and intrigued by connections between the apparently different worlds of religion, science and the mind. I began to see how we all contributed to the whole and that thoughts were powerful creations and even creat*ors* – if one mastered one's thoughts, reality itself was experienced differently.

I was set upon a spiritual path; one that I had always sensed but never known in such a tangible way. My quest was to find again and secure the same sense of oneness and connection I had claimed in that one sweet hour in Georgia's garden.

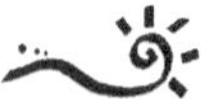

My quest for deeper spiritual learning led to a visit to a psychic a friend had recommended.

As I entered the small, neat bungalow on the far outskirts of the city, I was intrigued by the eclectic display of deities and icons from widely diverse religious and mystical practices that were dotted throughout the rooms. Here, Jesus sat next to a Buddha, who sat next to an image from the Tarot, which sat next to a quote from the Koran, which sat next to a range of Hindu gods.

'I need all the help I can get,' she explained as she noticed me surveying the clashing gurus.

Indeed, the help must have been flowing in because the session was quite remarkable.

'Your trials have been necessary in order to lead you to search deeply within yourself,' she said. 'You did not choose a quiet path.

'However, right now, your energy is very scattered from too many shocks and while several of your chakras are completely shut down, others are overheated. You need balancing, yes?'

I nodded.

'Yes, yes,' she went on. 'It is like you are wandering in the wilderness without a map and you don't know how to find your way home.'

She scribbled down a number on a piece of card and handed it to me. 'These people will help you with guidance, balancing and healing.'

I looked at the card. 'Yasmina – Invitation to Life', it said, along with a phone number.

She met my eyes and held them steadily and somewhat earnestly.

'You *are* going to be all right,' she said and smiled. 'You have a pure and loving heart and your spirit is very, very strong.'

I felt tears spring into my eyes and she handed me a tissue from the several boxes I saw scattered around. Obviously, crying was quite a common occurrence in her field.

She took my hands in hers and again looked deeply and fiercely into my eyes. 'I must warn you,' she said, 'you have chosen a difficult path and your strong nature will not always be appreciated or understood by those who are afraid to look within, for you shine a strong mirror upon them and they will blame you for the fact that you have shown them that which they do not want to see in themselves.

'You must learn to rise above the pain of these rejections and see the fear that directs them. You must accept and make peace with the fact that the path you have chosen is not an easy one and that you will need much guidance along the way. And this,' she tapped the card, 'will help you enormously.'

A few days later, I found myself standing at the door of an unremarkable 60s-style flat in a concrete-surrounded block of the kind to be found in every suburb; hardly a temple.

A woman answered the door, her luminous and gentle face surrounded by a thick black mane of cascading tendrils. 'Hello, I am Yasmina,' she said, in a thick French accent. 'Welcome to IVI.'

We talked for some time and I noticed that throughout our conversation, she held two fingers in a circle, which I would come to know as a means of keeping 'engaged' and in a state of grace during our exchanges. I was then invited to lie on a bed in the corner of the room for my first 'harmonisation'.

Once more, I felt myself sinking into a sweet oblivion under Yasmina's gentle touch, similar to but lighter than that which I had experienced with Georgia.

I registered a softer and more subtle quality to Yasmina's energy that I could only describe as a feeling of pure love. It was interesting to me that the energy *could* feel different, depending on who channelled it; nonetheless, it was blissful and I knew that I had found my spiritual guide and in turn, my spiritual 'family'.

I commenced regular harmonisations and joined a weekly group which involved 'sharing', prayer, phonetic singing (called 'Vibration') and the sharing of food together, headed by Yasmina, who, to me, was the most beautiful of women, both externally and internally, and the closest to the embodiment of an angel in human form that I had ever encountered.

Though non-denominational and with followers from all walks of life and a wide variety of belief systems, IVI (the French acronym for the group, which had begun in France) made use of conventional prayer and, given its religious connections, I, like many, struggled to embrace prayer as a component of the teachings.

However, when I dropped my intellectual resistance and agnostic arguments and surrendered to the process, I found that prayer, with its gentle rhythm and flow, created a stillness and focus for the mind, leading to an inner calm.

The 'sharing' also intrigued me. There was a strict rule that no-one was to intervene, even out of the best of intentions, while someone else was sharing. This meant that even if the person sharing was obviously distressed, they were to be left alone to work it through; there was to be no hand on the shoulder, no hug, no words of comfort. Instead, we were to hold a space of calm for that person. There was no time limit on the sharing.

By stepping back and allowing this flow, several things were happening. One came to recognise that the urge to intervene was often driven by one's *own* needs and discomfort at witnessing another in distress. To intervene may also interrupt a valuable insight or release which may lead to a form of resolution. And any sense of impatiently having to 'wait out' someone else's sharing often served to highlight one's own difficulty in being fully present for another or simply being able to 'be' with oneself.

I stayed with IVI for over a year. It was a time of great learning for me and I turned to the prayer as to a life-rope each morning when I found myself still wrestling with my anxiety demons and poor sleep; sitting on the back porch, dutifully reciting the rosary as I had been instructed.

I began to record my learnings in a notebook entitled *The Little Book of Wisdom* and I found that every day presented an opportunity to re-evaluate and re-interpret my responses from the IVI perspective:

Listen – There is no need to fill every space with words. If you are still, you will hear all you need to know
Use every human interaction as a means of learning more about the part you play in them
The quicker you get to gratitude and forgiveness, the quicker you get to peace
Stop blaming, start owning
You don't need pain to tell you you're alive
Get out of your head and into your heart
Care deeply about everything you do, think and say
Let go of the things that bind you; a little more each day
Avoid 'I am' statements such as 'I'm sick', 'I'm lonely'. You might just convince yourself that you are those things
When you begin the journey, you begin to be alone. We will sell our soul not to be alone, so we pull back. It is only by walking further that we come to know that ALONE is really ALL ONE

Living on the path is to live a life apart; within the world but not of it. Apart, in secret communion with the Beloved, returning to bring back to the world these secret gifts of love and peace, then returning once more to the Beloved to be replenished and cleansed of the world and its gravity

The weekly sharing was also an opportunity for me to release layers of old hurts and misconceptions in a safe and non-judgemental environment and the unconditional love and patient tolerance with which Yasmina responded to my occasional intemperate tantrums of frustration or lapses into self-pity, shone a quiet light on how far I had yet to go.

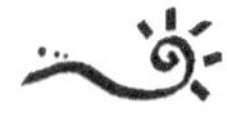

I was deeply involved with IVI when I met Owen*, a Vietnam veteran who had lost sight in one eye through ocular tuberculosis, supposedly through exposure to Agent Orange.

It was interesting that I had met a man who was blind in one eye. My father had suffered a similar fate when, as a twenty year old, he was building a chicken coop and a nail flew into his eye and lodged there. My father wore a glass eye, while Owen's was kept intact by a metal ring inserted into the cornea. In any case, this seemed like a fated connection.

Though a little rough around the edges and still a bit macho regarding sexual politics, Owen seemed companionable enough and I arrogantly thought that my more developed level of enlightenment would be enough to 'educate' him onto more equal footing – a common error of the novice … and the ego.

Owen was a willing student, having already dabbled in personal development via the route taken by many people beginning on this path – the 'MYF' or 'Manifest Your Fortune' (as I called it) path, which centred on attracting wealth or success through mental focus. It seemed to have been working fairly well for Owen so far – he had just purchased a brand-new red sports car, which I dubbed a 'wanker's car', much to his bemusement and surprise. After all, wouldn't every woman be impressed by this willie on wheels?

It was not long after I had started seeing Owen that I read *The Magic of Findhorn*, which tells the fascinating story of the establishment of the Findhorn Community in Scotland – a tale of blind faith if ever there was one.

Findhorn gained attention in the 60s for its gardens, which, though on the same latitude as Alaska, and on barren, sandy soil, nonetheless sprouted enormous vegetables of all types and impossible species for that climate which thrived and grew, including even tropical varieties. For over forty years, people had made the pilgrimage to Findhorn to attend classes in personal development and spirituality.

Owen was fascinated by this story; spellbound, in fact. 'I'm going to visit there one day,' he announced.

Within a matter of weeks he received a phone call from his elderly mother asking if he would accompany her to Wales to visit her sister and she offered to pay his airfare. Owen immediately booked in for two 'Experience Weeks' at Findhorn as part of his trip.

In fact, it would be *three months* before Owen returned, as he decided to remain longer at Findhorn.

Though I was pleased for him, my old fears were stirring, for here was another man who was leaving and I anxiously awaited his return in a month's time.

During Owen's trip I took a major leap into a new creative enterprise that I had secretly hoped he might join me in on his return, as we had tossed around ideas for new mutual ventures prior to his departure. I saw an invitation for proposals for the use of one of the warehouse areas at Gasworks Park in Albert Park, which was an arts complex on the site of the original gasworks plant that had stood there since the 1800s.

With only a week till the submissions deadline, I took the plunge and put forward what was really only the germ of an idea for a gallery dedicated to Australian Comic Art.

I aimed to gather artworks to sell from my colleagues at ABWAC and to help promote the status of cartooning as an art form in this country. As usual, I had not fully thought out the practicalities of this undertaking but was propelled by excitement about the possibilities of the venture.

My proposal was accepted so I quit the office I had shared with John for the past three years. The reality of actually making this new enterprise work then hit home, though I was promised support and promotion from the local council. However, in reality, the park was a somewhat obscure secret, given that it was hidden behind massive stone walls that bore no advertising, so it was only those in the know who ventured there.

Another unexpected problem was that obtaining artworks for display from the cartoonists was like pulling teeth. Why this was so was beyond me but I put some of it down to the strange and somewhat closeted nature of artists in general.

Added to this dilemma was the expense and sheer labour of converting the old building into a working gallery. Regina and Allen pitched in, working tirelessly over many weeks and giving their time freely until the great unveiling in June 1994. The Ha Ha Gallery of Comic Art was open for business. I excitedly sent photos of the opening to Owen, who was coming home in a few weeks' time.

The man I met at the airport was much changed. I immediately sensed a reserve in his greeting and a coolness in his embrace. His recent 'enlightenment' had made him inaccessible and his newly gained wisdom seemed to give him an air of conceit. Our once easy conversational exchanges were now more like therapy sessions, with me as the 'client' as he instructed, cajoled and lectured, riding roughshod over my own hard-won sagacity. Some of this information was helpful, of course. When I was open to listening, that is.

He told me about one particularly fractious Findhorn workshop based on money. Each person played with a set amount. This money could then be donated, stolen, borrowed or lent and may or may not be returned. So-called enlightened and non-material people were weeping and some were on the verge of fighting, Owen told me. This was by far the most emotional exercise he had done at Findhorn.

'Having someone just take your money or even give you money – it says a lot about you and how you are seen. Money is a symbol of love,' he said. 'Love given or taken away; whether you have enough or you lack it. Money signifies your worth – to yourself, others and the world.' He resumed his job, ironically in the gambling industry, which had been held over for him but only lasted there three days before he found it oppressive.

His initial air of cool detachment began to crumble into crabby outbursts and, yet again, I felt the cold hand of panic in the pit of my stomach. I knew Owen was leaving me; returning to his new love, Findhorn.

Within a matter of weeks he finalised his affairs, sold his sports car (for the full price that he had purchased it a year before) and, finally, at Christmas, said goodbye to me. In the spirit of the season and indeed in the spirit of the Findhorn money exercise, he left me a card. Inside was $1000.

A great gloom settled over me again after Owen left. The cold fact was that even devotion to a Higher Purpose was not enough to exclude me from abandonment and likewise, I could not exclude my own feelings from the equation.

As much as I tried to be selfless and happy for Owen, the truth was that I felt not only hurt and sad but also, to a degree, ripped off. It had been me who had initially fostered Owen's emerging spirituality, spending hours lovingly teaching him all that I had learned. I had taken him to Georgia and supported and comforted him later that evening when we had travelled down to Apollo Bay, where, on the lonely lookout, he gazed out to sea, wracked with sobs as the horrors of war that he had kept inside for twenty years were finally released. I had introduced him to IVI and as a result he was invited to participate in one of their seminars in France while en route.

I also noted, with some bitterness, the vast difference between adhering to the Path while living in the world and the cloistered experience Owen had enjoyed of emerging in an environment free of hostility and worldly demands, where hugs and support were in abundance and when all else failed, one could always go and hug a tree. I marvelled at how quickly his cool demeanour had disintegrated once exposed to the real world and yet he had had the temerity to behave like some guru, discounting my feelings and dismissing the gifts I had offered from my heart.

Winter had now set in and the gallery became a lonely, creaking place overlooking the windy and now almost empty park. My heart was no longer in the venture. I could barely keep up with the running costs and did not have the funds to better promote it and because of its location, visitors were few and far between. The lack of support from all but a few cartoonists was a disappointing factor and, cutting my losses but in considerable debt, I decided to continue my cartooning work from home and supplement my income with café work again. A journalist recorded the gallery's demise in the *Herald-Sun* with a headline that read 'Last Laugh for the Ha-Ha Gallery'.

While I turned to IVI for support through this time, I still had many unanswered questions, particularly about the nature of this mysterious deity I was praying to; the slightly 'religious' aspect of the group was something I could not fully get past. I still had something of a war going on with God who, I believed, had dealt me some raw deals.

I was not yet wise nor evolved enough to separate myself from the idea of God as an entity with human foibles, who, it seemed to me, was capable of disowning me as so many others had done before. I simply did not *feel* as much of a connection to God, nor comfort from the divine as I had hoped to and this caused my anger and frustration to surface frequently.

How could I have faith in the indifferent silence that greeted my petitions? I still experienced illness, unhappiness, loneliness and anxiety. I was praying my head off, yet my life remained perplexing. Why wasn't this God, who was supposed to *love* me, fixing my life? It seemed that the more I found answers, the more they were matched by questions and the more difficulties I rose above, the greater the challenges that followed.

Above all, it felt so *unfair.*

I decided that, while IVI was a path upon which good and loving people travelled, ultimately, it was not *my* path.

I had no idea what constituted my path; I knew only that I must find it my own way.

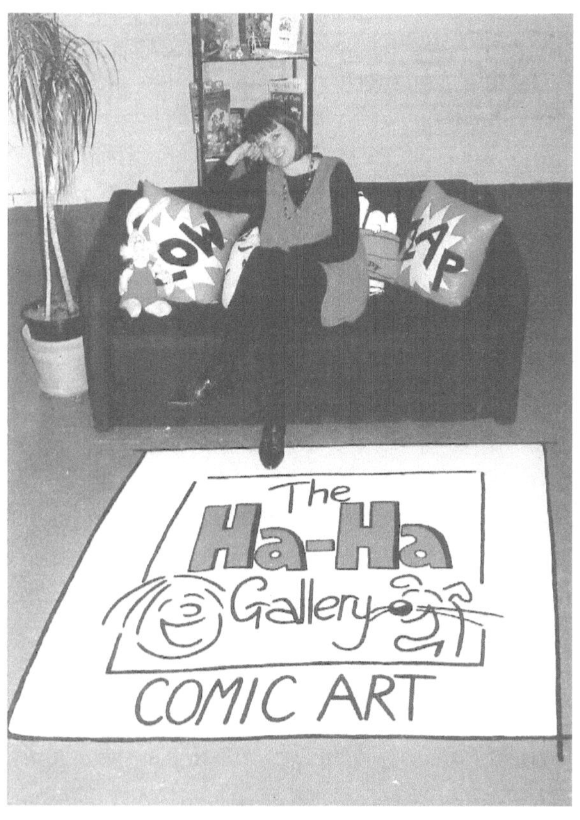

Tuesday 26 August 1993

Today was soft and golden – utterly beautiful. I am now noticing the beauty around me that I haven't noticed for so long.

I often sit in a cane rocker among the ferns in the 'sanctuary' I have constructed on the back porch and gaze out at the humble wonders of my garden, entranced by the way it changes subtly from day to day. Beyond is a lightning-blasted tree whose skeletal frame catches the morning light like some form of energy conductor.

I felt the edges of – joy? creeping in. A wonder in itself – how could I be alone and joyous? – But I was.

I tended to small tasks and felt that same joy in a muted magic in the doing, applying myself with tenderness and meditation to even the most mundane of daily enterprises and I was rewarded with a sense of quiet connectedness and order in their completion.

One of my most constant and adversarial companions of many years, Worry, seemed to be taking a rare vacation this day. It amazes me that I still worry so, as if worry is insurance against disaster. After all, things generally seem to sort themselves out anyway. If only I could trust more, as I have done today.

But these ecstatic glimpses of freedom are gradually becoming more than occasional. Little by little, they are weaving themselves into the fabric of my life; these tiny, golden, precious threads of hope where once there were none.

I see now that this process has its own time. It cannot be hurried. Rather, it is these contrasting lapses of faith that create the richness of a growing trust. In the manner of … a flower, perhaps, opening to light, then closing when a cloud passes – or an untamed creature making its first tentative steps towards a human hand – I am slowly learning how to just be *and that I am safe.*

Today, beauty was in me and around me. I felt a strong connection to something greater and I paused often to drink in the heady freedom of the seamless sky, the light, the day, the peace. I imbibed the mystery, the mystic, that was this simple Thursday over a sink in Richmond.

I had touched on bliss in solitude, on union in singularity and it was heady, powerful, yet soft as a lover's hand.

Perhaps, at last, I have begun to heal.

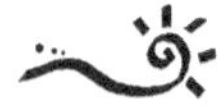

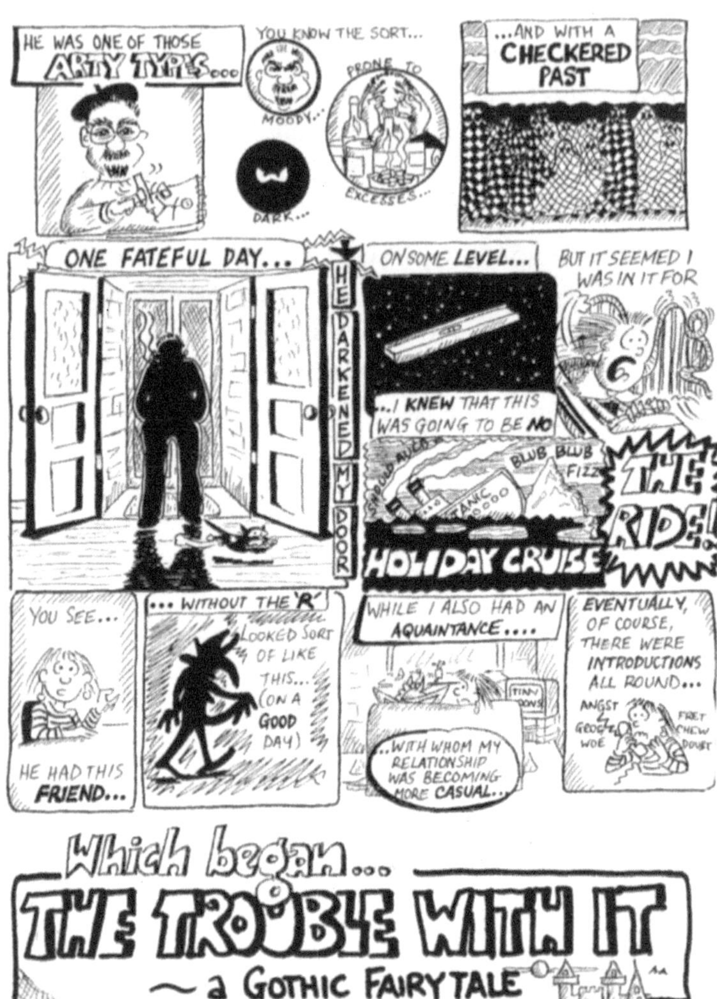

'Here's the thing,' BM* would say, sketching a rectangle in the air to resemble a blank page or an empty canvas upon which anything might be writ – an insight, idea, declaration or plan.

This gesture was symbolic of our relationship – anything and everything was writ there, over one of the most challenging and pivotal periods of my life.

A New Age tenet suggests that when there is true completion of one relationship, the next will follow quickly on its heels. My hard work on releasing Owen to his mystical journey had apparently been effective for, soon after, into my life strode this man who I would come to think of as my Beautiful Monster.

BM did not come alone but lugged with him the carcass of a second failed marriage, a romance with alcohol (which he claimed to have ended) and his own version of IT, which he referred to as *The Trouble*, comprised of guilt over his perceived failure as a husband and father and the product of childhood trauma with an abusive mother, who I would eventually meet.

Thursday 11 May 1996

On Mother's Day BM took me to meet his mother. I was a little nervous to meet this matriarch, who had been given some bad press, to say the least. According to BM, it was his mother who had done all the damage.

I tried to put any judgement on hold but the tight, unwelcoming face that looked me up and down at the door did little to dispel it. Despite BM's warnings, I was still unprepared for how soon she slugged me.

'I'm trying to put together some family photos, but it's so hard with all these separations and broken marriages,' she said and with that, plonked an album opened to a photo of BM's first wedding into my hands. 'And here's the other one,' she said, turning the page to reveal the 'ex' with whom I was by now uncomfortably familiar. 'And these are my grandchildren,' she indicated finally, with a knobby finger.

At one point, I used the toilet, which was situated next to the laundry, so I went to wash my hands there. 'Use the bathroom,' she called and I cheered briefly, thinking I was being treated as a guest worthy of more refined ablutions. 'I don't like people messing with my taps,' she added. Then 'Close the door. I don't want to heat the whole house.'

Later, mercifully, the rest of the family arrived and when we sat talking around the table, Mother all but disappeared into the background. Through the window, we saw a crow land in the garden.

'The Familiar,' I said, before I could stop myself and BM and his sisters roared.

Later BM told me that this had been the first time a group of people have ever sat around that table talking happily.

It seemed that at least some healing had taken place, if by a little witchcraft, though the evidence of damage had been clear. BM's sister ate from the moment we arrived and Paul matched her bite for bite with slug for slug.

This man was quite a package; one from which my instincts were telling me to flee, while my intuition was curiously urging me to stay.

I chose the latter. How could I not? For I was hooked from the start by this charming, funny, intelligent, gifted man; here at last was my longed-for artist, a philosopher of sorts and a thinker who stimulated me and challenged me to bravely face down my fears, like a warrior. 'Do it harder! Come on, be big!'

Tuesday 14 March 1996

My wiser self tells me I'm in for a rough ride, no matter how alluring that ride may be – but this time I have a greater intention. I can clearly see the potential for my old pattern of rescue and over-giving to repeat with this man but I have my eyes wide open and it is my aim to walk headfirst into this whole pattern with new awareness and give it a different outcome for myself. I want to finally heal that childish wound that has been my companion for so many years and I know that BM will challenge me to stand firm.

BM presents me with an opportunity for learning on a profound and intense level. I sense that this is somehow a fated relationship and I also know that it is unlikely to last – one day it will implode upon itself like a meteor that has burned too brightly and fiercely.

But I also sense that I am at an important crossroads in my life and that I must keep walking this path until I reach the very end. Besides, for now, I want to, for I have not felt as alive and inspired by anyone for many years, as I do now. At last, I have met an equal; someone who 'gets' me; someone who also operates on a deeper and more questioning and complex level than most people.

From our first encounter, when an editor friend referred him to me to discuss his idea for an illustrated book on divorce, I was intrigued and attracted to this puckish man, with the dark and mischievous look of a pirate. The cartoon illustrations for his book were exceptional, wherein he depicted himself as a shrunken, bearded child, engulfed by the things of the world he inhabited.

Sunday 19 February 1996

BM's arrival for our first 'date' marked out the unique nature of our connection that had been evident from the start. His first words were: 'I've never done this before.'

When I asked what he meant, he said that it was the first time he'd been in this kind of situation with full awareness, wanting to do it right, from the start.

From 'this kind of situation', I deduced that he meant the first time he'd been with someone to whom he was attracted.

It occurred to me that this was also true for me.

On our next outing, we went for dinner at an upstairs Greek restaurant. As we reached the top of the stairs, we realised that we had actually stumbled into a Greek wedding; however, the manager ushered us in, so we sat among the din of one hundred rowdy guests and a bride resembling a pavlova. We laughed at our attempts at conversation over bouzouki music, leaning across the table for our spontaneous first kiss.

As we passed shops en route from the restaurant he pointed out clothes he thought would suit me (and they would) and retro décor that he liked which I also liked and I enjoyed the way he noticed things; the way he was as aware of and intrigued by the details of the world as I was: the minutiae which passed by so many people.

And I enjoyed being able to share my art and my humour, finding, to my delight, that there was no need to explain little tags and phrases: BM sparred and parried with equal wit. But I also felt edgy about how much grog he had put away and the fact that he had lied about having quit drinking. Walking back to the car it was clear he was pissed and a small voice within me said, 'Beware.' I heard it of course, but it was too late. I just hoped I was up for it.

My inner searching had taught me much and very soon I was learning to apply these new rules to my life, with BM setting a new and challenging pace.

Tuesday 14 March 1995

> *The more I allow things to unfold naturally by surrendering control, the more I realise that it was this very need to control, which had, paradoxically, caused things to spiral* out *of control in my life.*
>
> *I am worrying less about where I am going and trusting that I will know what to do with whatever shows up. In fact, the ' I' I had identified with for so long has ceased to exist in so many ways. I am becoming a new 'I', who is now more of a spectator to my life, an observer, noticing what 'she' does, how 'she' thinks, pausing and considering my responses where once I would have just automatically reacted.*

It was occuring to me that with BM there were no set rules of relationship, other than the fundamental principles of being true to self and truthful with each other, no matter how painful that might be. I recognised that so much of my past turmoil had been because I was responding in the way that I had been taught – by society, my parents, movies, films, books, music – through examples that fostered an unhealthy attachment to romantic love: 'I'm nothing without you', 'Can't live without you', which in the main suggested that relationship was ownership.

BM was forcing me to choose between a rock and a hard place. 'Take me as I am' – the whole package, including unreliability, selfishness and even a cruel streak – 'or not at all'. He was saying: 'I cannot and will not change into who you might want me to be. I'm not here to please you. You must please *yourself*.'

Monday 17 April 1996

Perhaps I will catch up with this diary one day to record these turbulent, exciting, tricky, testing times but I have been too busy living them instead.

Besides, I would probably feel rather foolish if I had recorded all the on-again, off-again dynamics of this relationship, with BM feeding me just enough affection and declarations of love and just enough life, music and art to reel me in, then turning ugly enough to have me walk away in disgust, both at him and myself.

But I have to admit that there is an edge to this that is thrilling – the anticipation of days filled with surprises, pleasant or otherwise, is still more like living than the coma of routine.

There is something fierce and dynamic about this time that calls on all my learning to date – being tossed off balance and having to find a way to right myself again, living intuitively and calling on faith and focus, seeking self-reliance as well as unconditional love – these things have strengthened me as much as they have tested me.

No matter how sticky the scenario, we share an honesty that I have not previously experienced. I am constantly amazed at how co-operatively we work through issues together.

We are utterly frank, knowing that the other will not only wear it but will have listened and considered, without shutting down into the usual defensiveness of those who choose to live more carefully.

It is ruthless but exhilarating to peel back the layers of Shadow – fear, self-doubt, guilt, anger, blame, control – in such an accelerated way.

We are like coaches, encouraging each other to strength and resilience; shucking off the excuses for smallness that have kept us weak. Fellow warriors, we challenge each other on the emotional retreats of 'Poor Me' and 'I don't know'. We poke at expectations, prod at conventions, trample on 'old maps' as BM calls them.

Even so, this is no holiday cruise. Sometimes I am up for it; at other times, I feel too fragile, still.

BM will push it to the limit: that's inevitable but I no longer blame BM or life or circumstances or Fate for where I have firmly placed myself. *I am an equal player in this game and knowing that is empowering. I no longer feel like I am an unwitting plaything of the Universe.*

Despite my optimism, BM's *Trouble* was beginning to hog centre stage and my IT was again stirring uncomfortably in response. This ugly marriage of insecurities was slowly but surely unravelling my new-found calm and the joy in discovering my equal. We were telling ourselves that we wanted to help the other be strong but, in truth, this was the very thing we both feared, for strong people walk away.

The Trouble, bottle in hand, had the habit of loping onto the scene in hobnailed boots, the moment I lapsed into a sense of love and security.

Sunday 23 April 1995

We visited Broadford so that I could show BM my old hometown.

There was a cinematic unreality as I retraced the steps of my humble past as a woman who was now an author who was on the arm of an artist.

I took him to all my childhood places, and he was there one hundred percent with me.

On the trip back, I introduced him to 'Chinese Portraits' – 'What colour am I? What kind of animal/flower/food/ attire/musical instrument/building?' – and we played this game all the way home and he loved it and I loved him loving it.

And so, according to BM, I was the colour red – specifically 'autumnal red' – a bilby, orchids, pumpkin soup, a medieval gown, a violin, and a house by a lake and when it was my turn he was chocolate brown, a wombat, sunflowers, Cajun food, an old suede jacket, a saxophone and a New York tenement.

'You know you're a beautiful thing?' he suddenly declared. 'You're this most amazing thing! I love you very much.'

But my joy was short-lived. Over dinner back at BM's place, I found the ghost of his ex-wife again sitting between us as had become the norm, while BM, consumed by alcohol, guilt and regret, lapsed into heroic notions of reinventing himself enough to repair past damage and with this detour, his love for me was then incidental.

'I was with that woman for twenty years! *I'll show the bastards! I'll fix my life and then she'll have to take me back!'*

It would end in tears, of course; mine, of course, when he pushed too far as he too often did and then he would be chasing my car out of the driveway. 'No! Don't go! Come back! I love you!' and either then, or in a matter of days, I would be persuaded to return, for no-one had ever loved me hard enough to beg for me before.

Never were the contrasts more evident than in this gifted man. On one hand was a wonderful larrikin: 'Come over! I'm cooking dead animals! Come now!'; a gifted artist: *I was struck by a beautiful construction he had made which was comprised of heavy plinths of weathered wood that he had found and along this were arranged seven little towers of stones, each a totem with its own intrinsic meaning and poetry. This piece was beautifully calm, yet powerful and it revealed to me more than any words could convey, this man's soul and the beauty within that created this lovely thing*; and an unconventional teacher: 'Problems, losses, hurts: they're just cream pies, mate! Just big, messy cosmic cream pies going *Splat!* right in your face! Life – it's just a play, a game, a farce!'

On the other hand was a dark and troubled boozer, wracked by guilt, dragging the mess of his life onto my lounge-room rug like road-kill and playing nasty drunken mind-games to poke at my vulnerability.

But the truth was, to amputate the shadow side of him was to eliminate the genius of the other. These were the convoluted elements that made BM, BM. Take it, or leave it. It was only a matter of time before it went too far, of course. Our 'experiment' in truthfulness, acceptance and consciousness was pushing the boundaries of my endurance.

Tuesday 4 May 1996

> *We were invited to a farewell party on Saturday and it transpired that it was held right next door to BM's old home, wife and kids. I felt uneasy while he sat in the passenger seat, fidgeting and chain-smoking all the way there.*
>
> *On arrival, I found myself smack-bang in the middle of suburbia. Here was the wood veneer cabinet, the pods of framed family photos of brides and bridesmaids in ridiculous 80s hats and puffy dresses, the outdoor barbecue area festooned with 150 varieties of fuchsia and Celine Dion playing in the background.*

BM plonked himself in a corner with a drink, abandoning me to the fate of trying to negotiate the smallest of small talk with the gathering.

After three hours of superficial nonsense, I was suffocating in this world of grey vinyl couches and matching accessories. I turned to him and said, 'I have to go. Now!'

Surprisingly, he agreed. As we drove away, he told me that he'd seen a car he didn't recognise outside his ex-wife's place. I could see he was consumed by jealousy and braced myself for the ensuing fallout.

Again, the same spiel: he would prove the bastards wrong and show them he was the better man and that may require him going back to her and even though I was worth ten times more than her, he would do it for his kids.

I said, 'So where does that leave me?'

'Come on, we're above all that! We have this thing, you and me! No control, no ownership! It's all one big letting go, isn't it?'

'But aren't you *hanging on?'*

'Twenty *years!* Twenty *years! Children! Honour! No small thing!'*

As he ranted, he was working his way through a small cask of wine, on top of the God-knows-how-many glasses already downed at the party.

It was hopeless. I was beaten by this sick sham of a relationship. My feelings didn't count in this. After all, I was just a Girlfriend; *I wasn't a* Wife.

The web of family – invisible threads of blood and lineage, stretched thin as gossamer, yet made of robust substance – these things were not mine; how could I claim fierce loyalty?

I curled up into a foetal position on the rug, next to Midnight,

BM's cat, absorbing his soothing warmth and softness and feeling the gentle vibrations of his contented purr; I wanted comfort and love, not this cold place of exile.

Would there ever come a time when I wouldn't need it so much? I wondered. Would I ever find a love unsullied by such painful compromise? Did I really believe I would emerge from this triumphant?

I was drowning in helplessness, as if the core had been carved out of me: I no longer had the will to fight or even stand up for myself. I hardly knew how to live anymore; somewhere along the way, I had forgotten the rules, or mixed them up or lost the guidebook. I no longer knew what I wanted nor where I wanted to be – here or elsewhere – it all came down to the same lonely shit, no matter how brave I tried to be.

BM, suddenly tender, carried me to his bed like an invalid and I was too slumped to resist. I lay there for a long time, numb and blank; a woman of rags, staring past his stone sculptures on the windowsill to the leaden sky beyond.

He returned with a glass of wine. 'Medicine,' he said. I looked at his beautiful, weather-beaten face and wanted to kiss it and slap it at the same time. The more I fell in love with him, the more it hurt me. This was such a crippled love.

I sat up and put on my boots.

'Stay, I need you!' he begged.

'Yes, BM,' I said. 'You need me but you don't want me. Not really.'

I got into the car and lowered my head onto the steering wheel, utterly exhausted. I was not yet strong enough for this: it/he was too much for me and I had been foolish to think I could cope. My Beautiful Monster and his pet *Trouble* were eating me alive.

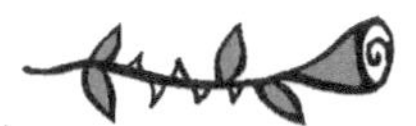

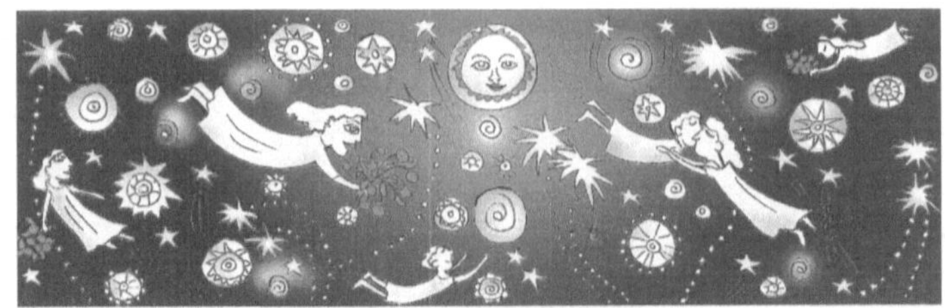

My troubles were compounded the following week when, in one fell swoop, I was hit with a tax bill that wiped out my savings, I lost my part-time job and had my weekly comic strip, *The Fletchers*, cut without warning – and with it, my regular income.

With minimum funds, I still had to service the loan for the gallery and the only payment due for an illustration job was weeks away. Without money I felt exposed and weakened and, as Owen had discovered at Findhorn, even more unloved. I felt my emotional wheels wobble on their tracks and I knew that it was only a matter of time before they fell off completely.

Feeling the old familiar panic rising, I called BM and asked him to come over but when he arrived, it was blatantly clear that he was not going to offer the emotional support that I needed so badly.

'Cream pies, mate!' After draining me dry, he was not going to return the favour.

Of course, why would he? Had he not shown me his narcissism from the start? But I had turned my back to the bleeding obvious, and childishly clung to the notion that if someone loved you (as he said he did) they would look after you.

I was very vulnerable and knew that I had to walk away from this man who had become increasingly toxic to me, yet I held on to the shred of hope that our bond would conquer all. I also knew on this day that I just did not have the strength to do it. It was a choice for the lesser of two evils: alone with him or alone without him.

I longed for a place to rest with loving arms around me, to help summon the strength to go on but BM had other plans and decided that I needed to 'Do it harder! Do it stronger! Get down to it!' The more he talked, the more overwhelmed I became. A darkness rolled over me in a clammy fog. Unable to summon even one thought to comfort me, I began to weep in great, wracking sobs that could not be stemmed but went on and on and on. BM seemed to soften a little and moved to hold me but I did not respond. I had shut down to everything and everyone.

For every two courageous steps I made forward, there was always a giant leap back, which just left me in the same hollow place. I could see no life for me that did not involve pain.

'Go away, BM,' I said. He hovered uncertainly. 'Just go!'

I heard the front door closing quietly, hesitantly, fearfully.

I cried all day and all night. I cried from the bottom of my soul; I cried from the scars and wefts in my poor brutalised heart.

BM called, again and again, his voice echoing on the answering machine through the adjacent room, trying on different appeals: humour, dares, flirtation, concern, but I did not, *could not*, respond. I had nothing to say to anyone. I had no answers, no insights, no wisdom to call on; there was only a white noise of nothingness in my head, as if I had slipped onto another frequency.

In a strange way, my psyche was rescuing me. For once, I heard my thoughts clank and clunk like a decelerating machine then halt to rare and exquisite silence. At last, I had stopped thinking; I was completely and soothingly numb. I wanted to stay in this silent blandness forever. Nothing could touch me there; nothing was asked of me, nor expected of me. I had no battles to fight, no wars to win, nothing to prove and nothing to lose.

It was peaceful in this mindless mist. I had no desire to return to the cruel world again; the world that demanded too much, pushed too far, that jarred and speared my sensitive spirit and offered no rest. I wanted to remain uncaring, unfeeling; so lost in my pain that I was beyond pain.

I then did something I've never done before. I simply went to bed. And there I stayed for the rest of that long, cold, miserable day, floating in my boat of a bed, vacantly riding the waves of wakefulness and unconsciousness. After several hours of silence, there was another message from BM: 'I'm worried about you.' But I was afraid to speak to him for he would want me to do something, say something, be something.

And so I inched my way through that lost week, seeing no-one and speaking to no-one.

After three days, I gingerly emerged into the main body of the house for longer than the few minutes it took to find food and use the bathroom. The phone had remained silent for two days now. Clearly, BM had got the message.

Showered and finally fully dressed, I sat staring out at the day beyond my window, wondering how to reconnect and of course, it was my art that I turned to. I spent the next few days easing my way back into the world with the execution of eight small, intricate paintings. The act of painting became a meditation as I allowed the images to unfold of their own accord and a medication as my mind set about licking its wounds.

Rather than depicting black despair, these paintings had a delicate tenderness to them: dreamy pictures of spirit people, secret gardens and angelic figures flying through skies filled with the fireworks of stars reclaimed my lost innocence.

Eventually, I was forced to re-emerge into the outside world, as I was booked to do a public talk on my book, but I felt ill-equipped to advise anyone on mental health.

In the end, I decided to do that which I did best – simply tell the truth – and talked openly about my collapse and subsequent retreat and how I'd learned that it was actually okay to not be okay and that if one stops fighting and allows a natural process to unfold, things will often right themselves of their own accord.

To my relief, the audience responded warmly to my disclosure, which taught me something powerful in itself.

The phone rang.

'I lasted a week,' he said.

'You've done well. I'm impressed.'

'Marry me, live with me, I *have* to see you!'

I didn't respond. I was resolved not to be beguiled by this.

'Come over!' he insisted. 'I want to see you. We'll talk, laugh, eat; we'll dance!'

'No, I don't think so,' I replied.

'Okay. Fine. Well, I guess we'll leave it another week then. See you later.' I heard him darken at the end of the line and my old fear kicked and with it, my will dissolved.

'I'm just sad. Lonely,' I said, despite myself.

He brightened immediately, 'Then I know a good cure for loneliness. Come over. Come *now*!'

'You have to be kinder, nicer, more gentle,' I said.

'I can do that!'

I heard myself say yes and wondered how the hell I would do this; why the hell I was doing this, but somehow I knew it had still not fully played out. There was another chapter to come.

The moment I arrived, heralded by my clattering Volkswagen, he tore open the door and wrapped me in his arms. 'I've missed you so much. It's so good to see you again!'

I didn't feel like saying much initially but it was not long before we were again talking for hours, just as we had always done so easily.

'What the hell, let's do lunch,' he said and within the hour, our peculiar magic had dissipated the shades of the week before.

Monday 17 April 1995

> *We were like a couple of kids, playing truant from school. We walked along Bridge Road, arm in arm, and I rapturously declared: 'This is joy! This is what joy feels like!' and he said. 'Yes, it is.'*
>
> *We wandered into a fairy shop and sat with our oversized adult bottoms perched on tiny stumps in the children's story-telling room, which had been decorated to resemble a forest glade.*
>
> *The floor was strewn with dry leaves mixed with millions of sparkles. From the moment we entered, I felt a shift of energy and a strange and beautiful coolness; it was heady, light and bright with the energy of young souls. I suddenly had the intoxicated feeling that everything was all right, after all.*

We had begun our strange affair again: the meeting of minds, an exotic, creative, artistic relationship, troubled and divinely complex. We were irreversibly intertwined.

At one stage he became lost in thought. I asked him what was on his mind and he said, 'It's just that I've never been so interested in what someone says, so involved with what they do, so stimulated by another. You've shown me another way.' And I thought, 'Yes, despite it all, it's the same for me, too.'

But by evening BM was back to his old ways and it was not long before belligerence cancelled out our beautiful day; it was already weird and I had only just returned. How much of a fool was I, to be sucked in like this, over and over again? It was classic co-dependency.

I decided to go home. 'Oh, don't do that!' BM whined. 'Why are you going? Stay, sleep on the couch, I'll lend you my pyjamas.'

But I had to get out.

'Okay,' he said, eventually. 'You win.' But I wasn't trying to *win* anything. I wasn't even competing. I was just trying to save myself from further heartache.

'You're a wonderful thing,' he said, as he was wont to say when full of wine, full of need.

'Yes, I am,' I said, more to myself than anyone. And I thought, 'Then why can't I get a better deal than this?'

I didn't have to wait much longer for BM to play his trump card, his coup de grâce.

In fact, it felt more like a fait accompli; as if he had deliberately mapped out a plan from the start – introducing me to his nice friend Buzz, knowing instinctively that we would click, then orchestrating the next moves to ensure that there was a climax and a finale – as in all the best dramas.

Sunday 28 June 1995

BM was hosting a 40th birthday party for Tracey, Buzz's ex, and invited me to come. I knew that he and Tracey had had a 'thing' some time before but that they were now good friends with a long history dating back through the surfing years.

The picture that Buzz had painted of Tracey and the private insight that she and BM had had a fling behind Buzz's back was making it difficult for me to imagine her in a positive light but I was determined to do my best not to judge her.

BM called me late Saturday afternoon. 'Where are you? I want to have you here! I want to see you!'

I told him I would be there in a few hours, at party time.

I proceeded to uncharacteristically 'girlify' myself for the event, to let everyone know what was what, I suppose.

Tracey approached me with a saccharine smile. 'I've been a bit nervous about meeting you,' she gushed, 'but you seem like a really lovely lady.'

I thanked her but could not bring myself to reciprocate as heartily. Something about this encounter felt tainted but I couldn't put my finger on it. The party only served to remind me of why I had come to dislike parties with such a passion.

Despite his earlier enthusiasm about my arrival, BM had now left me to fend for myself while he held court in the kitchen with old surfing buddies; I wandered self-consciously and aimlessly, nursing a drink and attempting and failing at faltering conversations with garishly painted women in short vinyl skirts and with billowing bosoms. At one point, a birthday card circulated and I was asked to write something.

'Thanks for having me,' I wrote, intending the double entendre but unsure what motivated it.

Around midnight, I admitted defeat and headed home.

Strangely, I woke at 4 a.m. with a migraine, which persisted for several hours till I gave up trying to sleep and got up to wait it out.

When it finally abated later in the morning, I drove to BM's with croissants and coffee and to help clean up.

There was an unsettling undercurrent fuelling this and when I arrived, I was taken aback to find that it was Tracey who opened the door. She quickly explained that she had been too drunk to drive home and had taken BM's bed.

I was relieved to find that, in line with her story, BM was asleep on the lounge-room floor, spawled out among the party litter. I half-registered the fact that there was an extra cushion next to him but he greeted me with such genuine warmth and affection, I dismissed it.

After the clean-up, Tracey departed and BM and I spent a lazy, timeless day together. It felt comfortable and easy: a 'kickin' cans' kind of day. We lit the barbie, and poked the remaining snags from the night before over the coals, talking and not talking, smiling and cuddling, best friends and lovers. We went for a long walk that nearly killed both of us, each with our different hangovers, carving a swathe through multi-hued autumn leaves, rugged up and snug, our arms linked together.

All was well; that is, till BM took a phone call that evening. Afterwards, his mood changed completely, as if a cloud had passed over the sun.

He didn't elaborate on what had transpired but he had clearly slipped into a mood that I was not keen to pursue, so I decided to leave.

'I've had a wonderful day,' he said, as he leaned in the car window to kiss me goodbye. He stood watching me reverse out of the driveway, palm raised in farewell and for some reason, that picture, that portrait of him floodlit in the headlights, was imprinted on my mind, as if he stood on a dock, waving to a ship upon which I was sailing away to another world, forever.

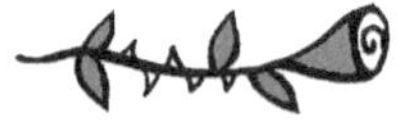

Tuesday 6 June 1995

I came home in the evening to find the answering machine tape full of beeps but no messages – someone had clearly been trying to reach me all day – calling, then hanging up, calling then hanging up, over and over.

The phone soon rang again and I picked it up. It was Buzz. He sounded breathless and flustered; either upset or angry or both.

'I really need a friend tonight,' he said. 'Can I come over?'

'Of course. What's up?'

'I'll tell you when I see you. I'm coming now,' he replied.

When he arrived, which seemed only minutes later – always a lead-foot, he must have virtually flown to my house – he looked ready to rip heads off.

'That mongrel! That bastard! And as for *her*!' he said, fuming.

I sat him down and brought him a drink and as he took it, he promptly burst into tears.

BM had invited him to a barbecue with some other old surfing mates. By the time he arrived, BM had been drinking for the entire day. BM addressed the gathering, bottle in hand. 'See this bloke?' he said, flinging an arm in Buzz's direction, 'He wanks himself off. His missus and I have been playing with each other's bits for years!'

I shut my eyes for a moment against the shock of BM's cruelty to his old friend. He would stop at nothing.

Then it hit me – the party, the cushion, Tracey at the door in the morning, the mysterious phone call. 'Thanks *for having me*' – I knew, I *knew*, of *course* I knew but had not wanted to know.

Buzz went on. 'I went home – Tracey was out, *as usual* – and I tipped out drawers and ripped through cupboards till I found her diary and I read it; I read the bloody thing and there it was: all this stuff about BM and her together. What a fucking fool I am! They took me for a ride and I let them. Those two scheming bastards!' and he began to cry again.

I sat next to him and put my arm around him and he melted against me.

It was time I conceded defeat. BM's problems were simply too big for me. I had been arrogant to think that I could help him overcome them. There was no more left to give; nothing more that I could do.

'Buzz, as hard as it is, we have to forgive them for their pathetic little game. There's no loyalty between them; they stab each other in the back. They're using each other as much as anyone else. It's a cheap soap opera and sadly, they've both lost their most loyal fans. It's they who are the fools, Buzz, not you, or me.'

'Why *you*?' he said. 'Has BM done something to you, too?'

'I think maybe he has,' I said, 'and I think he knew exactly what he was doing.'

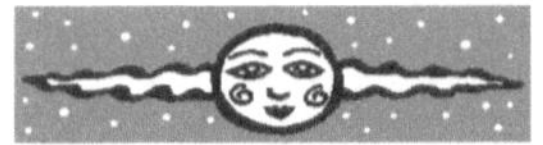

Thursday 8 June 1996

BM rang, mid-morning.

'I don't know quite how to tell you this ...' he began.

'You slept with Tracey.'

'Yeah ... well, I half-did. Then I changed my mind. I was pissed, I got abusive. I'm so sorry.'

'Jesus, BM. What the hell are you doing? You're better than this!'

'I know. I'm a jerk. Can we talk this through? That's how we do it, isn't it?'

'Yes, that is how we do it but this is huge, *BM. There's not just me, there's Buzz. You crucified him, you know.'*

'We'll talk. It'll be OK.'

'I wish I shared your confidence.'

BM called again early that evening. He'd been drinking.

He said: 'Regarding Buzz: he was asking for it. The stupid bastard wouldn't face the truth and it was up to me to enlighten him before Tracey went for the sucker punch. Whatever happens – if he is no longer my friend, then that's the way it goes. I did him a favour.

'And regarding you, most beautiful thing: if you leave, I'll miss you and I'll think of how wonderful you are forever. But hey, if that's what you have to do then you have to do it. This is what I do, this is how I am; this is who I am. Take it or leave it.'

'Why do you keep asking me to come back?' I asked.

'Because we have a destiny.'

'You're not a psychic. Why do you really *ask me to come back?'*

'Because we have so much in common, because I like you, because you're my friend.'

'What happened to I love you? Now it's just like?'

'Okay, I love you but you want a husband; that old map. I don't want that. I've done that, I've been that, I am that, still, in a way. I'm just not ready to give you what you want. At the end of this, if she says come back, I'll have to go. She and I have a history.'

'And what if that never happens? I have to get on with my life. It's not fair to me. You leave me no choice.'

'Will you dedicate your next book to me?' he asked, out of the blue. 'Would you do that?'

'All you need to know is that I love you and I will miss you. It's so bloody sad.'

'I'll never let you go,' he said, suddenly and bewilderingly.

I didn't answer.

Then he was begging and pleading: 'Don't leave me! Don't go! You're the only one who really gets me; knows what I'm trying to do!'

'You expect me to feel nothing while you roll around with this ghost of your ex? And now this stupid, drunken shit? Okay, here it is: I don't care – if that's what you want. I hope it works out for you both, whoever that may turn out to be. Or – you could decide to let all this old, dead stuff go and love me properly instead.'

'I do love you', he said. 'I adore you. Does it matter how *you're loved?'*

And I suddenly saw it.

'Yes. In a relationship; yes, it matters.'

I'd finally hit on the very thing that had eluded me: the realisation that I deserved *to be loved – wholly, exclusively, completely, not in bits and pieces, not as an afterthought, not with a feeling that I had to sacrifice so much of who I was and what I needed in order to be loved.*

In a way, I had arrived at the same destination as BM, only via a different route: this is who I am, this is what I do. Take it. Or leave it.

I now also knew what BM meant when he said, 'I've been saying sorry all my life.' Hadn't I been doing the same? Hadn't I been apologising, in one way or another, secretly or overtly, externally or internally, my entire lifetime, for simply being myself*?*

'You just want to control me …' BM began.

I reflected on this for a moment. Maybe I did. Or maybe I just wanted to believe that I was cherished.

A spiritual teacher's words came to me: 'Have you ever had your face cupped in someone's hands? Have you been cherished?' And I recalled how powerful those words had been to one particular woman in that workshop, who was ravaged by arthritis – her body twisted like a knotted tree, because her mother had called her ugly and pushed her away.

Hadn't I also seen myself as emotionally disfigured? Hadn't I deemed myself too ugly for love? Too difficult, too complex, too uncertain? Wasn't this, fittingly, a sick, crippled kind of love?

'I don't want to play this game anymore,' I said.

'Okay,' he said, 'then let's have a fight – I'm ready for that.'

'Not with me. I won't fight with you or for you anymore. I can't help you. I love you, but I can't stand by and watch you destroy yourself while I lose myself in the process. You need serious help.'

I began to cry.

'Stop it!' he yelled. 'Be the warrior!'

But I was tired of being the warrior. I'd been brave enough. I had vanquished enough dragons.

'No – you have to know how much this hurts. That's it,' I said, finally. 'That's all I can do.'

'You've done it,' he said. 'I love you very much. Let me take you to dinner tomorrow night.'

But there would be no dinner. It was Game Over. I had said goodbye to my Beautiful Monster. Once. And. For. All.

That night, I sent up a prayer to God, in case He was home, in case He was real, in case He was listening: 'Send me a good man; a kind man, the *right* man for me. Send me the one who *values* me; who will be proud to stand by me.'

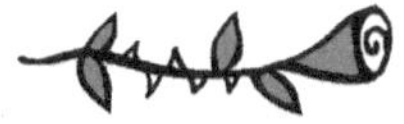

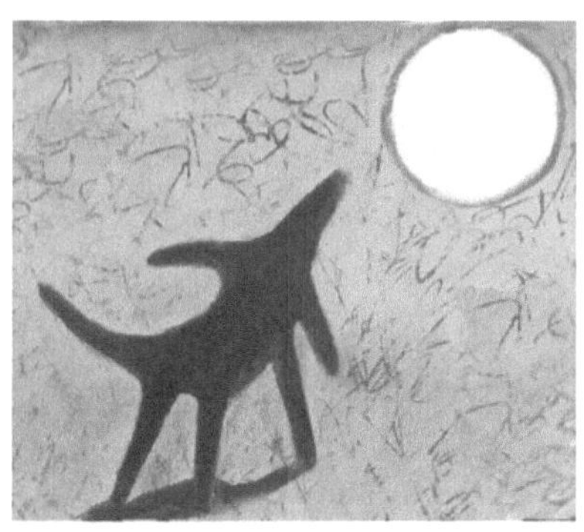

Wednesday 12 July 1995

The truth is I still miss him. I miss his rugged, scruffy pirate-ishness, his surprisingly tender touch, his mischievous humour, his art, his mind, his enthusiasm, his unique manner of speech. I miss it all.

And why wouldn't I? If I didn't, he wouldn't have meant anything to me.

This evening, I watched The Power of Myth, *a program on the philosopher Joseph Campbell. No wonder he has J.C. as his initials. He said: 'Life is a wonderful opera, and it hurts. The idea is to embrace* all *of life; not standing in good and defying evil but standing in the middle and seeing both as in accord. Horror is the foreground of a wonder. Get back to the wonder.'*

But for now, I've quested enough. Enough, enough; I've had enough. I'm tired, I'm whacked, I'm spent. I just want to mindlessly live for a while.

I've done my learning curve. I've taken on challenges, faced down fears, pushed through insecurities, owned my stuff, released resistance, loved unconditionally, rewired my brain, reprogrammed my thinking, surrendered to a Higher

Power and done my best to embrace a whole lot of shit from a whole lot of selfish bastards, so Enough.

I feel like I've been through a great war. I need nurture, rest, peace; buckets of it. I need looking after; nursing. I need salves of kindness and bandages of tenderness and swaddlings of affection.

I need love; generous love, not some sick, shabby, sordid, selfish, sad excuse for love. I need the banquet, not the crumbs.

I borrowed a book from the library: *Medicine Woman* by Lynn Andrews – the story of a New York gallery owner who'd gone in search of an Indian marriage basket, which led her on a transformational journey. She discovered that her spiritual identity was a black wolf. The old woman who had become her teacher described her as a lone wolf who is afraid to be alone, and this resonated deeply with me.

I looked at my own paradoxical nature – how I separated myself in many ways; how I had chosen a lonely path and needed a great deal of space, yet how I could only effectively use that space when I felt connected to a pack, a tribe, or a family. This was represented by the IVI group and also by my own longing for a mate and a home and a loving base from which to move out on my adventures and to which I would return for nurture and rest.

I realised why I spent so much time howling at the moon, for I was also the lone wolf separated by my own wanderings from the pack. I had lost my place somehow; had lost my way home, beached as I was between the tides of independence and belonging. And as the she-wolf with no children of my own, it was harder still to find a place for myself.

The men in my life had become my children, and I showered my love and care and protection on them, placing their needs first until they were strong enough to wander away. However, I had pushed this particular child out of the den. The separation was no less painful but I had the first inkling that through this eviction, I was taking the first great step towards my own freedom and another leap on my spiritual path.

It was not the first time I had encountered the idea of the wolf as an icon in my life. Earlier in the year, I had participated in a workshop conducted by a remarkable woman called Jennifer Lynn Cline.

Tuesday 4 April 1995

As she stood before us, motionless and contained, I found that one moment, I saw a woman, the next, a man – the two genders seemed to have blended into one being.

She did not lecture; instead, she asked questions: broad, sweeping questions that only we could answer internally and in our own way.

'How present for another are you in relationships? What are you indulging? Are you in your own truth or the other's?'

'Have you ever had your face cupped in someone's hands? Have you been cherished? Have you done this for another?'

'If you are unsure about someone, how do they smell *to you?'*

'If I show you my vulnerability, what do I risk? If I can't show you my vulnerability, what do I have?'

'If you're avoiding loss or pain are you playing it too safe?'

'Is courage really the issue? Or is it more a matter of acceptance of a situation?'

'If you walk into the darkness and it falls away, what then?'

On the first night, we were led through a meditation to the sound of a Tibetan Singing Bowl. A tone is sounded by a wooden pestle, which is then rotated around the rim, keeping the tone ringing, on and on.

The vibration reached the deepest part of me. I again experienced a sense of time disappearing, then suddenly, I felt someone leaning warmly against me and holding me in an embrace. I opened my eyes but incredibly, saw only the other seated participants a distance away and Jennifer at the far side of the room.

Tonight, Jennifer filled an entire whiteboard with a list of our reported aches and pains that had surfaced overnight. Mine was aching shins, which represents the breaking down of rigid ideals and standards, allowing flexibility.

She then asked us to send out a request, or a command, to the Universe – a clear and sincere message that would define our quest in this life – with a caution that it would be manifested.

'I invoke fearless love,' I said.

Finally, we did a long meditation, this time accompanied by drumming. Almost immediately, I heard a loud snuffling, grunting noise which I mistook for snoring and I wondered how someone could have fallen asleep in what had only been a matter of seconds; then I realised that the sound I was hearing was that of an animal.

Immediately, I sensed a heavy, musky, animalistic presence behind me. I heard hot, panting breaths and when I felt fur against my back as it moved past, I knew it was a wolf.

At the end of the meditation, every person in that room had seen, felt or heard an animal.

The wolf still wanders through my life. She appears in my art as a black dog, a symbol of companionship and the spirit guide who visited me that night but also, the 'Black Dog' of depression and anxiety that threatens, yet is familiar; that shadows, yet informs the art that springs from it.

In real life, the black dog walks with me as Senna, my nervous little Kelpie friend and reminds me, by example, of the nature of truly selfless love, as did her predecessor, Tao, who died at the age of seventeen, two years ago.

On this day, my old friend faltered on legs that could no longer carry her to my side. She could no longer lift her head to the flawless sky, or her eyes to mine; she quivered with a pain that could not be spoken but through which she silently told me that this was a good day to die.

As the minutes unkindly raced towards the fateful hour, I sat with her as the sunshine warmed her old bones for the last time and I stroked her faithful, pretty head and cupped her tender paws in my hands.

In this exchange there was the simple and familiar transference of love and trust which had so naturally described our years, now made profound in farewell, now outlined and underlined and significant and important because this was the last time.

Later, phone calls to friends; to those who could not countenance sadness, who waxed philosophical, who spoke of her good life but failed to see the burden of my own without her, and those who knew, who deeply knew, that this was the bond of soul-mates; a loss which transcended species.

That night, I wandered through my home and my life, now filled with dog-sized spaces, which quivered with the ghost of her energy where she had sat or trotted – with the reassuring clatter of nails on the kitchen tiles – or slept, with her head draped in complete abandon or with her paws twitching in somnolent pursuit; and for a while, it was I who had become the ghost, earthbound but unanchored.

Excerpt from 'The Transcendence of Species'

Bev Aisbett 2009

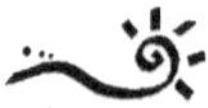

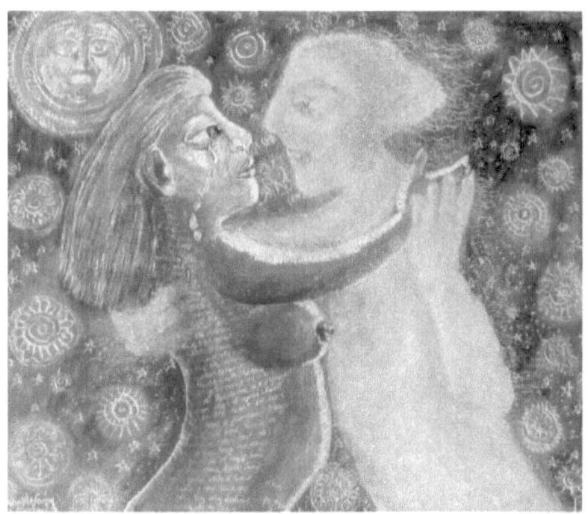

An onlooker might consider the union between Buzz and me as a rebound romance. It was and yet it so wasn't, because in fact, we were soul-mates, if a soul-mate is defined by a conspiracy of Fate and a shared destiny, that is.

Though flung together by the fickleness of our respective partners, there was a deep knowing that we were destined to come together; even the calculating BM could sense this from the start and, in fact, had orchestrated it to a degree.

I recall BM's strange glee when he had first introduced us, several months before Tracey's party; as if, even then, he took secret delight in the prospect of passing the baton of our burdensome relationship to another. Perhaps he saw himself as a master draughtsman consigned to render the next step in some divine plan that would thrust two similarly sensitive souls, with similar wounds, into a healing union that, godlike, only he could stage manage.

Though later I recognised BM's private conspiracy, it did not consciously register at the time, passing me by until much later, when all the dastardly deeds were done and the dust had finally settled on the inflammatory ending of our troubled relationship.

BM had invited Buzz to visit while I was at his place one night, having told him that I had written a book to help people with anxiety; something which was of interest to Buzz, because Tracey had experienced several episodes in the past. I was not exactly pleased to see Buzz arrive, having planned a serious talk with BM that night, when the doorbell rang.

'It'll be okay,' BM said, grinning knowingly as he went to answer it.

BM sat in state, the ever-present glass of wine in hand, smiling benevolently at his two charges as Buzz and I talked for hours; yet I had no glimpse of what was to come, instead seeing this as just a pleasant evening with one of BM's more pleasant friends.

However, the next time I saw Buzz, he was strangely subdued, as if a light had gone out inside. I asked BM for Buzz's number, saying that I had the feeling that he needed a friend, and BM was happy to oblige.

A sensitive and unassertive man, Buzz was struggling through the final stages of his marriage – and with it, the dissolution of his family life, which involved four young children. His guilt was similar to BM's but was of gentler stuff and he was struggling with his feelings.

Meanwhile, in the flotsam of the days with BM, I was wrestling with my own demons again. I had reached a much improved level of recovery through sheer courage and enormous self-work and, in the main, I had been fairly stable. The three years of unremitting insomnia had finally eased and episodes of strong anxiety were now months apart.

Even so, I could feel anxiety lurking at the edges and nudging me with its icy spikes as I faced the reality of myself alone again with only the company of my renegade thoughts, which were precariously close to rebellion.

BM had been a distraction from much of my anxiety because the attention was mainly outside of myself. Despite the pressure he brought to bear, in many ways he highlighted the fact of my internal strength. Now I returned to the sole company of my miscreant thoughts, which muttered and sneered and rattled their cages, for in the new silence they could be more clearly heard.

Over the coming weeks, Buzz's friendship and gentle presence provided great comfort and he called regularly and visited often. Though I saw him as a friend and ally, our mateship appeared to be changing into something I hadn't planned on.

Tuesday 4 July 1995

> *Buzz called. 'I was thinking about you,' he said. We talked for a long time. I feel so at ease with him. It is wonderful to not be living on my nerves, watching my back, working out strategies. I can be totally myself with him.*
>
> *Strangely, when I went to bed, I spent the first hour tossing and turning with this particular man in my head. Why? Is this just my loneliness and need for comfort? Probably.*
>
> *I'm in no hurry to hook up with anyone for quite some time and certainly not with all the overtones of this liaison. It's ridiculous, but he is haunting my thoughts nonetheless.*

Because Buzz was minding his children that weekend we were not in touch, so I was left to myself. I felt, once again, the vacancy and aimlessness of another 'Long Sunday': the day of the week that I had always dreaded spending alone: the closed shops and sparsely populated streets underlining loneliness and highlighting any lingering sense of alienation and residual anxiety.

Having wandered, unfocused and procrastinating for several hours, tinkering at the edges of the old, fear-bound paralysis that I knew too well, I eventually threw myself into the execution of a large painting, using the same etched oil pastel technique I had used for my earlier *Age* illustrations.

An image emerged of a sad woman dancing with a man made entirely of light; an angel of a man, or the spirit of a man; a beautiful man with a face of deep kindness. A single tear coursed down the woman's cheek and over her body I etched tattoos of graffiti which expressed her dream of a kind and noble love.

I called this painting *Thought-form of Longing* and it was only when I had done the final stroke and stepped back to look at it from a distance, that I realised how much the man looked like Buzz.

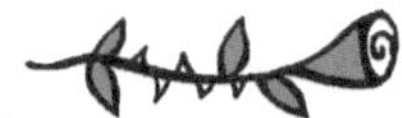

Tuesday 18 July 1996

A strangely spooky sort of day. I mooched around feeling sort of sad and stuck most of the afternoon and incredibly tired, despite not having achieved anything in particular.

I just wanted to curl up in some loving arms, and strangely, gentle Buzz was the one I thought of.

On the way home, I sent up a whimsical request to the heavens: 'If possible, please send me some love and affection tonight.'

I was home by 4.30. At ten minutes to five, the phone rang: Buzz.

'How are you?' he said.

'Okay … no, what am I saying? I feel lousy. I'm not having a great day.'

'Want some company?' Buzz asked.

And so we shared a lovely night of food, wine and lazy, comfortable talk. Again, I was struck by the ease of his company. His gentle, patient presence was a healing balm under which I dropped all defences. I felt myself lifting out of my greyness and his infectious, wonderful laughter soon had me feeling bright, happy, and light.

I showed him a new cartoon strip I had been working on – Hercule Parrot *– and he could barely get through three pages because he was laughing so hard, tears were streaming down his face. I told him I would take him with me any time I wanted to show the new work to an editor.*

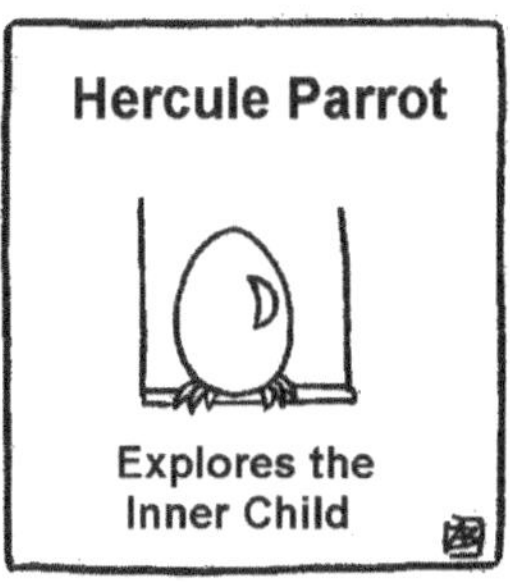

We sat by the fire, talking well into the night.

He confessed that last night, he had such a longing to see me, he had actually started to walk to my place in Richmond from Box Hill North, a 40-minute trip by car.

He'd walked several kilometres before deciding that the venture was sheer insanity and turned around and headed home.

I told him that if he had finally made it, I probably would have opened the door and said 'Why the hell didn't you just drive*?'*

But the image of him pounding the footpath, led by his heart, touched my own.

I leaned against him, wanting to feel small and comforted, and his arms welcomed me completely.

The next day, I worked away quite happily, thinking about the fact of this man in my life. The nature of our union was still somewhat undefined but whatever it was, it felt destined and wonderfully, naturally right.

While my relationship with Buzz was budding, my quest for inner peace and empowerment continued, possibly more so, because as my feelings for Buzz deepened, so did my desire to free myself of any risk of sabotaging my stability or prospects for long-sought happiness.

I enrolled in weekly meditation classes conducted by Pauline McKinnon, who had overcome her own anxiety through meditation. Her mentor had been Dr Ainslie Meares, author of *Relief Without Drugs*.

Ironically, in a few years' time, Pauline and I would both be speakers and workshop facilitators with the Anxiety Disorders Association of Victoria (ADAVIC).

I rang Buzz. 'What are you doing tonight?' he asked.

'Well, I was about to start dinner. Shall I make it for two?'

'I'll be there shortly,' he said.

We sat by the fire, curled up together in a cocoon of tenderness. Here, at last, was solace; was comfort. I draped against him and let myself completely sink into his warmth with the abandon of a child. I was observing this new self; this trusting, loving self, from afar; the way that it looked to be a woman dissolved into a man and realising how seldom I had been able to do this without being on guard.

I could ask this man for anything and it would be given wholeheartedly and without question. I was not being asked to prove myself nor jump through hoops to be worthy of his love.

Buzz stroked my hair.

'Boy, you just melt away, don't you?' he said.

After my first blissful session at Pauline's meditation centre, I emerged in a beautifully floating state and decided to visit Buzz on the way home. I found him hunched over a 'candlelit dinner' which comprised a charcoaled chop and instant noodles. The candle was stuck to a tin lid – which, along with incense, was something he seemed to have adopted from our nights together.

He listened with enthusiastic interest as I told him about the meditation session during which a vision had come to me wherein I crested a hill that overlooked a most exquisite valley that banked onto a cove nestled between high cliffs. The entire scene was suffused in dusky pastels of evening, which lit the calm water with soft metallic tones. Below, lights gently glowed from a scattering of small cottages and there was such welcome and comfort to this scene and, with it, an overwhelming sense of homecoming, that it had actually brought tears to my eyes.

As I recounted my experience, I saw that Buzz was feeling it with me; his face soft and full of tender engrossment as he listened. I looked into his face and saw my painted angel-man.

It was late and as I stood to leave, I leant over and kissed him tenderly on the head. 'Goodnight, beautiful Buzz,' I said.

So it was with some astonishment that, two days later, when we set off for a weekend at Phillip Island, I found him strangely remote: closed and cool and deep inside his protective Cancerian shell. My heart sank. Not again.

En route the conversation was stilted and formal and I found myself fighting a black dread as it was clear that even though he was sitting next to me, he was not with me in spirit. Eventually, I screwed up the courage to ask him what was going on.

He took an agonisingly long time to respond, during which all manner of horror scenarios played out in my mind but finally he revealed that he had disliked my calling him 'Dear little Buzz' when I last saw him.

I laughed with sheer relief. 'Good grief! Is that what you think I said?' and set him straight and then he was laughing too and no doubt, it was with the same relief.

Unburdened, we were now free to be happy and excited and we wound out of gloomy winter Melbourne, with our talk quickly erasing the tortured silence that had begun our trip. I felt a wonderful sense of freedom and a humming, giddy anticipation that made me feel childlike and enticingly nervous.

Our destination was a delightful hideaway tucked among lush vegetation with a trailing vine on the veranda, big soft couches, a wood fire, a 1920s cabinet lined with leather-bound books, and the room decorated with rugs and paintings as perfectly chosen as if we had furnished the home ourselves.

And so began an evening of quiet, then wild, embraces that lingered on throughout the night. Here at last were the loving arms and boundless affection we had both ached for. A golden seam of trust ran through those two days, releasing us from any lingering reserve and allowing the sharing of our deepest selves. There was no longer that old insecure watchfulness: the thread of tension that had kept us on our guard in the past.

We *knew* what the other was thinking, feeling, sensing, as if we were parts of the same spirit. The energy of each was in and of the other and it was at once soft, healing and intense.

On Sunday morning Buzz woke to the freezing dawn and headed to the beach to worship at his temple: the sea. I dozed on and off, waiting for his return. I pictured him surfing the icy water and for a little while I was there with him, seeing it through his eyes and riding the wave with him, sliding effortlessly in towards the shore.

Then I saw him from above: a small, single figure on the grey waves and his dark-swathed outline as he climbed the dunes; then I saw his old Torana, driving too fast back along the winding road as he came home to me as naturally as if it had always been so and I had made the house warm and welcoming for him, with all happiness in the world to be doing so.

Monday 30 July 1995

> *We drove into Cowes for a wonderful late lunch at a little pasta place overlooking the water. This whole day was more than I had ever dreamed. In a timeless swoon we shared wine and a meal, snug and lost in each other, gazing out at the colours of the day: the dark, fringed green of Norfolk pines on the foreshore, the backdrop of pewter sea and a strip of pale orange/pink light as the watery sun pushed through the ashen winter sky.*

Then, too soon it was nightfall and our enchanted Sunday was ending and the thought of returning from our shared dream was almost too painful to bear.

For some reason, no-one had appeared to check that we had vacated the cottage, which presented us with a daring choice: to leave or break all the rules and stay one more night. We tossed a coin: *Heads – Leave.*

We both visibly slumped, almost as if someone had died. Silently, we started to pack and clean up; silently, we loaded the car and even then, neither of us had uttered a word by the time we entered San Remo fifteen minutes later.

I turned to Buzz. 'I guess one of us had better start talking, unless we're going to remain mute forever!' Buzz laughed and with that, the floodgates opened to conversation again.

Everything and anything seemed possible. We were now completely, obviously, overwhelmingly, beautifully in love.

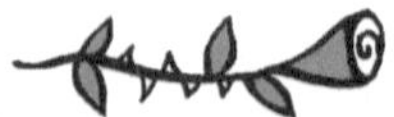

And I did love him – *wholeheartedly* – basking in the softness of his devotion, revelling in his agile physicality which had been forged by the seas he so gracefully commandeered in all weathers: a devoted disciple to the watery hymn that lured him to the tides. I felt a swell of love and pride to see him work so deftly at masculine things: sawing, chopping, mending, building, in the confident and efficient way of my father.

Beginning as friends, we became best friends with a common language and understanding, even though our worlds were far apart, in terms of the cultural things that were dear to me; for Buzz was just as dear.

But, like BM, he also came with a package – and though of a less traumatic nature, it was nonetheless a challenge for which I was ill-prepared.

Yet again I said 'Yes' then attempted to make it fit, though how could I not, for this cargo was indivisible from its vessel and took the form of four children; young at that time, ages ranging between three and eight – girls at either end; boys in the middle.

And so it was, that one day this strange quartet stood on my doorstep, regarding me with inscrutable blankness, as if I, or they, had just stepped from a spaceship.

Sunday 3 September 1995

> *Buzz brought the kids around for the big introduction. I was so nervous! I felt as though I was in a scene from* The Midwich Cuckoos *as four sets of eyes as big as saucers regarded me with unblinking stares that gave nothing away.*

This was going to be tough! I took them to see my fish pond, which received absolutely no reaction; I told them that they were there just in time to help me sort out my 'treasure chest', which contained cartoon mementos from the Ha Ha Gallery. This loosened them up a bit but it wasn't exactly excitement triple plus and I was fast running out of ideas.

Buzz then suggested that they go and play on the building site next door. I sagged onto the couch next to him. 'They hate me!' He took my hand. 'Of course they don't. Just relax and ignore them.'

Eventually, I suggested that I do a caricature of each of them and slowly, more out of curiosity than anything, they gathered around me and I drew the eldest, Josie, with her thick mane of tangerine hair, Callum*, with horns and a tail, capturing his reputation Anthony*; and finally, beautiful but cautious Elizabeth*, known as Lizzy*.*

I looked up to see Buzz beaming at me as all parties finally began to relax. Soon after, the kids were bundled into the car and were waving goodbye.

'I want a full report,' I told Buzz as we sneaked a goodbye kiss. An hour later, he rang to tell me I had been a smash hit and that Josie had taped her drawing to the fridge. Whether this was entirely true or not remains to be seen. Nonetheless, I felt hugely relieved.

Towards the end of the year, Buzz and I decided to set up a home together and moved into a house behind a high fence on a busy road in Richmond. The property backed onto businesses along Victoria Street, including a nearby brothel. The 'girls' parked their cars in an empty lot behind our back fence and we were often treated to the sight of long legs in fishnets under tiny fragments of fabric which barely skimmed thighs, as they teetered from their cars in high heels which were nothing short of engineering feats.

Our first night as a 'family', with the kids staying over, was a disaster. It was stiflingly hot and the kids were fretful and tearful and demanding to be taken home. I sat moping on the front veranda thinking, 'Are you out of your bloody *mind*?' The dynamics of part-time parenting would remain an ongoing challenge for me and while the sense of 'family' and 'home' was stabilising, at times it was an unsettling influence.

Though I could still be easily thrown emotionally, Buzz's calming influence and the need to be more focused, generous and adult for the children in my care honed a greater maturity in me as I released more of the child in myself by necessity.

But, unaccustomed to parenting – which was fraught with perils as it also involved taking on the mercurial Tracey, with her own somewhat erratic style of mothering – I made many mistakes. The greatest challenge was the impact of the children's presence on my relationship with Buzz; the most difficult gulf for an insecure would-be parent to bridge when the children are not one's own.

Sunday 1 October 1995

Being a de facto stepmother has presented its own extreme challenges, and yet again, I find myself climbing a mountain. When Buzz is in 'Dad' mode, there is a matter-of-fact, dismissive air that is a cold contrast to the downy bed of tenderness whenever it is just the two of us.

There is no easing into this – at 6 p.m. every second Friday, the car doors slam and with that, the door slams shut on my life with Buzz.

This separation from him has less of a sting when I am granted the rare and delicious wonder of small arms that reach for me but these occasions are few and far between.

These children are guarded and distant and are not, by nature, greatly demonstrative. The gifts I have to offer, which I long to share – my art, my cartooning and indeed, my affection – are shunned in the main.

Their wariness is understandable; their own mother has shown herself to be changeable and erratic and has threatened to leave them on occasion, which can only have carved the deepest of wounds. No wonder they cling so to the one reliable font of love.

But as I watch Buzz being unconditionally adored while I sit by, ignored, it is difficult to be generous and not slump into hurt; but after all, I am the adult and the adult must tend to her own needs, and rightly so.

Nonetheless, the child in me feels the alienation so greatly that my fears that I am irrevelant, that I am passed over in this equation, play impishly around me in concert with the antics of the children that now alienate me from the man I love.

I fight hard to be noble and grown-up, yet it is as if he is emotionally gone from me; as if a switch is turned off at the moment of their rowdy arrival. For the next two days, I will wander around the edges of my own home, accompanied only by the background blare of breakfast television, biting my tongue against complaints about discarded odoriferous sneakers splayed around the room, the invasion of necessary quiet and calm and the sheer tyranny of the energy of four children.

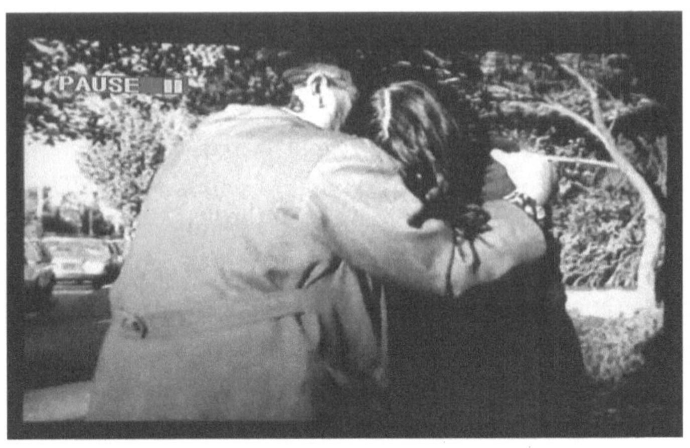

For all I was being tested, my IT was by now mostly manageable, which showed how far I had come. In the main IT was an occasional rumble when I allowed stress to take hold and I felt confident enough to consider that I may have something to offer to those experiencing anxiety; I enrolled in a certificate course in counselling.

Having completed my second book on anxiety, *Living IT Up*, which explored the minimisation of stress in general, I commenced work on *Letting IT Go*, which introduced a more philosophical perspective on life's challenges, derived from my own spiritual growth, which I now saw as an essential component in recovery.

It was also during this time that a film crew invaded our home, much to the delight of the kids. I was filmed in my minute office, which Buzz had converted from a neglected shed in the back yard, for an SBS documentary on anxiety disorders, named *Secret Fear*. The film featured interviews and re-enactments (including a revisit to my night with Jeffe Jefari) with fellow 'anxiety ambassadors' such as author Bronwyn Fox and actor Garry McDonald of Norman Gunston fame.

I was now ready to see clients one on one.

My first client was John, who was suffering with anxiety. Though I was somewhat feeling my way (I'm not sure who was more nervous on our first session – my client or me!) John and I made considerable headway in a relatively short time. It appeared that I was the one offering help to John, but in fact he was to contribute to my own life in ways that neither of us could have predicted but which would set me on a new path to my destiny.

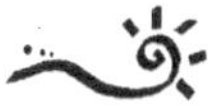

Despite Georgia's and then IVI's interventions, my ongoing dedication to spiritual growth and my love of Buzz as healing forces in my life, the clusters continued in the same gruelling pattern over the next six years.

Eventually, around 2003, the attacks would finally peter out but whether this was as a result of my greater acceptance, or simply hormonal changes, I cannot say. Perhaps I had learned all that I was to learn from the experience and was now done with them.

Ironically, this miserable ailment opened up a whole new and exciting world to me. My illness, like my anxiety, was a powerful motivator for change and also the means by which my wisdom expanded; albeit via a diabolical path in both cases.

One such enormous learning experience was a weekend workshop in 1996 called Turning Point.

I had been referred by a friend to a GP/naturopath who she thought might be helpful for the clusters. His surgery was right across town, a significant fact as it would transpire.

When I told him about the clusters he looked at me levelly and asked: 'So what are you doing about your anger?'

I stared, or rather, glared at him. 'What do you mean, my *anger*? I've got cluster headaches. The pain is indescribable. You'd be feeling angry, too!' I retorted.

Unfazed, he reached for a brochure and handed it to me. 'Nonetheless,' he said, 'it might be helpful for you to explore this. It starts tomorrow night.'

I stomped out to the car, muttering. Now and then, I glanced at the pamphlet as I crawled through peak hour traffic on the way home. 'Bloody New Age guilt trip,' I thought. Even so, the pamphlet, with its beautiful photograph of a lotus on a calm and pristine pool, kept grabbing my attention.

'Okay,' I thought, 'if I'm home by the 6.00 p.m. enquiry deadline, I'll call.'

Of course, this was impossible. It was already 5.20 p.m. and I was virtually stalled in a snag of homeward-bound cars, buses and trucks. Then as if by magic, the traffic suddenly parted like the Red Sea. I was home by 5.45.

'Bugger it!' I thought, but kept my bargain with the Universe.

I reported to the Zoeros organisation to begin Turning Point the next night.

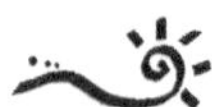

'Fake it till you make it,' our instructor said. It was some time on the Saturday of the Turning Point weekend and we were about to do *anger.*

We had been in this room for hours. Just how many hours was anyone's guess because no timepieces were allowed. It could have been anywhere between 11 a.m. and evening. Judging by my hunger pangs, I guessed it was around lunchtime. That would come soon – at 5.30 p.m.

Since morning, the group of fifty people had slowly opened up. Some shared their stories, cried a little or a lot; some said only a few words; and others simply wouldn't shut up. Some I liked and some set my teeth on edge; as is the way of the world.

We had explored childhood and its enormous impact on our experience of life. We had meditated, worked through complex diagrams exploring the ego's traps, studied notes and done group sharing. Now we were getting down to it. Now we were *feeling*.

'Mars' from Holst's 'The Planets' suite issued at full volume from the speakers, stomping darkly and formidably across the room in a musical portrait of war. I checked within myself. I didn't feel especially angry … perhaps just a little … perhaps there was some in there … it was building but it wasn't like I was feeling *enraged* or anything; just a bit *annoyed*, really; a bit *edgy*, a bit …

The music was now a percussive red pulse in my veins. I felt something dense and lurid congealing like lava in the very core of my being; then it was rising up and up in a volcanic surge: an ancient, roaring, flailing spew of rage that flung itself from me like a living thing; a demon, an infernal, unfurling fury that, now freed from its confinement, erupted in a diabolical roar.

I was not alone in this; around me was the Dante-esque bellowing of those who had also dared to fling open the latch and allow their beasties full flight: stuffed-down helplessness, clogged-up shame, unspoken frustration; their silenced heartbreak came hurtling out in yells and cries and rasping sobs.

Over the weekend, we opened and aired the dank cellars of the past, experiencing a full range of emotions in the process – anger, sadness, hope and even euphoria – till we finally arrived at a clean and joyful quietude. It was one hell of a ride.

My Turning Point was conducted in a large office block in Brunswick. Later, Zoeros moved to new rooms in St Kilda and the original venue was taken over by the head office of NQR or Not Quite Right stores; further proof that the Universe has a wry sense of humour at times.

Within two years, I would be teaching at Zoeros.

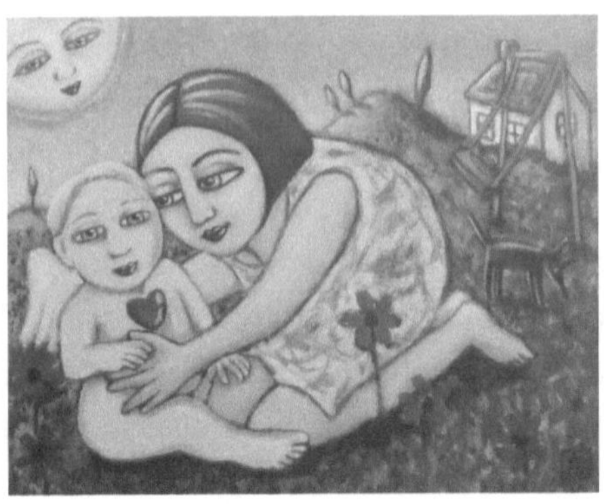

Buzz worked as a mechanical designer and was also an excellent handyman.

In 1998, we bought a run-down house in the leafy suburb of Box Hill, which we threw ourselves into renovating. An inner city girl by nature, my move to the 'burbs was going against the grain but the house was near Buzz's children, his work and our price range.

The house was a post-war commission house built of reinforced concrete ('The Hiroshima House', I dubbed it). No glamour-puss, it was in dire need of a makeover but the setting was superb: on an elevated block, it overlooked the grounds of Kingswood College, glimpsed through a border of majestic oak trees with the Dandenongs a distant backdrop.

In time, Buzz built a deck at the rear of the house where I would sit to start my day; high up in the trees, with birdlife all around.

My project was an 'artist's garden', with winding paths revealing hidden oases. My own sculptures, carved out of Hebel (aerated concrete), were dotted among the foliage, as were water features and stone and wood constructions made from found objects; echoes of BM's influence. Surrounded by lush vegetation and set well back from the street, it was our own magical hideaway from the world.

Though a hideaway, it was also a retreat from the stimulation of inner-city life, and, with territorially inhospitable neighbours, bland and unimaginative streets and clusters of outsized commercial outlets in a DIY paradise, I was slightly 'marooned' in suburbia, no matter how beautiful our oasis. To counteract this, I did my best to bring life and colour into our home by hosting dinners, lunches and parties to animate the house with the energy of people, which I craved in the isolation of self-employment.

It did not seem to matter greatly in the early years that Buzz did not foster friendships of his own, for he was welcoming and pleasant company for my friends, by whom he was well-loved. Content with home-life, his reclusive nature meant that the onus was on me to maintain and nurture friendships.

However, to those who knew us, we were a 'perfect couple' and our bond was deep and loving. We shared a love of the sea and I often accompanied him on his surfing trips, watching him from the shore as he glided over the waves with such nonchalant grace.

We travelled to Bali in 1996, hiring a 'Jimmy Jumper' to tour the island with the surfboard slung in the back and then to Thailand in 1998, within weeks of my having discovered, to my dismay, that I was pregnant.

Having often spoken of his love for children, in contrast to my own ambivalence on the subject, our reactions were surprisingly reversed when I broke the news. Buzz turned white. The twin blue bars had registered positive only minutes before we were leaving for a weekend in Gippsland for a 'family' visit to Buzz's mother, Erin.* With the kids on board, we were unable to discuss the situation and spent most of the journey in stunned silence, each lost in our own thoughts.

The next morning, finally alone with Buzz before the kids woke, I was shedding a few tears which were a combination of awe and dismay that, late in my life, I had been presented with this momentous event.

True to my complex life-script, I struggled to know what to do about the pregnancy; this was not a clear-cut nor pragmatic decision. After all, my own life had begun under a similar cloud. My studies of recent years had taught me that things were 'meant to be' and the mysteries of hormones were already beginning to weave a bond between me and the tiny bud sprouting within me. More importantly, this was my last and only chance to be a mother; there would never be another. I wondered what sort of mother I might be: firm but fair, generous and caring but unavoidably enigmatic, given my strange alchemy.

But we'd be okay, wouldn't we? We'd sort it out – my practice run at parenthood had shown me that.

How could anyone ever be sure of such a decision? I understood, then, my own parents' agonies prior to my birth. In the end, I could only follow my heart and, despite all odds, just like my mother, I said 'yes' to my fate. When I saw the tiny beating heart in the ultrasound, I knew there was no turning back. I somehow knew it was a girl. I called her Grace.

I was ten weeks' pregnant when we travelled to Thailand. One day, I was struck by the most terrible pain and I was shocked to discover that I had started to bleed. We rushed to a local doctor who ordered me to bed for the remaining two days before our flight home.

Buzz had planned to go on a boat trip to Ko Tapu, known as the 'James Bond Island' that day. I encouraged him to go but secretly, I wished he had insisted on staying. I felt alone and frightened as I lay there through the long day, listening to the distant, whirling hubbub of life out on the busy streets.

Sometime in the afternoon, I heard a chilling banshee wail resounding along the hotel corridors. This eerie keening continued for hours and sent chills up my spine. I shuffled to the window to find its source and discovered a black cat, howling below our very room.

By the time we landed in Melbourne, I was in agony. Grace was gone. She was never to be.

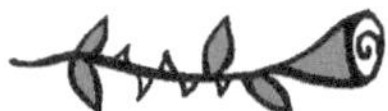

After months of weekly sessions, my counselling client, John, had made significant progress and as a 'graduation', I suggested that he also do Turning Point. He did and loved it so much, he ended up taking leave from his work in advertising to volunteer for admin work at Zoeros.

John rang me one day with an idea. 'I think that your approach would be ideal for a workshop at Zoeros,' he said.

There were many clients who would have benefited from doing the weekend but were too overwhelmed by their anxiety to take on such a challenging experience. My workshop would help them to build a foundation of inner safety and act as a bridge for any deeper work they wished to pursue from the insights they gained.

I put together a format designed to enlighten and inform sufferers, as well as equipping them with a raft of strategies with which they could steer their own recovery, or at least speed the process, if working with a therapist, by being more pro-active in building their recovery. My aim had been and remains firmly resolved to empower those who might have been led to believe that they were helpless in the face of an 'enemy' comprised of errant genes or wonky chemicals. My quest was and is to discourage a 'victim' mentality and remind people that they have much more impact on their own wellbeing and circumstances than they may have previously believed.

I commenced my workshops at Zoeros in 1998; then, after a change of administration, I moved to the Anxiety Disorders Association of Victoria (ADAVIC) for the next twelve years till an undignified squabble over money brought this to an abrupt halt in recent months.

Though a somewhat inglorious and initially upsetting end to a long relationship, this incident afforded an opportunity to adopt a spiritual perspective, even in conflict.

I sought inner guidance and the message was clear: 'Honour your worth, take the most basic practical steps, then let it go. The Universe will sort it out.'

The real work was to release anger, fretfulness and self-pity and to shove my ego out of the way.

In the end the true rewards were beyond the material: peace of mind and freedom from bitterness. The Universe had served me well in this and in my time with ADAVIC.

'There were only two people who had objections to your talk last night,' Anna reported by email, as if this was good news.

'Love hearing about the ones who didn't like me,' I replied.

I know Anna worried about my notorious renegade streak. Her other lecturers at ADAVIC were far better behaved.

Two out of sixty. Not too bad. This is usually how it goes; one or two people protesting that I have been confronting or insensitive while others declare that they have been inspired and uplifted.

Interestingly, it is seldom the people I have challenged who take issue, but someone completely unrelated to the recipient who feels moved to express outrage on their behalf. Of course, this speaks reams about people's patterns. These people are most likely to be rescuers in real life, leaping in for others, to ease their own discomfort.

But the recipient of the comment has usually got it; has been slightly shocked into wakefulness at last.

I see them suddenly more alert, more present, as the sliver of anger in the moment finally opens a door of insight into their stuckness, sparking an energy that has lain in a leaden blanket of immobility and despair for years.

It has become part of my job to take the bullet. I'm the one pointing to the elephant in the room, the spinach in the teeth or the open fly. They may not be thrilled to hear it but they can now do something about it.

My quest is to empower people to move out of their inertia; to take one crucial step towards reclaiming the power that they have relinquished to others, to the past, to hurts and injustices, all stuffed down like the filling in a rag doll that is now splitting its seams and spewing anxiety.

How little do they know of how much I love them. If they only knew how earnestly I long for their freedom and how I can hardly bear to witness the smallness of their vision of themselves in comparison to the vision I hold of them as strong, capable, truthful and free.

Too many people have by now patted their limp hands and poured sympathy into their wounded lives, thereby unwittingly nursing and fostering helplessness.

Of course, if helplessness becomes too comfortable there will inevitably be resentment for anyone who challenges them to embrace the truth, which is: you chose this.

This is the hardest truth, the one I, like many, have struggled to embrace. I still ask, 'How could I have chosen this?' knowing that I have and I did, for no-one else could choose for me.

I chose to leave or stay; to hang on or let go. I chose him, I chose her. I chose this helpful thought or that harmful belief. I chose resentment when I could have chosen empathy; I chose to be the victim until I chose to be the victor.

Some are ready; tentatively brave enough to let me hold a mirror to their lives to show that suffering is a choice and they have chosen me because that same unyielding mirror has been shown to me – and when I was willing to gaze upon that which was reflected back with honesty and compassion, I saw that there was nothing binding me except the very notion that I was in bondage; that I was somehow subject to the capriciousness of life and others, rather than my own will.

I love to watch their faces; in fact, their whole bodies change through this process: grimaces, frowns, tears and angry, hurt faces, arms defiantly crossed or legs coiled into contorted pretzels, all slowly unfolding to a new openness.

I often surprise myself, too, as I bow to my intuition. I may be tough on one person or tender toward another; lightheartedly cracking jokes or passionately intense.

I will often secretly ask myself, 'Where did that come from?'

But this healing is not my doing; not entirely. En route to these events, I do a small ritual which involves letting things unfold as they will by getting out of my own way.

I ask that I am given the right words to say, that I will hear that which I need to, that I will be gentle when it is best and forthright when necessary.

I ask that I be the best help that I can be for those who have come for my aid, no matter what that might entail.

I am not sure who or what I am invoking. Perhaps I am just aligning with a natural flow. Does it matter where healing comes from?

I feel no uncertainty or stage fright and, apart from the ritual, do very little preparation. I am able to enter a level of trust that I so often wish I could carry more into daily life.

When I do this work, I know who I am and what I am doing and ironically, it is because I have learned to step aside that I can be my best.

And it is through this work that I have come to see what my soul contract was really all about – that every moment of anguish, every gram of tearful frustration, every gut-wrenching fear, every long night of futile beseeching, every piercing hurt, every down-on-my-knees defeat was my training for this.

How else could I know what to say? How else could I stand before a crowd of strangers and know with conviction that I will answer any question that is asked of me?

It is here that I know what to do. It is here that I am in Grace. Here I can know unconditional love.

My role is to hold a place for others that says:

'I'm here if you care to join me but I can't help you by sanctioning your misery. I've been in that place and though it might be temporarily appeasing to share misfortune, if one wishes to overcome misfortune, a choice must be made to move on and with that choice, come consequences.'

One step in front of the other, one day at a time, day after day. Being big when it was so tempting to stay small, hurting and then releasing the hurt, loving self when everything and everyone seems to say otherwise, choosing and choosing again: thoughts, beliefs, reactions, emotions; getting it right, getting it wrong; realising that it was neither of these things.

But this is no penance; it is instead, a great and necessary opening of the heart; unshackling it from the false security of fear and claiming the unfettered fearlessness of love.

As more clients were entrusting themselves to my care in those early days at Zoeros, I felt a strong responsibility to continue my own personal evolution. Turning Point had given me a taste to do more experiential work on myself. Through all that I had explored to date, I was slowly and surely peeling back layer upon layer of the resistance that kept me from the deep inner peace and clarity I aspired to.

My emotional graph still registered relatively high mountains and valleys and though I now had the knowledge and insight to pull myself quickly out of nosedives, nonetheless the nosedives were still too unsettling for my liking. There was clearly more work to do.

Avatar was a nine-day intensive which actually took me twelve days to complete, such was my resistance. I didn't recognise this, of course. Instead, I blamed this 'stupid' course and the 'infuriating' teachers who sent me out each day with a set of obtuse instructions that at the time made absolutely no sense to me.

The most exasperating of these assignments was a daily walk to local gardens where I was instructed to *feel* the park. No further explanation was offered, nor, I now realise, could there be any, but it was doing my head in big time, because I had absolutely no idea of what was required of me.

What did *feel* the park mean? How does one *feel* it? It's a park. It's there. It's trees and grass. What's there to *feel*?

Day after day, I trudged to the park and wandered, frustrated and miserable, for hours, trying to grasp the hidden meaning of this task. I tried physically touching the trees, bushes and flowers but that didn't seem to enlighten me any further.

While the other trainees were happily feeling, not only the park, but the street, the city and even each other and, as a result, had moved onto the next stage of the program, I was still on my bench seat, cursing the park, the trees and the innocent folk who were having such a lovely time lying on the grass, pushing their strollers and walking their dogs, while I was sat on, stuck and suffering and cursing the day I had begun this Avatar business.

Now and then, I reported back to base, where my trainer attempted to steer me in other directions to my enlightenment, such as getting me to count the bricks in her paved backyard, which only served to send me into even more of a tailspin. The one thing that was slowly sinking in was the concept that we each create our own reality, though I wasn't too keen on taking the blame for the unpleasant things that had been done to me.

The rest of the group had graduated but I was still down at the park. I had no idea how long this was going to take me and had visions of being there for the rest of my life and dying without ever finding the answer to the puzzle.

By now, I had sunk into a kind of glum passivity, like a prisoner who finally gives up all will, when suddenly it hit me: *No-one* was *making me* come to this park! I didn't *have* to be here! I didn't even *have* to do this course! And most of all, I could have been *enjoying* this park! *No-one* was making it an *ordeal*, except me!

I started to laugh. I laughed at myself and my ridiculous, mulish, indignant, foolish insistence on suffering. I laughed at my childish pouting and small tantrums as the teacher sent me on my way each day. I laughed at the fact that I had made this woman, who was the same age as me, such an *authority* in my life. I laughed at the ridiculous notion that I *had to do what I was told*! Good grief, how *old* was I?

I laughed all the way home and Buzz, puzzled, yet swept up in my mirth, laughed with me. Things that had seemed so earnest, desperate and serious were now ridiculous and farcical. I laughed at the instructions on how to make a taco on the packaging for taco shells – 'As if any fool couldn't figure that out!' I had tears streaming down my face at the papier mâché shark in *Jaws*, which was showing that night, and I was still giggling when I climbed into bed.

A week later, I was back at the park for a follow-up, only this time I was feeling the park beautifully, sitting on a bench and soaking up the sun. So in the groove was I, that I was only subliminally aware of a jogger passing close by me in a pair of tight, white shorts à la Olivia Newton-John in 'Physical'. It was only when I looked up a minute later that I saw the jogger emerge from a nearby bush, completely naked and wiggling his tragic little penis at me like an uncooked sausage.

I looked at the flasher in bewilderment for a moment, then it struck me: I created *this*?!

I swooned from the park bench, bent double with laughter, tears streaming down my cheeks as I reeled down the path, leaving the poor, pathetic bastard staring in disbelief after me, his manhood now shrivelled to a deflated balloon.

I probably cured him for life.

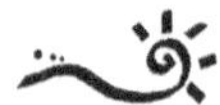

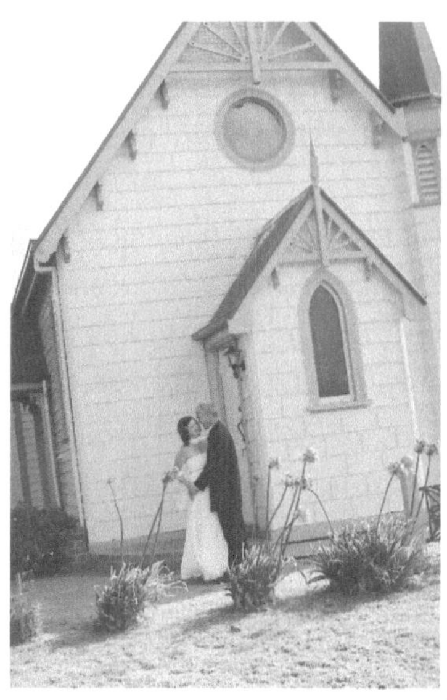

The agreeable and obliging nature that had endeared Buzz to me in our early days had devolved into a slightly alarming and excessive acquiescence which was becoming a source of tension in our otherwise happy union. From the start there had been indications of this but they had been easier to ignore in the early days of our relationship.

Friday 29 September 1998

A tricky phase but I sense that it will pass.

I can no longer picture life without him, yet the differences between us now and then rise starkly and spook me.

He has a tender heart, like mine and we are equally sensitive but he lacks my warrior spirit and determination, and willingness to confront fears and concerns. Instead, he simply caves.

I don't want a 'Yes man' any more than I wanted a 'No man' and I am disturbed by these flashes of 'weakness' through an inordinate compliance to the wishes of others, including myself.

I wish he would just stand his ground sometimes.

Yet he is too precious, too beautiful and too hard-won to allow these petty things to place our love in jeopardy.

But we're okay, Buzz and I. There is real love between us: love at the deepest level; it is my own fractured sense of self that is revealing itself in these carping concerns.

This man loves me with such open trust that I am shamed by these secret misgivings. What do they mean?

I reprimand myself: 'Did you think you wouldn't be tested? Just love him for who he is. So you're stronger, so what? You've always had a big dose of male energy. Feisty Scorpio, gentle Cancer. He teaches you peace, you teach him 'How to live my life', as he said last night.

In a way that is also what he teaches you by example: how to be trusting and childlike in a world that's tough on children. Go, play, love. All is well.

As a sensitive child, Buzz had been distressed by his parents' regular arguments, which had led him to fear and avoid conflict in any form; no matter how mild. In adulthood, Dale Carnegie's *How to Win Friends and Influence People* cemented an idea that the best strategy for an easy life was to simply agree with everyone – and Buzz had taken that message completely and excessively to heart, with the result that I seldom knew if he felt negatively on any subject because he did not tell me; nor did I have any idea of his personal preferences because he usually complied with mine.

It was usually a mystery to me whether he was happy, sad, hungry, cold, angry or bored; whether he wanted to watch the program on Channel A or the one on Channel B – so in the end, I saw no point in asking and decided for both of us.

Should there be an unavoidable unpleasantness, he procrastinated; stalling on fear at both ends of the process: fear of commitment, then fear of having left it too late. Attempts to bring important matters to the table were like trying to grab air; always eliciting the same 'agreeable' responses: 'You're right' or 'Whatever you think' or 'Yes, I'm wrong', dead-ending potential negotiations.

At times, these passive–aggressive delays and stone-wallings ignited my short fuse and I would hear my own voice becoming ever more shrewish, as I turned into that most hateful of creatures – the 'nagging spouse'.

In the heat of these one-sided arguments, Buzz would simply disappear; driving off into the night and no doubt cursing me to the four winds, while I remained behind within four walls; fuming, frightened and fretful that I had driven him away.

In essence, he *gave* himself but he did not *share* himself, holding pain or sickness or worry to himself in secret, sealing himself off from my care inside his own skin. *Just like my father had.*

Years on and too late to rectify this toxic pattern, I would come to better understand the trap we had fallen into, namely: if the thing we do best, which is initially appreciated, is no longer appreciated, we will just do it more.

Buzz's gift to me was his calm and easygoing nature and mine to him was my drive and ability to focus. These were our specialties and other qualities we lacked were provided by the other. However, in time, easygoing Buzz, now inviting criticism for laxity or procrastination, feels that his gift has lost power and ramps it up. Likewise, as the organiser and problem-solver, I was now more frequently perceived as 'controlling' because I was best when I knew where I stood.

The more I pressed for order and reliability, the more Buzz quietly revolted through small passive–aggressive sabotages – being 'late' or 'forgetting' – designed to create subtle chaos through which he might assert some personal power.

Yet these things were, at the time, simply undercurrents to a love that still ran deep. Every relationship has its Achilles heel, I reasoned, and this was ours.

When we were in harmony, we were wonderful – Yin and Yang in perfect balance – he patient and yielding to my headstrong zeal; I the spark who urged him out of the hermitage of his safe shell. We were in such harmony on our second holiday in Bali, in 2001, for, after six years together, we became engaged.

Well, perhaps not in *complete* harmony, for it was a bungled proposal.

We sat cross-legged under the thatched pergolas of the Lotus Inn in the mountain village of Ubud, dining in our favourite place in a breathtakingly beautiful setting overlooking ponds fed by carved stone fountainheads and festooned with quilts of water lilies.

After our meal, we leaned over the bamboo railings, replete and happy in the warm, soft night. As we gazed at a bloated Bali moon and the galaxy of lights draped from the surrounding trees, I commented playfully, 'This would be the perfect setting for a proposal, Buzz.'

'I was going to,' he said, then fell silent, apparently withdrawing the unspoken offer.

An awkward day ensued, with the 'elephant in the room' plodding behind us around the streets of Kuta, till finally that night, Buzz proposed but, given the previous night's faux pas, this time it felt as though it had come a little under sufferance.

Reason told me that marriage didn't matter; that it was an outmoded institution with scant bearing on a committed relationship. The pledges, though full of good intentions, were hardly more than wishful thinking – how could one promise to change in total accord with another till death? – but on some level it *did* matter: it was an affirmation, a proclamation, a declaration and, above all, a celebration; a happy day to outshine old sadness; a raft of hope and optimism to buoy us through the inevitable storms of life.

Buzz and I married on 9 February 2002.

We had discovered a perfect little chapel for our ceremony, perched on a cliff overlooking the sea on a beautiful estate on Phillip Island, the place where our love had first awakened. It was a tiny wooden structure which had been trucked from nearby San Remo onto the site on the back of a semitrailer a few years before.

Though it was the height of summer, that year was unseasonably cold. The day of the wedding dawned gloomily with a howling, bitter wind and sulking sky. Despite brief, heartening swatches of sunshine earlier in the day by afternoon the weather had completely disintegrated.

As I walked with my attendants – my brother, Michelle and Tori – from the shelter of the gardens into the open area leading to the chapel, I gasped as we were swept by a bullying, icy gale that shredded my hundred-dollar hairdo into horizontal rags.

However, I was soon proceeding along the short aisle in the snug comfort of the church, smiling randomly at the congregation in a myopic haze (vanity prevented me from wearing my glasses) towards my beloved Buzz, who, smiling ear to ear, leaned over to kiss me the minute I was at his side and at impromptu intervals throughout the ceremony, as the impulse struck him.

The ominous gale rattling the windows and the chapel creaking like a small boat lashed by a storm were simply a contrasting backdrop to the warmth and love within the room and there was no sign, apart from the weather, that this was anything other than the happiest of days.

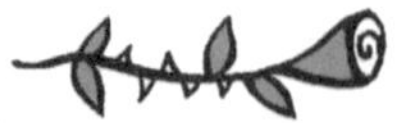

Wednesday 6 April 2011

> *Today I did a presentation at an anxiety conference at the Melbourne Hilton.*
>
> *Heading there, I was actually feeling quite nervous, which is unusual. Having done public speaking for over a decade now, the most I'm likely to experience is a pleasant little fizz of edgy anticipation, rather than stage fright.*
>
> *Then it hits me – the* Hilton *– the ill-fated 1991 Stanley Awards were held at the Sydney Hilton.*
>
> *Amazing how the body remembers – how the cells retain their own minute memory banks – long after the mind has been trained to forget.*

Now, here's a secret. Through all these years, through all I've done – writing books, presenting lectures and workshops, where I show up and smile and speak with confidence – I have been unwell.

Not visibly unwell – in fact, that would somehow make it easier, for to look *normal* and suffer physically is to suffer twice over – but a low-energy, dragging thing, like a permanent flu. Few get it when I try to explain – they shrug when I say, 'I'm ill,' thinking in terms of that small sniffle last spring or even the full blast of last winter's flu, where in fact, my body is in considerable chaos at times.

'But you do so much!' they say. 'You can't be that sick!'

But a lot of the time, I am, pretty much; for nine years now – longer, really, but nine years of the worst of it. I just hide it well.

This is the last big mountain for me to climb: to think myself well. It's probably nothing that a few months' complete rest wouldn't heal but I am 'it': I am the boss and the breadwinner and there is no paid sick leave.

However, it is well that I work for myself, for it is difficult to honour a set routine. I am fretful about appointments earlier than 11 a.m. or later than 6 p.m. because any earlier or later, it is likely that I will be sleep-deprived, with a head full of cotton wool and a bewildering brain-fog to match.

Too much Yin, my Chinese doctor says; poor digestion according to the naturopath; allergies guesses the GP; too many surgeries says the ENT specialist; and unresolved grief says the psychic – this last probably being the most accurate.

For a while, I became 'Bubble Beverley', reacting wildly and annoyingly with sweats and palpitations to anything from dust to a passerby's aftershave, whiteboard markers or even the chemical smell of a plastic raincoat. Food – a thing of nurture – became treacherous, with too wide a spectrum of culprits to eliminate all offenders without turning into a cave-dwelling yogi.

I felt envious of the casual ease of others – to eat any and all things; to drink wine; to peacefully drift into sleep and wake rested in the arms of a lover; to say, with assurance, 'I'll be there', without then having to summon the wherewithal to honour that agreement.

Of course, illness is a metaphor and mine was clear in its definition. The world and those who trod in it, had become toxic to me; I was exhausted by the sheer effort of trying too hard to be loved. It was easier to retreat; emerging only for the brief hours without the worst of the unsociable symptoms; squashing as much living as I could through that small window of relative wellness; like stuffing a too-fat parcel into the slot of a tiny letterbox.

Still, I learned a lot from my body in that time; the most significant and too-late lesson being that unless you are kind to it, it has a mean streak and believe me, you don't want it cranky with you, for the simple reason that you can't move out if your temple turns into a dive.

I could write a directory of healers, conventional and otherwise, whose bank accounts I have boosted in an effort to be healed. Some were downright goofy: a man speaking in tongues brandishing the Bible against the dark forces that had apparently invaded my living room; a 70s refugee, still time-locked in a ponytail and kaftan, applying to my head a cube constructed of matchboxes containing magnets and held fast by red insulation tape, claiming that it would channel invisible healing forces to assuage my flagging spirit.

But there were others, like Doreen, an energy healer who had cured herself of a mysterious paralysis, who understood the distress and isolation that I was experiencing and provided me with valuable guidance on the journey to attaining physical, emotional and spiritual healing; however, I did note that, even though Doreen was now fully ambulant, she was also morbidly obese – but I guess you can't win 'em all. At least her wisdom was as well-rounded as her body:

> *Nurture* ***of*** *you must come* ***from*** *you. Seeking beyond yourself for this is asking for disappointment.*
>
> *Embrace limitations – do what you* can *and make that enough. Let go of everything else.*
>
> *Listen to the body and respond* immediately *to its needs – if thirsty, drink; if hungry, eat; if tired, rest; if stressed, relax. If you want to pee,* pee *– not in half an hour's time when you 'just finish this'. The body then doesn't have to scream to get your attention.*
>
> *Say NO. Walk away from anyone who tries to pressure, push or guilt you into doing more than you are able.*
>
> *Focus on what* is *working, rather than what is not.*

No matter what *is going on, love and accept yourself anyway.*

All the weeping and wailing in the world isn't going to change a thing about the situation – it just makes whatever it is harder to bear.

Accept the situation as it is for now. *Accept there are limitations for now and strangely, try to love it: love it to* death *(or is that love it to* life*?)*

Name the (emotional) beast driving the illness, thank it for its efforts to compensate, protect or right the body's imbalance (even if it's overdone it a tad), then tell it to skedaddle, because now you're *the one driving the bus, thanks.*

But how could I possibly *love* this? How could I love it to death? Love is hard to find when the cost has been considerable; the cost of normalcy, energy, enjoyment and spontaneity as well as the burden added to trying to make a living alone.

What was the true face of this beastie? Was it my IT, finally evicted from my psyche but now taking up residence in my body? Or was it buried grief after all? Was it one too many blows to the heart, blows to the ego; too many 'cell-shocks'?

There was that last big 'cell-shock': the seismic tremor that finally unhinged my immune system and sent it tumbling into a nosedive, the one that led it to fall in a heap: 'I'm outta here! I give up!' – the one that sent me into my cave for a while – to rest, retreat, release, recover, re-evaluate.

On the third day of our honeymoon, Buzz told me he didn't want to be married anymore, didn't want to be in my beloved Bali, wanted to fly home the next day and declared that it had all been a mistake – that wildly windy wedding on the cliff at Phillip Island, with the disturbed weather a portent – had I been paying attention, only weeks before.

'You are too strong for me,' he said, which felt so far from the truth in this moment, caught as I was in the midst of a raging panic which was suddenly arrested by a sharp stillness of certainty as I looked into his eyes and saw that for once, at long last, he had stepped into his own strength; that which I so much wanted for him, that which he had never before fully claimed, not till now, the worst possible time.

There are moments in time when life divides suddenly and shockingly into *before this* and *after this*. The first of those moments for me was anxiety; the second was this. I instinctively knew that there would be no way back for us, because Buzz had finally spoken the truth: the whole truth and nothing but the truth, so help me God.

I staggered upstairs, panic rising and in a hurt so fierce, I could hardly think, hardly breathe. I rang my niece, Michelle, and declared, for no particular purpose – save that I could not carry this alone – that Buzz was leaving me right now, right here on our honeymoon. I heard her incredulous silence at the end of the line, and the groping for words, where there were none – as I well knew would be the case – but I needed someone with whom to share the burden of this awful moment.

I could not stay another minute in the place that had suddenly transformed into a monument to this terrible event. I threw clothes into a bag with no regard and, sobbing, demanded that Buzz help me to relocate to another hotel, for I was incapable of rational thought.

We stumbled past the bewildered staff at our villa. 'Where are you going? What's wrong with you?' they asked with their childlike lack of discretion. I could not answer.

As we exited the taxi at my new accommodation, I handed money for the fare to the driver, who held up his hand to stop me.

'Your husband has already paid,' he said.

'*Ex*-husband!' I spat.

At reception, I collapsed into paroxysms of weeping so profound that Buzz had to sign in for me. The staff stared uncomprehendingly at the spectacle of this Westerner's hysterical public display – all this flailing about – so undisciplined, so *gila*.

Buzz dropped off my bag at my room and then was gone into the night. I was alone on my honeymoon, in Paradise.

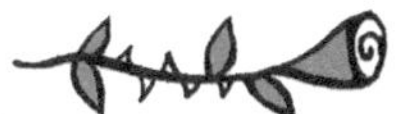

The next morning, I staggered blearily out into the street to buy water, only to see Buzz walking towards me, unshaven, sheepish and contrite. We talked for several hours but my hurt ran deep and I needed more time to process the shock and gather my thoughts. I wandered through Kuta, trying to adjust my perspective to that of a single person; rehearsing for that possibility and trying it on for size.

We reunited for the last days of our holiday but it felt forced and unnatural and the fact remained that even though Buzz had finally stepped up, he had also immediately stepped down again. Nothing had really changed; in fact, it had worsened. Deep in my heart, I intuitively knew the damage had been done, though I longed for it to be otherwise.

As the plane for home lifted into the night sky, I looked back down at the lights of Bali – like my life, now forever changed for me – and I began to weep, blind to the concerned glances of my fellow passengers. The old scar on my heart had been rent open and I knew that it would never quite heal this time.

Sometimes I have wondered how it might have been if I had just swallowed my bloody pride and a desire to 'punish' and thrown my arms around Buzz with relief and forgiveness as he approached that morning. Sometimes I wonder whether it would have happened at all, had I been less forceful; had I just coaxed him more gently to express himself; had I just made it safer for him to speak up over time. Sometimes I imagine the wonderful life we might have had, if he had stood his ground earlier and more often and more definitely.

If only we had yielded our defences, which had become our weapons: I, my prickly barbs of frustration; he, his impenetrable shell with the painted smile.

But 'If only' and 'What if?' – those futile mantras of the depressed and anxious – are dead-end streets. The reality is, I didn't, he didn't, we didn't and 'What if?' can only be answered by events unfolding as they inevitably will and they unfolded over the following painful months as we packed up our things, along with our life together and sold the home into which we had poured so much love and care.

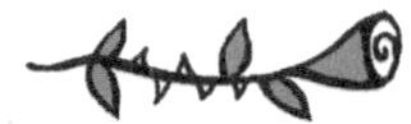

Friday 17 January 2003

I'm down on my knees. I can't take any more. I feel damned, doomed to walk this earth for the rest of my days as this weary, fretful, invisible ghost – through day after day of intolerable unrest, pain and loneliness like a bitter fog that obscures all joy.

There is no respite; all is gone from me, even hope. All gone. I cannot see a tomorrow; cannot see past this now: this stuck, stuck 'nowness' that shambles on and on, polluting my dreams of anything beyond.

I am marooned on an atoll of anxiety. I see life on the other shore, so simple in its unfolding, so known, so accepted, just so, while I am chained by discord to this damned place, condemned to be a spectator to the 'normal' course of things.

I am too difficult, too lost, too complex, too demanding, too wretched, too broken, too contradictory, too judgemental, too selfish, too unkind, and above all, too consumed by guilt (the irony of this does not escape me) to any longer bridge that gap.

Yet how I long to belong. How I long to be known and embraced despite the knowing, forgiven despite the unforgiveable, accepted despite the unacceptable, loved despite the unlovable.

I cry out from this cold place of exile. I cry out for release, I cry out to a silent God, to fictions called angels, to fairytales called guides, to anyone, anything, to deliver me from this afflicted life of mine.

I long to believe in something, anything, *yet have no evidence for belief and so I am thrust deeper into a faithless abyss. There is no mercy. There is no fairness, only this arduous journey of days, indistinguishable one from another, save for the weather and the degree of difficulty.*

Where is my help? Where is the miracle manifestation, the big, fat angel in the middle of my lounge room, smiling at me beatifically, benignly embracing me in a wing-draped arm to soothe my sorrow and my fear?

'Where are you?' I cry, but no-one is listening. There is only the night and the sleeping city, ignorant and impartial to this lonely torment, this single light in a street of darkness that burns on and on till the weak relief of dawn.

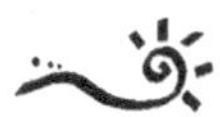

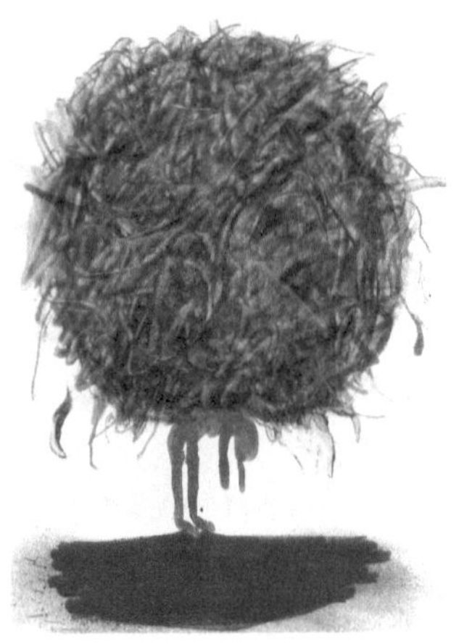

Saturday 8 March 2003

> *Again, I feel as though I have momentarily tipped over into madness, but what is madness other than emotions gone awry?*
>
> *I once saw an interview with a man suffering with severe schizophrenia. When asked to define his illness, he replied, 'An extreme sensitivity to stress.'*

The same paralysing fear I had experienced when I had stepped away from my life with Harry had reared up again in the face of my parting from Buzz.

In the first days of our separation, a frightening bitterness, long-buried and muted by years of passivity, now surfaced in Buzz, revealing a sinister edge: *'I hate all women,' he sneered. 'I hate the way they look, the way they walk, the way they talk, the way they smell. I hate 'em!'*

'Am I included in that?' I asked, shocked by the venom in his words.

'All women,' he replied.

His anger had become an impenetrable armour which deflected even the possibility of a friendship I had hoped we might sustain. I knew that this aggression came from hurt but he was no longer the man I once knew and I did not know how to reach this hostile, seemingly misogynous stranger.

Even had this not been a barrier; having now stepped outside the ranks of our 'family', I no longer had the wherewithal to take on, not only our mortally wounded marriage, but also the war zone of two angry and confused boys entering teenage years, as well as the crossfire (and occasional direct hit) of the ongoing hostilities of their parents.

I had lost my man, my 'family' and my beautiful home and, like Buzz, I now burned with silent and impotent rage at my lot and against myself.

One fitful night of personal witchcraft, I gathered the icons of shared hope, the tokens of united dreams and the symbols of naive promises and tossed them onto the fire in a ritual I hoped, I prayed, would exorcise such diabolical pain.

I saved for the grand finale the cremation of my wedding dress.

In one irreversible gesture, I threw it onto the pyre, observing myself performing this momentous act with eerie detachment and from afar; as if I were watching a woman I did not know.

I looked on with a mixture of exquisite hurt and something verging on awe, as I witnessed the dress curling and charring – white to black, and finally melting, like a beautiful, beaded marshmallow upon the tongues of flames; within the dark mouth of the hearth.

Extract from 'Western Beaches' (revised version)
Original version shortlisted for Ida Cambridge
Literary Award
Bev Aisbett 2005

My old terror of solitude was now sharpened by my temporary relocation to a house owned by a medical clinic that was next door. Though the house ideally served my immediate needs of cheap rent, an inbuilt office and a short lease, it was hardly a perfect environment to promote peace and healing.

Tagged for demolition to make way for development, and with the surrounding land already in the process of being converted to a staff car park, the house sat like a lonely, grounded ship in a dusty and barren desert of graded earth. Devoid of foliage, the area was scuttled by winds which met no resistance and on weekends, when the clinic was closed, it became an isolated, dusty wasteland in the heart of suburbia.

My most loyal friends – JB, who worked nearby and dropped in regularly for long philosophical chats that sometimes helped and frequently hindered, and Angelo, along with a relatively new friend, Suzanne, were three of the few visitors who braved my haunted house and my haunted self on a regular basis.

In the main, I faced down innumerable hours without a single encounter with a fellow human being, save for fleeting engagements with the local shopkeepers. My old demons of abandonment skulked around this discomfited place and loomed largest at nightfall when the hum of day subsided to the lonely echo of my own footsteps in the long, unpopulated hours of darkness.

And long they were, for my health had now taken its nosedive and anxiety played out in new and sadistic ways which sabotaged the slim sleep that I already struggled to find; my light burned and my television flickered into the small hours, night after terrible night.

I was wrestling with something profound which felt like a fight of my life – huge, grotesque, wild, and all-consuming. In desperation, I turned to my art for refuge, as I had done before; only this time, it would take a new direction.

Suzanne, who had recently been studying art therapy, had discussed the principles involved with me and, out of interest, I searched out a book on the subject at the local library. Glancing through the book I found that a few things were connecting – flickering strands of something trying to coalesce; I had no idea what, but I realised how much of my self-expression – save for the free-flow of a few previous occasions – had been stifled by practicality, bread-winning and over-concern about neat results.

I had held back, reluctant to experiment too wildly under the gaze of an imagined and critical audience. Even when I used my art for release – as I had done during my time with BM – polite, pretty little pictures had emerged while inside remained an unreleased stream of emotion that ran deep within.

The book gave me new directions on opening up and pouring forth: it said *feel*, don't think; let whatever wants to come, come. There is no right or wrong way to do this; create the way a child does: and express, with less care for results. Above all, it said: be willing to make a *mess.*

This final clue spoke deeply to me, for life itself was neither neat nor predictable; life was a mess, a changeable, beautiful mess that defied constraint and mocked our feeble, futile human attempts to control that which could never be controlled. And here was my mess, boiling up within me; waiting to pour forth and away.

That night, I opened a fresh, untouched sketchbook and dedicated it to this next stage of my healing. This virgin book – this blank, white path upon which I was about to embark – was the beginning of a deeper journey into myself.

Letting my hand, and not my head, guide me for once, I began the first rendering and was surprised to find that quite a bright, colourful and optimistic picture emerged.

Was I still being 'polite'? Restrained? I wondered. Was I still so afraid of my own Shadow?

Then I did another; this one monochrome – winter, not so much bleak but stripped of colour: the bare bones of things.

Finally, she spewed forth, in pinks and reds: a howling warrior woman bellowing out magenta rage.

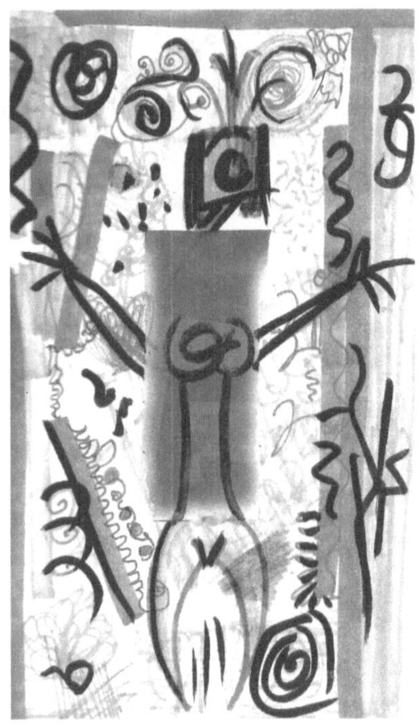

Night after night, when sleep eluded me, when loneliness was a physical pain, I turned to my sketchbook and layer by layer, I released the hurt that bound me as, one after the other, I channelled images from the deepest part of my being.

Always surprising, they revealed a hidden world, sometimes fierce and sour: a tight, a frustrated, repeated rendering of the word **and**; sometimes heartbreakingly tender and raw, a female Atlas, bent double by the weight of the world – but with each new image I was untying one more knot, cleaning out one more crevice, emptying out one more emotional cupboard.

I gathered together every possible art material I could find for this purpose. The book had become not only a release, but also an adventure and there was now a small fizz of excitement as I wondered what would pop out next. I bought sparkle pens, blow pens, crayons, pastels, textas, watercolours, pencils; anything I could lay my hands on. I *had* to draw!

This book was my refuge on sleepless nights. It was my friend when I felt friendless. It was my counsellor and my guide and, above all, it saved me.

Ninety-six pages in two weeks. My art was the breath of life that gave me new reasons to keep breathing in the first place.

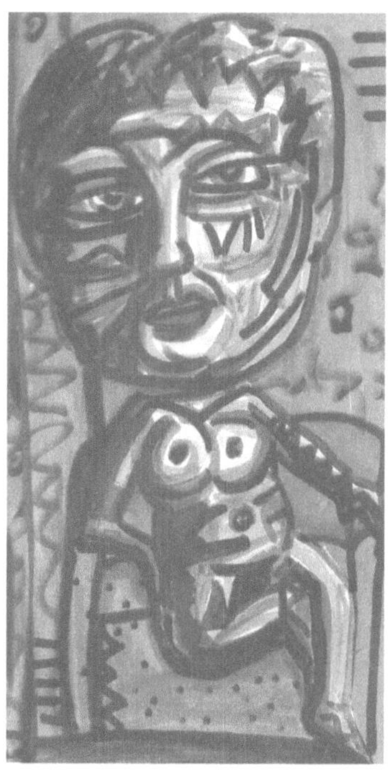

At the end of 2004, while Libby was vacationing with friends in Queensland, my brother took out a pen and paper, wrote a note marked 'Libby', which he propped against a vase on the kitchen table, packed his bags and left.

After seventeen years of complaint and compliance, he finally summoned the nerve to walk away.

But not the nerve to do it in person; something I saw as cowardly and cruel. Having felt the sting of the silent departures in my life of those who simply 'disappeared', too weak-willed to explain, I felt Libby deserved the respect of a face-to-face goodbye.

Monday 13 December 2004

A strange turn of events yesterday. Libby called to say that she'd seen Aisie outside her house at all hours.

I'm not sure what she wants me to do with this information but it does raise some concerns about his emotional state.

On Christmas Day at my niece's new home in the Dandenongs, after holding my tongue the entire day, a glass of champagne and Aisie's constant shadowing of me, telling me how miserable he felt, along with tall tales of fending off lusting menopausal women on a yacht cruise, my resolve loosened, then fell overboard and I finally confronted him.

'What the hell are you doing, Aisie? First, you leave Libby with just a lousy note, which, to be honest, I think is really gutless, then she tells me you've been hanging around her house!'

'I was not hanging around!' he flared, his face darkening.

'Then what were you doing there at all hours?'

'I was just looking at the house I'd put so much work into.'

We left it at that but the air was thick and I called him that evening. After a shaky start, it eventually settled into a calm and productive discussion. He expressed disappointment that I had believed Libby's version over his own; an irony, as it would turn out, through future events.

'Well, you can be hard work, mate! Do you know why you don't get sympathy? Because you need it too much!'

He gave a small laugh of recognition. 'I guess you're right,' he said.

'I'll try to smooth off my sharp tongue a bit,' I added. 'OK?'

Wednesday 12 January 2005

I had just started a painting today when a phone call from Michelle informed me that Aisie was in hospital with an abscess on the spine, of all things.

Out of curiosity, I looked up 'Abscess' in the listings of emotional origins of illness in Louise Hay's book Heal Your Body *and local author Annette Noontil's lengthily titled* Your Body Is the Barometer of Your Soul, So Be Your Own Doctor.

It seemed such an extreme and angry ailment, there must be a huge emotional block behind it. Sure enough, there it was.

Noontil listed 'abscess' as: 'Stagnation, festering emotions, holding onto old concepts' and Hay: 'Fermenting thoughts over hurts, slights and revenge', while the spine indicates one's flexibility and a sense of feeling supported.

It seemed my brother was wrestling with more than just physical demons. Since his split with Libby he had been staying with Michelle and her partner, Charlie, and his behaviour had been odd, to say the least, echoing how lost he had seemed when I returned from England. Michelle reported that several times she or Charlie had risen in the night to find Aisie standing like a ghost outside their room.

Charlie, who until Aisie's tenancy had found Michelle's dismissive air towards her father to be somewhat unfair had, within a week, likewise had enough and this would be repeated later, with my younger niece's partner.

Charlie found himself shadowed by Aisie in the precious early hours before work while the family slept, when, instead of quiet reflection, he was regaled with smutty jokes and stories of sexual conquests in Aisie's attempts to be convivially 'blokey'.

'For Pete's sake, this is my partner's *father*!' said the normally unshockable Charlie, in dismay.

That afternoon I drove to the hospital to see my brother. I was dragging my feet, knowing his destitute energy would engulf me. When I arrived, I simply could not go straight to his room, nor could I stave off the bitter thought running through my head: 'My God he'll do *anything* to get attention!'

Instead, I bought a coffee and worked on centring myself into a more gracious attitude and asked the Universe for loving guidance.

His back was to me when I entered the room; he was dozing in a foetal position with his toes curling upwards in their distinctive way. Wearing the short 'nightdress' of the hospital gown, he looked at once a small boy and a man much older than the one I knew.

He woke as I approached and struggled to focus glassily at me through the fog of morphine as if he, or indeed I, were in an alien land. His energy was difficult to be around: a lost and beaten quality hung like a dank mist over him. We attempted conversation but he kept losing sentences in the haze of the drugs, so I searched for some other way to connect.

Intuitively, I came up with a solution: I would give him Reiki. It was at least something that I could offer that was not in jeopardy of intemperate words. As I placed my hand on his chest, I was struck by the force of a dreadful, palpable sadness that I felt around his heart and in that moment, I felt only pity for the poor, hapless, deeply lonely human being that he had become. I knew that the one thing he needed most of all was the very thing that none of us could give him. And I wondered why we couldn't; yet I knew that if we did, no amount of love or attention or confirmation of his worth would ever be enough.

So I held his clammy hand, looked into his big, sad, bleary eyes and sent him as much as I could of that precious gift of love, if only by proxy. I left soon after, and hit by a surge of emotion, tears came as I walked down the hallway – for him, for me, for life that taunted both of us so with its harsh lessons.

From the car, I rang Michelle and asked her, 'Why can't we just love him, Michelle?' but she sighed, and I could almost hear her shrug her shoulders on the end of the line.

'Because he makes it so hard,' she said.

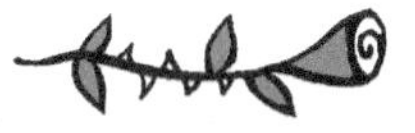

Sunday 5 March 2006

The big news is my brother. Being away on holiday I had missed my great-niece's birthday party, three weeks ago. Apparently Aisie appeared with a woman that no-one had met and whom he had met only a week before – at the council tip! He introduced her as the 'love of his life'!

We are all reeling over this rapid development; though we knew it was inevitable that Aisie would fall in love again as soon as possible.

I was curious to meet this woman and as it is his birthday tomorrow, I invited them to lunch today.

However, Aisie called me on Friday. 'Do you have your diary handy?'

'Why?'

'Well, I want you to keep 11th of November free. Trish and I are getting married!'

Before I could stop myself, I blurted: 'Well that's just bloody insane, Aisie!'

My frustration with his foolhardiness had me tossing and turning till 3 a.m.

It wasn't only Aisie that I had concerns for; but also his new fiancee. Did she have any idea of what a naive romantic he was? No matter how I looked at it, I found it hard to be enthusiastic. So it was with these mixed emotions that I opened the door to them this morning.

I noted that Trish* seemed to be bracing herself, like a boxer about to step into the ring. A tiny but sturdy woman, she gave the impression of someone who had a fair bit of living under her belt: a tough survivor. Though half Aisie's height, she clearly towered over him in pluck.

Buying time, I spent the first few minutes steering the conversation *around* the Big Event, despite all Aisie's attempts to drag it back, but eventually, it was unavoidable when Trish opened with: 'I know what you're all thinking, but I love Aisie, and it's just right.'

I said, 'I don't know whether Aisie's told you that I'm a straight talker and to be honest, I really don't get this great need to rush into marriage. I don't think you can really know anyone in four weeks.'

'It just feels right,' she repeated, adamantly.

As we had arranged to meet my friend Pete to go to the Sydney Road Festival, we were forced to leave soon after, but the air was still thick with my unspoken concerns.

As we walked through the crowds at the festival, I finally had an opportunity to talk to Trish on her own. 'It's not only Aisie I'm worried about,' I said.

I took a deep breath and went on.

'I'm sure you've noticed the family dynamics – and I just want you to know that there is a good reason for that.'

I explained that we had been quite concerned about Aisie's mental health for some time and he had been behaving quite strangely of late and that my nieces and I had some serious misgivings about his ability to make a sensible decision about himself. 'Personally,' I said, 'I am worried that Aisie is rushing into this.'

Having begun, I decided to tell it as straight as possible and to her credit, Trish was just as straight in response.

She said, 'I see him at a soul level. He gets it that he is unlovable. I just want to help him heal and teach him how to be whole.'

I suddenly found my heart melting and before I knew it, I was giving her a hug. I felt a dawning respect for her feisty, no-nonsense spirit, which was, in many ways, like my own.

'Well then,' I said, 'we will all gladly hand him over to your care.'

I came away from this meeting feeling that if anyone could reinvent my poor, lost brother, maybe this woman could and I surmised that if one wanted to be adored, then Aisie was the man for the job. Perhaps it was a perfect match, after all. Above all, I was pleased that we had both had the courage to be candid and as a result, the previous tension lifted and we ended up having an enjoyable day together.

Friday 31 March 2006

Last weekend was Casey's (my other great niece's) *birthday party. I was mildly curious about how it would unfold and it was an opportunity to observe the interactions of the family with Trish present. I had decided to be supportive of her; after all, the existing tensions weren't her fault.*

As it transpired, she didn't come – apparently, she couldn't quite face it. However, Aisie arrived and I saw him with new eyes: the way Trish might see him. He looked terribly lost as the rest of the family all but ignored him and, despite my being in concert with their exhaustion of sympathy for Aisie, I felt that their behaviour towards him was bordering on cruel this day.

What had been his crime except to try too hard, and get it wrong? Okay, he is hard work but I'm not sure he deserves this.

I sat and spoke with him and he brightened up a bit.

How sad it is to witness this disintegration of family – I think of the bonds of family and friends in my early life and how much they meant and how my mother, being the glue for all of us, fostered and nurtured those connections, which have now loosened almost to the point of drifting away entirely.

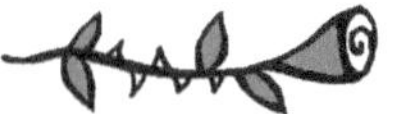

I remained close to my nieces, though not as close as we had once been, when we were like sisters in their single years. Partners, motherhood and geography had intervened and though still bonded, we were not in touch as much as before but we knew we would always stand by each other in the end. My nephew had long ago retreated to Perth, appearing only for major family events, such as Kym's wedding.

In the winter of 2006, my youngest niece, Kym, was married on an icy, wild, saturated day that threatened snow in the chilly mountains of the Dandenong Ranges. Despite the weather, the wedding was a happy affair. Kim had met her beloved Chris after many years of solitude and they were perfect for each other.

I stood waiting for the bride to enter on the arms of both her parents, and I was happy and excited for her. As she entered the room, I was stunned by how beautiful she looked. In a glamorous, understated swathe of a gown she bore some resemblance to the actress Julia Roberts, her poise in stark contrast to the chubby, unrefined girl I had known in previous years.

As the procession neared me, I caught my brother's eye and smiled at him, which he returned with a withering scowl. I was stunned. I simply could not understand what was going on. Clearly something was up, but neither was this the occasion, nor was I concerned enough to investigate too deeply, given that Aisie was prone to changeable moods.

I made a few small attempts at conversation with him during the night, and even ventured at one point later in the evening to ask if anything was up, to which he muttered a vague reply that didn't really explain anything. I left it, concentrating instead on enjoying the happy event. Indeed it was one of the happiest weddings I had been to.

A few days later, I decided to find out what was going on and rang my brother. He was icy cold but vague about details, saying only, 'You hurt Trish.'

I wracked my brains but could think of nothing extraordinary that had transpired. I decided to let it go for the moment. Perhaps things would be clearer in time.

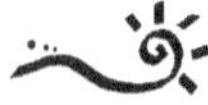

I decided to begin the new year of 2007 with a fresh start and enrolled for the challenging Landmark Forum weekend in January.

I had previous interest in the Landmark approach, having stumbled upon an account of the workshop titled *The Book of est* by Luke Rhinehart, author of the 70s cult classic *The Dice Man*, a controversial book which was purported to have been based on some of the est concepts. I had happened upon *The Book of est* while on a strange and brooding holiday on the Gold Coast soon after Owen's final departure in 1995.

At the time this book was something of a salvation, and I related strongly to some of the no-nonsense strategies that were outlined within. In fact, I was so intrigued by the est concepts, I then read the biography of the founder, Werner Erhard.

The Book of est is a fictionalised account of the entire workshop and it is clear from the description of the experience that est, as Landmark was then known in its original format, was not for the fainthearted. Participants were harangued and bullied into 'enlightenment', firstly through a stringent set of rules (known as Agreements), laboriously detailed for over an hour at the commencement of the course: 'NO WATCHES ARE

TO BE BROUGHT INTO THE ROOM, THERE ARE TO BE NO BATHROOM BREAKS' and so on, followed by a series of insults and invective from the facilitator: 'YOU ARE A BUNCH OF ASSHOLES! YOUR LIVES DON'T WORK!' directed in an attempt to ultimately break down defences by bludgeoning participants out of their 'rackets'.

Despite this, or even *because* of this, I felt that the methods, though extreme, had considerable merit in their pure and original form.

So often – too often – I, like so many others, had hidden behind excuses for helplessness or blamed circumstances, when it was only I who stood in my own way. And, like so many others, I had lived to a 'story' about myself which was really no more than a construction that I chose to continue to invest in and that story was entitled 'Abandonment'.

The Book of est explained the seduction of the victim mentality and how one creates one's own experience through personalising otherwise neutral experiences, demonstrated in an interesting exchange between a woman called Linda and the trainer.

'I wish you wouldn't shout ...'

'You don't like my shouting? ...'

'No ... it makes me nervous. I wish you would communicate to people in a gentler voice.'

'WHY DON'T YOU LIKE SHOUTING, LINDA?'

'DON'T SHOUT!'

'WHY DON'T YOU LIKE SHOUTING?'

'STOP IT! STOP IT!'

'Who shouted, Linda?'

She stares steadily at him with anger.

'Who shouted, Linda?'

'My father ... he shouted at everyone.'

The woman finally 'got it' that the trainer's shouting in itself was neither here nor there, good nor bad, but that she had placed her own *meaning* on the shouting, which, without her 'story' was just loud noise.

In another section, I read: 'I've been calling you assholes. Fine! Get it and note what you add to it: resentment, anger, bewilderment, depression, amusement, hatred, shame – whatever it is that you add to being called an asshole. Whatever you add; that's part of your assholeness; your mechanicalness ... I give you the words "You're an asshole". The rest is your creation.'

A final example of obvious interest concerned anxiety.

'... My item is anxiety,' he said.

'That's pretty vague, Robert,' said the trainer.

'All the time. I think I'm anxious all the time.'

'BULLSHIT!' snaps the trainer. 'Anything you think you're experiencing *all the time* is obviously a concept. I want to know a specific *place* and *time* when you really *experience* anxiety.'

'Okay,' says Robert '... when I go for an audition ... my whole body is tense.'

'That's CRAP, Robert. When your whole body is tense it's called *rigor mortis* [which means] you're *dead*!'

Although toned down in its current form, the process remains a confronting one but I felt that I was up for it by now, having borne many a sling and arrow over the years.

At some point in the proceedings, 'trainees' are required to call someone with whom we have unfinished business. Naturally, I thought of my brother, though a small inner voice was warning me that this was probably not a good idea.

However, the Landmark approach is very insistent that the onus is upon the trainee to resolve issues and valiantly push through any defences encountered in the process. With shaking hands, I rang my brother's number.

'I am doing a workshop this weekend and we are asked to call anyone with whom we need to sort out things,' I said. 'If

I have said or done anything to hurt you, then I'm sorry (was I?). Can you please tell me what it is that you are angry about, because I still don't know.'

'You upset Trish and I can't forgive that,' was the reply. The conversation was short, terse and unenlightening – on any level.

I was to make two further attempts, once more during the workshop, then another the following week when Aisie was visiting Michelle on his own. I had hoped that with just the two of us he might be more open to reconciliation, but this was not to be.

'I will never forgive you,' he said.

Despite the gravity of his statement, for a moment it conjured in me an impish mental picture:

> *'Ah can* nevah *forgive you, Sapphire/Diamond/Ruby/*
> *Pearl/Cubic Zirconium! Yo hurt the woman I love!'*
> *'But Rack/Torso/Pec/Hunk, ah'm yo sistah!'*

But what I said was, 'Well, Aisie, you've said it. You can never forgive. And that's going to fester away for the rest of your life.'

When Michelle came on the line afterwards, she said, 'Geez mate, I reckon *one* try would have been enough for me!'

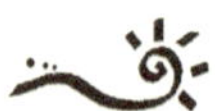

Of *course* writing of Aisie has been painful.

When your own brother sends you a text that says *'You are contemptable'* (sic) as Aisie did during the Landmark weekend, it is hard not to believe that of yourself; even momentarily.

For all my flaws, shying away from the painful truth (if, indeed, it *is* the truth) is not one of them but I simply could not recall anything that would warrant such a dramatic stand.

Whatever, as they say; it was done, with each party convinced that their own take on reality was the only 'real' reality. Even so, here comes my old friend Shame, shuffling onto centre-stage in her drab Dickensian rags, trailing my past of rejections and accusations in her wake. I am tired of her; tired of feeling like a bad person trying (and failing) to be good.

I want for myself that which I want for my brother, for my clients, for all who are shamed – to be free of that sick feeling of wrong, wrong, wrong that keeps appearing in my life as others who represent the disowned aspects of myself – for as I disown myself, so am I disowned. I want to learn to love in a way that sees no wrong in the first place but only hurt, fear and sorrow. I want to be myself without apology, without having to sidestep the landmines of my own and others' insecurities.

Despite my brother's or anyone's opinion of me, it is my duty to myself to love myself regardless; to see myself as Source sees us all – as blameless children, doing all that we know to do.

And I must become extremely adept at self-love, for there will be those who will try to convince me that I do not deserve love as much as they do. Loving myself is a skill and, like any other, mastering it takes practice and involves making mistakes, such as over-reaching.

Clearly, it served Aisie and Trish to see me as the bad guy! – there is strong currency in taking the moral high ground as the 'wounded party'; but I was rapidly learning that there really is no such thing. We *attract* that which comes our way. We teach people how to treat us.

So, in this context, what had I attracted and why had I attracted it?

In seeking the answer, I am led to an interesting book called *The Disappearance of the Universe* by Gary Renard.

Based on the teachings of a book by Dr Helen Schucman called *A Course in Miracles* – regarded as a profound and essential modern guide to the spiritual path – Renard's interpretation makes the following propositions:

- There is no-one out there. You are alone. Everything you see is your own projection.
- Those we perceive as 'others' are merely thought-forms of aspects of ourselves, reflected back to us.
- These thought-forms present as others in our lives in order to be 'absolved' and in doing so, we 'absolve' ourselves.

In simpler terms: letting others off the hook means letting oneself off the hook; likewise for accepting, appreciating and letting others be.

I pondered these concepts – indeed, how can there be any 'reality' that is not an individual's 'creation', perceived through layer upon layer of fears, prejudices, impressions, expectations and vulnerabilities and filtered through one's own unique history?

There really *is* no-one out there – others are no more (nor less) than who or what one *thinks* they are, influenced by a naturally biased viewpoint. One cannot really *know* another but only have an *opinion* of how they are. So, if one changes the way one sees others – preferably in a more positive light – others will appear to change as a result.

By seeing others as versions of *myself* – especially those who challenged me – I could detect aspects of myself that needed the greatest healing or, conversely, aspects that I wished to develop or that I appreciated.

Author John Bradshaw's work comes to mind – where he explains that when we feel a strong reaction against someone's behaviour, we are being shown an aspect of ourselves that has been disowned. Often the behaviour we react against is opposite to our own and therefore indicates a part of ourselves that needs reclaiming. So an *intolerance* of arrogance in another may indicate that one is being overly humble; aggression indicates people-pleasing; opportunism indicates rescuing and weakness the need to be strong. When we are willing to own and explore our reactions in this way, our 'enemy' becomes our teacher.

Clearly, an intolerance of weakness is first on my list and it is true that I most value courage and strength. What if I embrace the disowned self? What can it teach me? Perhaps that what I have construed as 'weakness' is instead a softness that, if developed, will balance my warrior zeal for truth.

So Aisie had presented me with my own vulnerability and, disliking what I saw, I denied it in myself and instead tried to fix it in him, or made it his fault.

I can only guess what it was that I presented to Aisie, but perhaps I popped up as an embodiment of his own harshest critic – himself – and it was easier to make me a culprit.

And what of Trish? Well, she and I both presumed to know what was best for Aisie and were trying to protect him – and perhaps control as much as caring, was the true motivator.

'I will never forgive you!' said my brother, which is interesting in this context, as was my 'apology' and I wanted to examine both. The concept of 'forgiveness' to me smacks of self-righteousness, given the necessity of a judgement of wrongdoing in the first place.

What if someone is simply presenting an unpalatable truth? Does that make them 'bad'? And if it is not true, why would it offend?

Perhaps a more enlightened approach to forgiveness might be: 'I absolve you of any responsibility for the way I feel, for that is *my* problem.'

This led me to question even more deeply. Should one say sorry? Should one be sorry? Perhaps, if one really *is* sorry. Again, a more insightful question may be 'What am I sorry *for*?'

Am I sorry because:

I fear another's disapproval?
I fear confrontation?
I might appear to be cruel/nasty/callous/unkind/not nice if I don't?
It is expected that I should?
I've been 'caught out'?

One friend, when visiting – by invitation – would utter 'Sorry' the moment I opened the door to him and this would be repeated, like a stutter, throughout the visit. His 'sorry' was revealing. What was he sorry for? Being here? Taking up some other, more worthy person's air?

Isn't this at the heart of anxiety? Fearful of speaking our truth, fearful of offending, fearful of being *real*, we allow ourselves to be shamed into compliance, second-guessing others' needs because we fear their disapproval. Not only this, but expecting the same of others: wanting them to be this, that or the other to make *ourselves* feel better.

EGO, EGO, EGO – 'IT' is the threatened ego, saying *me*, *me*, *me*, look at me, be careful of me, look after me: I'm *special*!

This was the ground collapsing under me during my 'mushroom epiphany' all those years ago: the ego cracking and crumbling like a fragile egg with the realisation that I wasn't 'special' after all.

I once read an interview with a community-minded celebrity who nonetheless had quite a reputation for terseness. She said: 'If you appreciate me for my gifts, then that includes the whole package that makes me, *me*. I refuse to apologise for being myself. I'm not here to look after your ego. How can I? That's *your* job.'

You can't change the buggers. You can't get them to do what you want. You can't get them to say what you want to hear. You can't please them or get them to make it all better.

You can only accept them – and yourself – *as they are*, leave them to it and let everybody off the hook. That's *freedom*.

Be who you are
And say what you feel
For those who mind, don't matter
And those who matter don't mind.
Source: A note stuck to a teenager's window I happened to read in passing one night

And thanks, inadvertently, to Aisie, I wrote *I Love Me*.

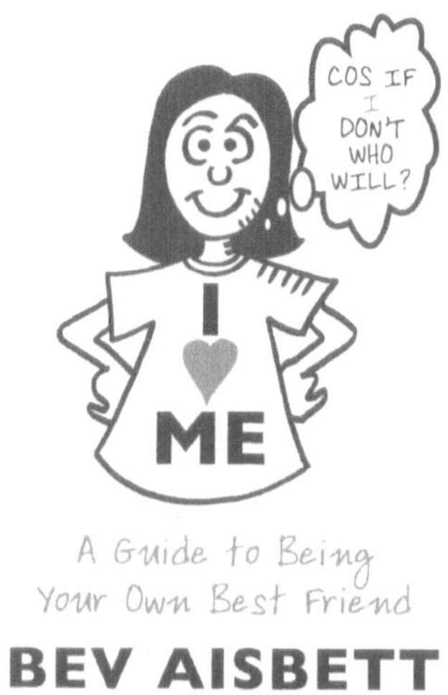

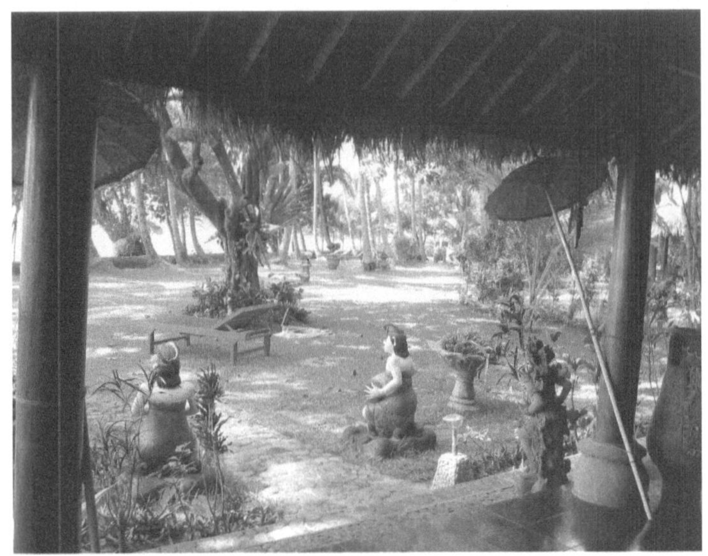

A year after Buzz, the diary entries slowly trickled down to erratic and occasional puddles of venting or an odd insightful reflection and eventually almost ceased entirely. And, I was pleased to note, my anxiety had gone much the same way.

My life slowed for a while; a long while, to allow me to draw breath.

There was no longer the need for great outpourings. My life was necessarily pared down by exhaustion; stripped of any but the most necessary of stresses, as it finally occurred to me – and I could only be amazed that I had missed this most obvious of revelations for all these years – that I did not handle stress well and that the greatest stressor for me had been trying to take on too-large doses of other people.

I gave up striving for intimacy and, save for a handful of loyal and abiding friendships within which I felt accepted and appreciated, I contented myself with more lightweight and fleeting exchanges. My life was now more restful and made simpler by retreat and, as a week, then a month, then a year folded seamlessly into more weeks, months and years, I discovered that retreat had become a habit a little too hard to break. The line had become blurred between giving up and surrender, loneliness and solitude, but my exhausted heart could do no more than seek rest and peace by stepping out of the arena for a while.

My art was now my Dreamtime and I lived more peacefully in my head – once the site of such warfare – as I now drifted from thought to thought like a leaf floating on a stream. My creativity flourished in this quietude as I told my stories of love and loss in brushstrokes in place of caresses, upon canvases which were now the beds upon which I surrendered to passion.

At the end of 2003, enticed by the sea, I moved across the Westgate Bridge to begin a new life in a side of the city that was entirely new territory to me.

> *We came here to begin again, she and I, both with our war-wounds; she with a serrated ear (ruined her looks in a previous altercation with a passing Ridgeback) and I with my heart held together with bandaids and glue.*
>
> *We came from East to West, from one side of the city to the other, trailing in the wake of a truck loaded with what remained of the cargo of my life ...*
>
> *... There was something optimistic about the way the bridge curved up and around in a concrete smile and the glimpse of blue from its summit offered a tinge of hope that managed to eclipse even the visual assault of the west's gateway of industrial gargoyles. Perhaps the sun might shine a little more here, perhaps there might be good souls and like-minded people to erase the loneliness and perhaps there might be a healing in this new world of sea and fisherfolk and boats and beginnings ...*
>
> **Excerpt from 'Western Beaches' (revised version)**
> **Bev Aisbett 2005**

One might think that I would have learned my lesson from the Ha Ha Gallery but I spotted an old shop for rent and decided to have another try; I opened Salmay Gallery soon after.

In truth, my intention for the gallery was little more than an opportunity to meet like-minded friends and foster my love of art. But a pestering and eccentric landlady, a break-in by one of the many 'Westie' desperados who still haunt the area, and the pressure of covering costs became too much for my limited energy so I moved back home to work.

I returned to Bali in 2004; back to the same resort which was the setting of my ill-fated honeymoon. The receptionist conducted me to my room and produced the key to the very same villa that Buzz and I had stayed in on that fateful night. I looked upward to the sky and silently said, 'Yep, thanks for that. Let's make it as tough as possible, shall we?' But in the end, it was just a room. There were no ghosts here; only the ghosts I chose to conjure with my memories and now I was freeing myself to make new ones.

Besides, this was just the final gesture in reclaiming Bali, having prepared myself at a retreat in a tiny village on the far north coast of the island where Elijah owned a villa and it was just as he had said it would be: a little touch of heaven. Away from all the touristy madness there was peace and the natural sedatives of heat and lazy, unstructured hours.

Elijah, a masseur and body-worker I had met in Melbourne and an occasional painter himself, had built a small art studio at the rear of the villa, which I was free to use. I whiled away the hours painting, surrounded by a Balinese garden set against the tinkling soundtrack of a tiny trickling moat filtering through the open doors.

I recalled one session with Elijah soon after the fall-out with my brother when I had wept over this most hurtful rejection, lamenting: 'The trouble is, I care too much.'

'Can I suggest a way to say that which *supports* you?' asked Elijah, hauling my leg somewhere near my ear and then he offered, 'The beauty is, I care *so* much.' And I did care; enough to fear for him.

One day I sat on the front porch, gazing out to sea, the view fringed with frangipani and hibiscus and before me, a skeletal, winged sail-boat like a bat drifted on the horizon.

Soon, a lunch of fish and several salads appeared in the dining pavilion and those who were staying at the retreat emerged from various villas hidden among the palm trees as we gathered to eat together, lured by the gorgeous smells emanating from Made's kitchen.

The yielding of the Balinese to life in all its colours is infectious. Almost from the moment I step from the plane into the swoon of heat and the mildewy aroma of the airport, I find myself casting off the burden of cares and pressures that are so 'normal' in my Western life. I slow down and embrace the quiet, natural pace that defines each Balinese day. I could live here; I really could, and I wonder why I don't, but big changes are still hard for me, even though, or perhaps because, I have hurled myself into so many in the past.

Metres away, the thunderous Balinese surf dashed itself inelegantly onto the pebbled shore in short, impatient and percussive dumps; unlike the sea at home, which rolled proudly towards the shore like drapery, swathing the sand with the lace of its long, luxurious exhalations.

Recently, I had the honour of participating in the very last Turning Point, twelve years after I had experienced it for the first time. This time, I did it for the sheer thrill of the ride. There was little anger this time – there was sadness but also a hard-won clarity and wisdom that could only have come from all that I had lived in the intervening years.

As a finale, participants were asked to visualise every person we had known who had been significant to us and imagine them lined up before us, to be greeted one by one.

I looked into every face; of those I once thought had hurt me, those who had once loved me and moved on and those who have loved me, no matter what. I felt a new appreciation even for my 'enemies' because I went *here* because of this person, I did *that* because of that person, I healed *this* because of him and *that* because of her. I suddenly saw in a way I could never have imagined, all of the connections; the beautiful logic of things: the divine, cosmic choreography behind the dance of my life leading me to this point.

And as I came upon each person, I was able to thank them for being part of my story; each an essential component in my life's journey, no matter how painful that might have seemed at the time.

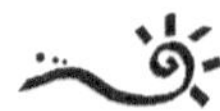

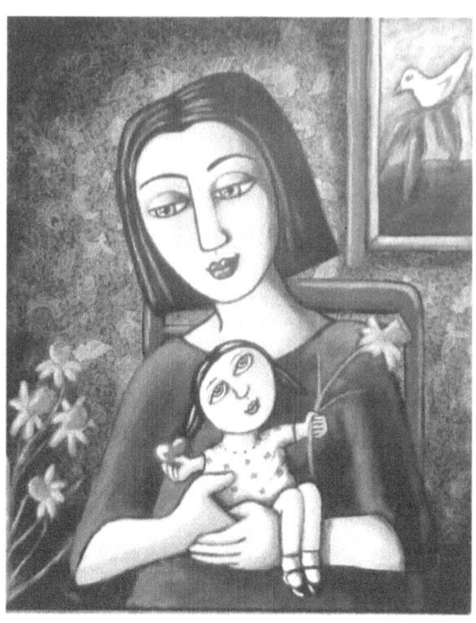

Slowly, she comes towards me, this child. She is wearing the pinny with the tiny red flowers and she is carrying Margarine, the big rag doll her mother made for her, named after her imaginary friend.

Moving warily, she is looking up at me from under her fringe in that shy way of hers. I'm not sure how I feel about her – the gap between us is so great, even though she has ruled my life for most of it.

We do not entirely trust each other yet: I left her unprotected and she kept me afraid, along with her other sabotages. But *I* was the one who left her driving the bus when she could barely reach the pedals. Yet I see now, how small and innocent she is: that little body, little arms, little legs. How could she know any better?

Finally, she speaks and she is angry: berating me for giving her too much responsibility when she didn't know what to do and making life such hard work so that she forgot how to play.

'Where did all the wonder go?' she asks and now I am crying, weeping. 'I was scared,' she says, 'and you didn't comfort me. You *hated* me.'

And I cannot deny it, for it is true. I hated her fear, her neediness.

'I'm sorry,' I say, because I am. 'I wish I had made it easier for you. I wish I had been more adult and made you feel safe. I wish I had given you nurture instead of hoping others would. I'm sorry I didn't stand up for you more.'

'I was scared. I kept telling you but you weren't hearing me right. You thought I wanted to hurt you. I just wanted you to listen to me; look after me.'

'You're my IT, aren't you?' I ask.

'Yes, that's all I am – a child, a wounded child. Not a monster.'

'I'm sorry,' I say again.

''S okay,' she says and hands me a gift of a blade of grass.

I search for something to give her; something to make up for all that she missed. It is a book; a beautiful, thick, gold-bound book and its cover simply reads: 'Life'.

'I give you life,' I say. 'The life you were supposed to have. I will not allow you to be shamed anymore.'

'You'll rescue us?' she says.

'There's no-one else who can.'

She runs to me and we hug.

I have made the child safe. There is nothing to fear.

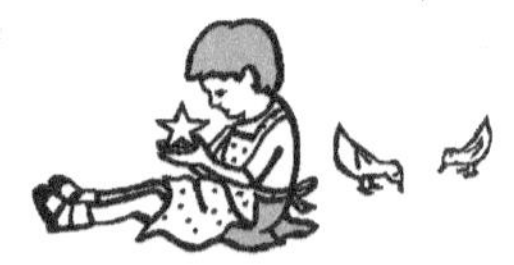

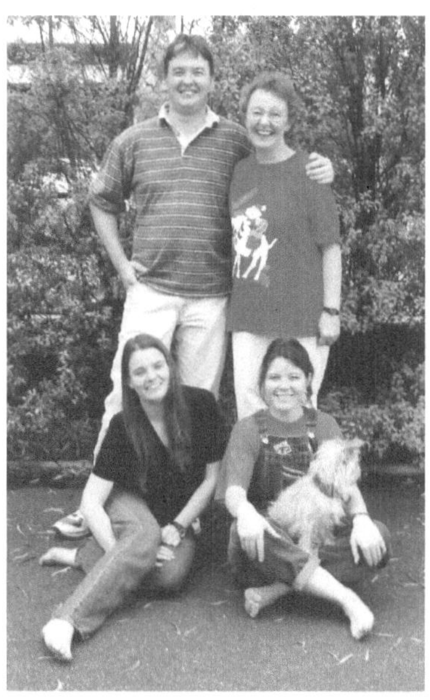

Saturday 19 March 2011

Beautiful weather today, finally making up a little for the summer that seems to have passed us by this year.

Out in the world there have been earthquakes, floods, cyclones, tsunamis, wars and despots. At least the locust plague, predicted to be of biblical proportions, has fizzled out, so I guess Armageddon is still on hold for a while.

For now it is just a beautiful day.

I drive to the seaside to see Michelle and my two great-nieces and great-nephew.

Casey's birthday was last Friday and on the passenger seat is a bag containing her gift and one for Michelle – two weeks late for hers but that's how it goes these days.

This is the same freeway that used to take me to my parents' home, all those years ago.

On the left is the Dromana Drive-In, where Julian and I smuggled in Geraldine and Rob in the boot of my Vauxhaul Standard Super 8, in 1972; the same car that later took us to the Sunbury Festival and the same four-seater that drove seven hippies all the way to Wilson's Promontory, when the muffler fell off en route.

That old car; my first car; such memories – driving from Broadford to Lorne one night on a whim and when it started raining, I had to thread string through the windscreen wipers and have my passenger work the pulley system all the way there. My mother would have had a fit.

And here's the turnoff to Hastings, which, if I turned left, would take me past the house where I hung in the hammock on that summer's day, listening to Van the Man, and then further is my brother's old home.

The kids run down the steep driveway to greet me. Michelle trails behind, a little tired because of too many kid things happening and a little sad because life is not so great at the moment.

We sit side-by-side on the couch as she shows me a video of Casey's 'disco party' from Friday night and Ashley, the middle child, a true 'Little Miss Sunshine' of a kid, bright as a button, sits next to me and snuggles up in an 'accidental' way which I dare not exaggerate; I must just let it happen: this closeness, this trust. The kilometres that separate us mean that we are only just getting to know each other.

I realise just how hungry I am for touch; a skin hunger that is now awakened by this small person who later almost incidentally threads her chilly fingers into my palm after a swim and there is a small twinge of loneliness for a moment. I idly wonder how much longer I will be by myself. I'm okay but it's been a while.

Is all that over now? Can it be that this is the end of the line of all those loves?

After Buzz, or more likely because of a 'certain' birthday, I developed a magical skill: I became invisible to men.

A strange experience, to have been loved and desired deeply and passionately; then 'click', the spotlight goes off, along with the hormones. I still reckon I've got it but hey, women have always had the big challenges. Besides, strong women are a bit scary, aren't they?

Oh, there have been a couple of old duffers who, still confusing sex with love, think that their own randiness is sufficient to compensate for small inconveniences like a complete lack of attraction or compatibility, but you can't blame a bloke for havin' a go, can ya?

And there have been some kind men, good men, who show love by being helpful and see me as a 'buddy' and you tell a 'buddy' about attractive women you fancy, don't you?

My artist still eludes me but let's face it, most artists are shocking narcissists. We can't help ourselves.

My ex-sister-in-law arrives with a beautiful cake, decorated with a figure 8 to mark Casey's years on the planet. A great dessert cook, Eileen. Should open a bakery.

Kym is carrying one of her twin two-year-old boys – Jack or Justin, I can never tell which – who is limp against her. 'You feel so helpless when they're ill,' she says.

Apparently Tony will be moving back from Perth soon. That's good.

This is my family and though the threads have loosened a little, I still feel that tug of love and those humble connections that give life meaning.

On the way home, I stop at the beach and Senna runs and romps in the shallows with fervent and unabashed glee; bouncing through the water as if she is on springs and grinning her doggie grin from ear to ear. The sea is a superb temperature and silken on my skin and I wish I had brought my bathers for what is likely to be the last chance for a swim this year.

Already there is a tweaking of the air that says autumn is fast approaching and with it, that sweet poignancy at the turning of the seasons.

Tonight, I watch the last episode of a BBC drama about a young man wrongly imprisoned for murder who has been exonerated after two years imprisonment.

After the long and bitter battle for his release, he visits his solicitor, resentful of the injustice that has been served upon him; full of angry questions: 'What if?', 'Why didn't?' and remonstrations: 'If only', 'Should have'.

The solicitor says: 'Does it really matter, Ben? You're free. *Do you get it? You're* free. *Just go and live your life!'*

And, like this young man, I am free. I am so free I could even choose to believe I was a prisoner if I wished.

All of it happened and that's just the way it happened.
It could have happened another way but it didn't.
I could have been someone else but I wasn't.
I might have done better but I didn't.
Or worse, for that matter.

I now close the diaries and in doing so, I also close the chapters of my life they have recorded.

I have walked back through each step and I have seen that there is another and yet another way of seeing each step; depending on where and when you're looking; depending on what you're expecting to find; depending on time and wisdom and release and *forgiveness.*

My life: this eccentric, multifarious life, is one unique yet tiny droplet in the great breathing sea of life, that surges and sighs with all of us in tow. It could not have existed without me; nor I without it. I am essential and incidental.

I am. I AM.

I carry the journals to the wooden chest my brother made for me years ago and into which JB's son carved his initials one afternoon while JB had his back turned, sermonising as usual about art or life or love; I can't recall.

I place the books in the chest and close the lid and walk away. It is done.

I now go and live the rest of my life.

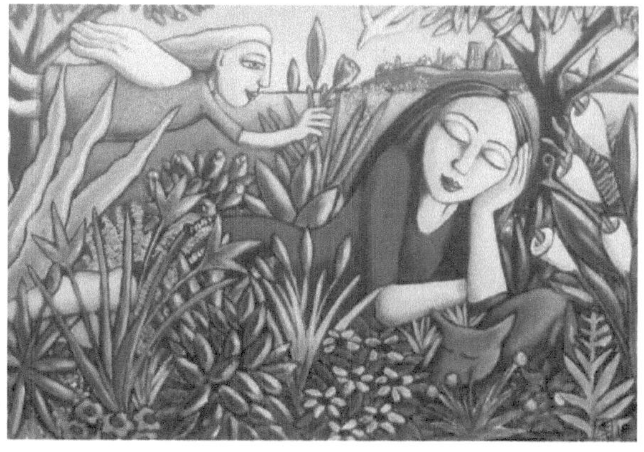

Epilogue

When I die

This is how the day will be

It will be a blue day, I like to think
The bridge will arc the sky in a concrete bow
Cars will flash and glisten on its loop
Eucalypts will flutter like faded bunting in the heat
The ocean will sag and spit at the shore

Almost at the stroke of noon
Will come the first tick of cicadas rising, rising
Like a stuttering machine

But perhaps I will make a grand exit, on a storm

It will roll over the city, the sky in collision, purple-black
The windows of high rises
Will become meaningless yellow squares in the gloom
An old, brown blind will tap in Morse against the window frame
Urgent Urgent Urgent

Or evening, on a cloudy day when all is quicksilver

The nervous systems of leafless trees
Will jitter and fidget against the glass
My cat will curl into a seashell and dream
Two birds will drop away in falling brackets
Just so, falling

Perhaps night

And in the fall-off of neons may come the ricochet of heels
Somewhere in the darkness a hand will pluck at paper with a
scratching pen
A ball of noise will bulge through an opening door
Then collapse to silence
A siren will shred the air far away

But this I do know

The day will be blithe and glib and undismayed
Someone will make love in a blind-drawn room
Someone will begin to sing, thinking they are alone
Someone will turn once more towards a closing door
And hesitate

Someone will be yelling down a spit-wet phone
Someone will be born
Someone will say ... no

And I will be gone

As simply and as difficultly as that

And then it will only matter
To a writer, or a bride, or silent friends

Just what the day is like
'The Day', Bev Aisbett 1988

I report back to the CEO of All Things.

'How did you go?' He asks.

'Well, I'm pretty tired. It was a big ride.'

'What's your assessment of your performance?'

'I think I did quite well with the entity I had to work with. She was a complex puzzle and often quite stubborn. Not easy to work with but she did come a long way.'

'Anything you would have changed?'

'I'd like to say no but that wouldn't be entirely true. There is a lot she could have done differently from the start.'

'Such as?'

'More fun, less drama, more flexibility, less work, work, work, worry, worry, worry.'

'In other words – the usual.'

I nod. 'Yes.'

'Anything else you'd like to add?'

'Just one thing ... can I have something a bit cruisier next time?'

The CEO of All Things laughs.

'Sure, whatever you want; you know that. It's your choice; just as this was.'

'I must have been out of my mind,' I say.

'Only for a little while.'

We both smile at that and head towards the rest area. I'm so zonked, I think I'll sit out a good few generations.

'WELCOME HOME' says the sign over the entrance.

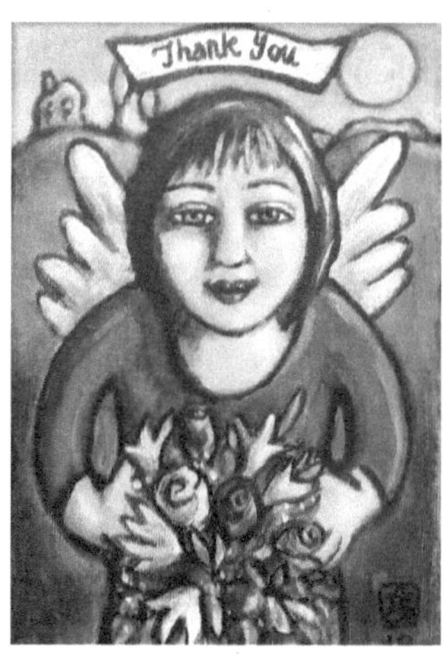

Acknowledgements

Three different captains have been at the helm for the journey of this book and my deepest gratitude goes to Mel Cain, the first of my trio of publishers, who championed an unrefined, meagre 40-page submission hastily emailed to her days before she departed these shores and publishing, forever.

Next, my thanks to the delightful, cheeky Sandy Weir, who became a sort of mate when we met in Sydney and shared a delightful day at Paddo Market, where she seduced me into spending way too much of my and her money: 'I would never allow you to buy a less than perfect dress!'

Thirdly, my current, overworked publisher, Roz, who I am sure will be relieved that my emails will finally have ceased (for *now*, Roz, for *now*!).

Special and affectionate thanks to Doug A, who generously volunteered his time and ex-English teacher qualifications to casting an eagle eye over punctuation and grammar – not a colon was missed!

Thanks also to Russell Thomson for his sensitive edit and to Anne Reilly for invaluable guidance and support in the finer points of the final edit.

A special mention to the wonderful staff at my local library and to my pals, who have been so supportive through this process.

Finally, to the chorus of players who, for the sake of economy were not able to be given walk-on roles in this version of my story, thank you for the parts you played, great and small, in the real-life version. I may not have always felt inclined to thank some of you as much as others then but I do most heartily now.

We are, indeed, all one.

BEV'S BEST SELLING BOOKS

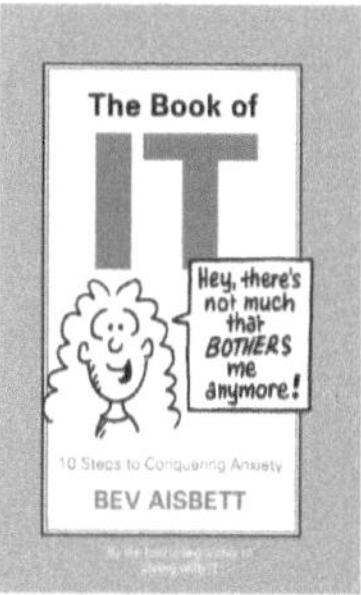

THE BOOK OF IT

Using 10 steps from her popular workshops, counsellor Bev Aisbett provides you with practical, sound advice on how to recognise and tame anxiety, whether it affects you just occasionally or every single day.

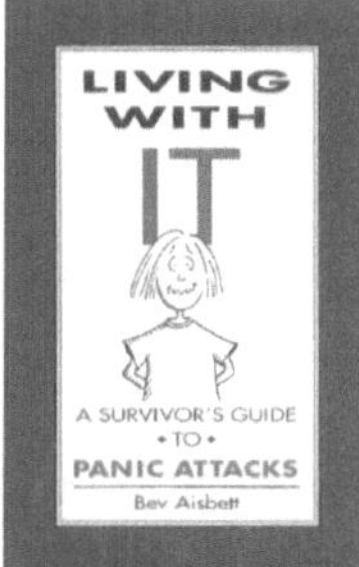

LIVING WITH IT

Living With It provides much-needed reassurance and support, showing the way out of the maze of panic with humour and the insight of first-hand experience. You can beat this

- You can beat this
- You are not alone
- You will recover

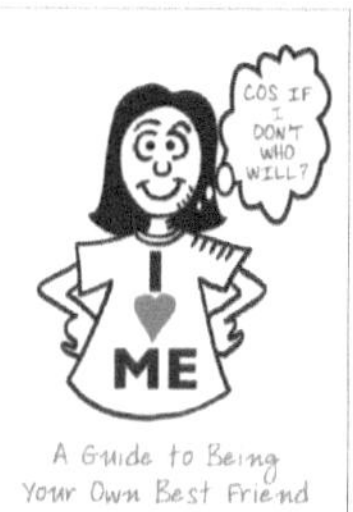

I LOVE ME

There are times in our lives when we seem to have no-one in our corner, and so we feel depressed, lonely, hurt or angry. Bev Aisbett now shows you how to find the most loyal friend of all ...YOU!

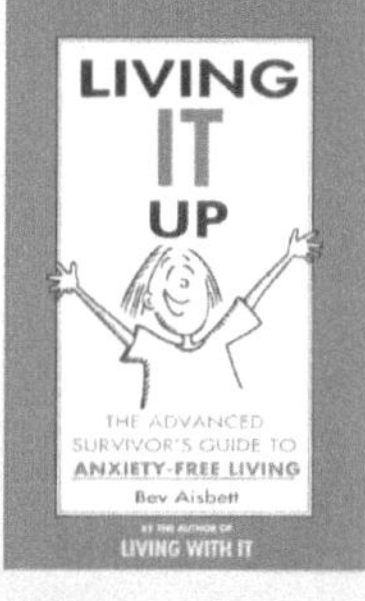

LIVING IT UP

Living IT Up offers further hope and guidance for sufferers of anxiety disorders, and valuable insights for those interested in personal development. *Living IT Up*, a sequel to the popular *Living with IT: A Survivor's Guide to Panic Attacks* is a guide to surviving anxiety.

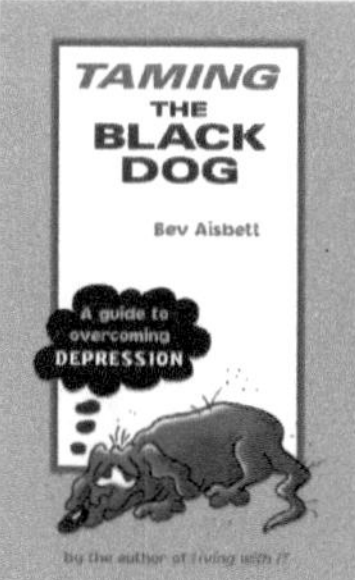

TAMING THE BLACK DOG

Taming the Black Dog has a unique blend of wit and information and is an invaluable guide for both chronic sufferers of depression as well as anyone experiencing a fit of the blues.

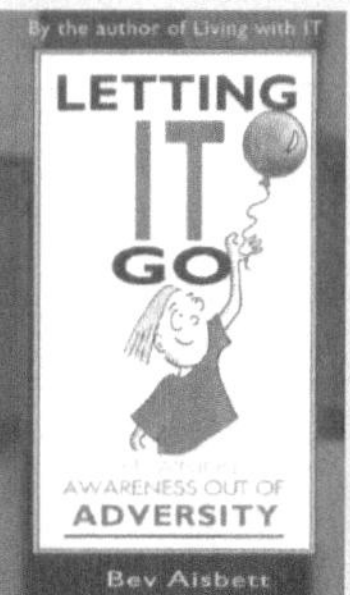

LETTING IT GO

Bev Aisbett shows you how to use the strategies learned in her journey of self discovery to achieve change and growth in your life. Now Bev Aisbett has a lot to live for. And you can too!

HarperCollins*Publishers*
harpercollins.com.au

www.ingramcontent.com/pod-product-compliance
Lightning Source LLC
LaVergne TN
LVHW041106080826
845145LV00007B/1709